WELCOME TO OUR BOOKLET STUFFED FULL OF SAVINGS, DISCOUNTS & ADVENTURE...

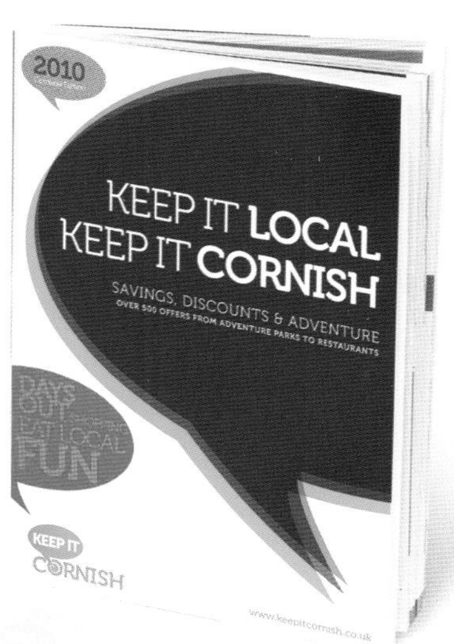

The Keep it Cornish booklet was created not only to save you hundreds of pounds, but to promote local independent businesses around Cornwall. The local way of life is so unique we feel it's important to protect all things Cornish and ensure it maintains the character and charm that it is renowned for on a worldwide scale.

In addition Keep it Cornish was set up with the aim to raise funds for charities in the local community. This year we are supporting two fantastic charities the Precious Lives Appeal and Cornwall Hospice Care. As well as making an annual donation to each charity we have participated in several sponsored events, including the Eden Project half marathon, and are on our way to raising £1000 from these events alone. For more information regarding these worthy causes please see pages 186 -187.

www.keepitcornish.co.uk

CONTENTS

We cover all areas of Cornwall from Penzance to Newquay, to St Ives and Falmouth.

We are supporting two great charities, the Precious Lives Appeal and Cornwall Hospice Care. To find out more information about these please turn to pages 186 -187.

Remember you can keep up to date with all the latest events and news happening in Cornwall on our website. Also join our news letter to find out all the latest offers and savings.

Photo: Paul Watts/VisitCornwall

www.**keepitcornish**.co.uk

SAVING YOU HUNDREDS OF POUNDS ON GOING OUT IN YOUR LOCAL AREA

WELCOME TO KEEP IT CORNISH

YOUR COMPLETE GUIDE TO ENJOYING THE SITES, SOUNDS AND TASTES OF CORNWALL BUT WITH ALL THE LATEST DISCOUNTS

The 2010 Keep it Cornish booklet will provide you with over 300 offers and savings from local businesses around the county saving you hundreds of pounds. From restaurants to theme parks, boutiques to bodyboarding, we really do have something for everyone. Use it only once or twice and the book will have paid for itself. With so many great deals why not support local businesses and Keep it Cornish.

SEE HOW MUCH THIS BOOK COULD SAVE YOU...

Lunch at Mannings	£20
Visit to Blue Reef Aquarium	£8
Lingerie from Blushhh	£6
Surf lesson at Breakers Surf School	£24
Dinner at the Bakehouse	£10
Total Savings	**£68**

...OR ANOTHER DAY OF SAVINGS...

Lunch at Townhouse	£12
Visit the Isles of Scilly	£20
Fancy dress from Ribticklers	£5
Movie at Merlin Cinemas	£8
Dinner at Onshore	£10
Total Savings	**£55**

Savings based on 4 people using one book.

EXPLORE CORNWALL

IN THE LAST DECADE CORNWALL HAS EMERGED AS ONE OF THE WORLD'S ICONIC DESTINATIONS.

Assured of a warm welcome, and a friendly word, time spent in Cornwall, whether you are a resident or visitor, has even more to offer than the typical stereotype of golden beaches, pasties and clotted cream.

Stand on the towering cliffs of the north coast, and view the rolling breakers as they crash below onto remote beaches harbouring newly born seals. Walk along the tranquil inlets of the south coast, and find a surprise around each bend.

Look through the arch of a derelict engine house, perched on the edge of a cliff, with the ghosts of miners passed singing as if rehearsing in a male voice choir.

Pick up your surfboard and wade excitedly into the surging surf at Newquay, alongside the best wave riders from all over the world.

Stroll along the narrow, cobbled streets of St Ives, and as you look out to sea, wonder at the clarity of light beloved by artists through the ages.

At Falmouth visit the Maritime Museum, and see all around you evidence of Cornwall's links to the sea, from giant vessels being repaired to racing boats from dinghies to yachts.

Shop in our cathedral city of Truro and enjoy a safe, relaxed atmosphere.

At Penzance, the gateway to the Isles of Scilly, stroll along the promenade and consider a trip by boat or helicopter to the magical islands.

Wherever you travel, take your Keep it Cornish book with you, and make a wonderful day affordable and complete.

USEFUL LINKS

www.keepitcornish.co.uk
www.visitcornwall.co.uk

Photos by:
Walker Photographs, VisitCornwall

OUR KEEP IT SECTIONS EXPLAINED

WE COVER EVERYTHING FROM TOP CLASS GRUB TO PUBS, BOUTIQUES TO BOOKSHOPS AND SURFING TO SALONS...

The Keep it Cornish booklet really does have something for everyone and we have even broken it down into easy to follow sections helping you to find exactly what you're looking for with minimal effort!

Don't forget to check out our website for more information...

www.keepitcornish.co.uk

We cover restaurants, pubs, cafes, bistros and much more. So if you're looking for a romantic meal for two in the cobbled streets of St Ives, a welcoming pub for all the family, or just a quick bite to eat for lunch, then look no further because we have it all!

Why not catch up with friends over a coffee, enjoy a freshly blended smoothie, or even hit the local bars and clubs that Cornwall has to offer.

Treat yourself to a relaxing massage, enjoy a full manicure, or get the latest cut and colour. We have everything you need to leave you looking and feeling great… you can even top up your tan!

We have activities for everyone from surfing for the whole family to coasteering around the beautiful Cornish coastline. For those adrenaline junkies why not take to the skies and jump from a plane at 10,000 feet!

Whether you want to see the creatures of the ocean, birds of paradise or farmyard animals, we have days out that everyone will enjoy no matter your age. From bowling to paintball, the cinema to go-karting. Make an enjoyable day an affordable day.

This section showcases Cornwall's unique range of local shops. Covering lingerie, sportswear, toys, designer clothing, cycling, surf wear, florists, gifts, photography, kids wear, jewellery, cakes, delis… the list is endless!

WHERE WE COVER

NE

PERRAN

ST IVES

REDRUT

CAMBORNE

HAYLE

FALMOUTH

PENZANCE

LAND'S END

THE LIZARD

Photos by:
VisitCornwall, Paul Watts / VisitCornwall,
www.gardensofcornwall.com/VisitCornwall

LAUNCESTON

PADSTOW

WADEBRIDGE

BODMIN

ST AUSTELL

LOOE

More towns added every day! Keep up to date on our website.

WE HAVE OFFERS IN THE FOLLOWING TOWNS

Penzance
Hayle
Falmouth
Newquay
Redruth
Helston
St Ives
Truro
Camborne
Sennen
And many more...

ENJOY SAVINGS
DISCOUNTS
& ADVENTURE

HOW TO USE THE VOUCHERS

TEAR OUT, POP ALONG & ENJOY THE BENEFITS OF KEEPING IT CORNISH!

The Keep it Cornish booklet is filled with hundreds of offers from 20% off to 2-for-1 discounts on the things you do everyday like dining, shopping, attractions and much more!

PLEASE READ VOUCHERS FOR INDIVIDUAL TERMS AND CONDITIONS

To receive your discount present your voucher to the participating business. Unless otherwise stated you may only use the offer once, and may only use one voucher per transaction. You may not combine the voucher with any other promotion or offer.

HOW TO USE YOUR 'KEEP IT FOOD' VOUCHERS

In order to use your '**Keep it Food**' vouchers you must follow these simple steps:

You must make a reservation with the restaurant in advance and advise them that you are using a 'Keep it Cornish' voucher.

You must present the voucher when ordering your meal.

Restrictions

Each restaurant allocates a number of tables for 'Keep it Cornish' customers. During busy times, such as weekends, these will be more limited so it is always best to book as far in advance as possible.

Please read the terms of each offer carefully to check if a restaurant has included any restrictions on usage.

All restaurant offers exclude certain dates throughout the year. They are Valentine's Day, Mother's Day, Father's Day, Easter Sunday, Christmas Eve / Day and New Year's Eve / Day.

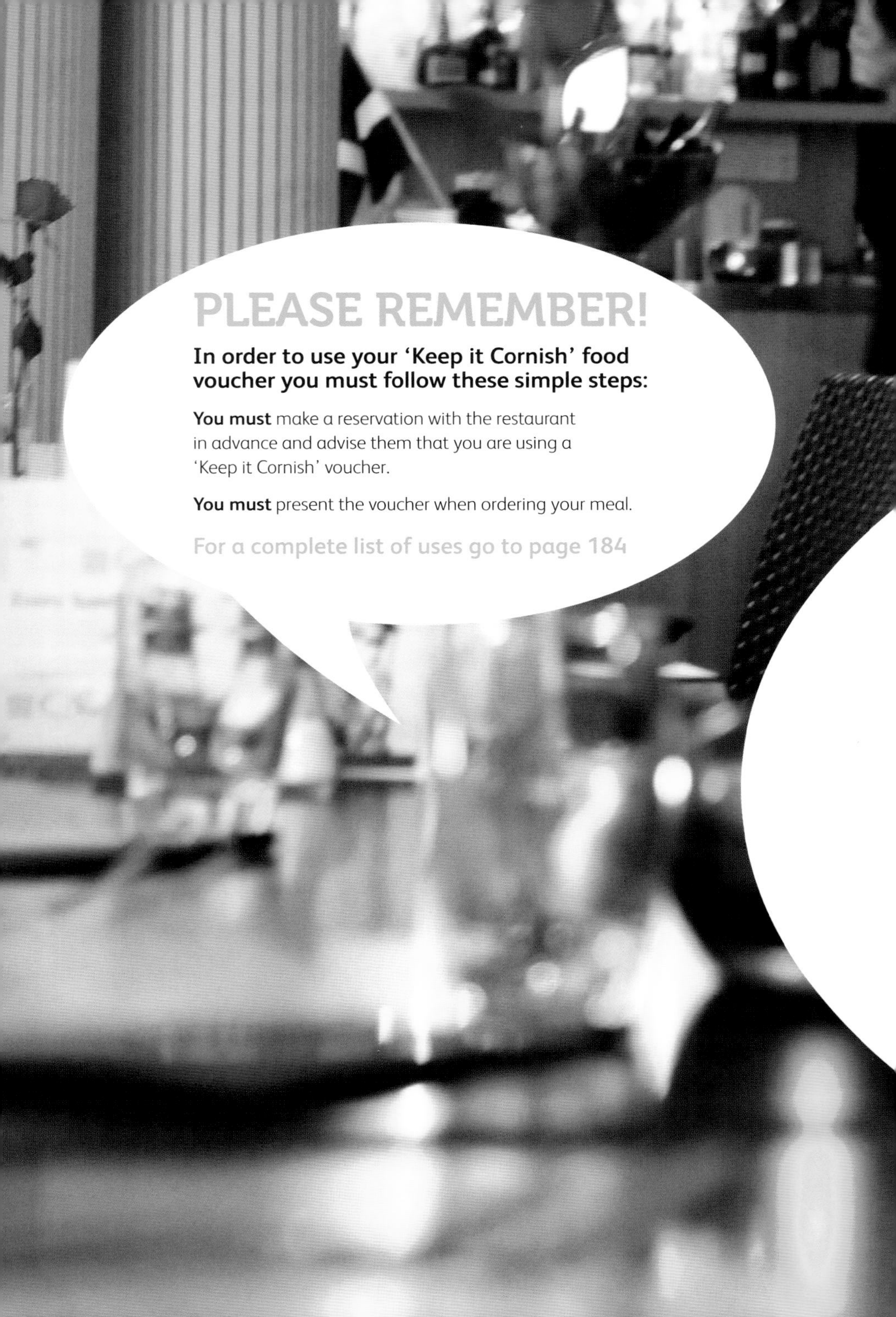
PLEASE REMEMBER!
In order to use your 'Keep it Cornish' food voucher you must follow these simple steps:
You must make a reservation with the restaurant in advance and advise them that you are using a 'Keep it Cornish' voucher.
You must present the voucher when ordering your meal.
For a complete list of uses go to page 184

KEEP IT FOOD

Penzance
Blue Bay Café F6
Blue Snappa F7
Cape Cornwall Golf & Leisure Resort F12
Exchange F18
Honey Pot F22
Lugger Hotel & Wheelhouse Restaurant F27
Olive Farm Restaurant F37
Renaissance F42
Savoy Restaurant & Bar F45
Turks Head/White Hart F53-57

Hayle
Johnny's Cafe F23
Lamb & Flag Inn F25

St Ives
7even F2-3
Beach Restaurant F5
Cornish Deli F16
Tyringham Arms F59
Watermill F61

Newquay
Butchers Bistro F8-9
Buzios F10
Café Irie F11
Chy Bar F13
Senor Dicks F46
St Pirans Inn F48
Tavern Inn F49

Truro
Astons F4
Explorers Café F19
Gallery Café F20
La Bevanda – Casa Fina F24
Larder Deli F26
Mannings F33
MI Bar F35
Shanghai Lounge F47
Truro Cathedral Restaurant & Coffee Shop F51-52
Zafiros F63

Falmouth
5 Degrees West F1
CK Catering F14
De Wynns F17
Falmouth Townhouse F50
Harveys Wharf F21
Marine Bar & Restaurant F34
Miss Peapod F36
Pea Souk F37-39
Phoenix Café/Bar F40
Roseland Inn F43
Victory Inn F60

Porthlevan
Corner Deli F15
Sandbar F44

Sennen
Little Barn F27
Whitesands Hotel Seafood Restaurant & Grill F62

Camborne/Redruth
Regal Restaurant & Bar F41
Tyacks Hotel F58

2 Meals for £10

miss peapod's kitchen cafe

Jubilee Wharf, Penryn,
Cornwall, TR10 8FG

T 01326 374424
www.misspeapod.co.uk

Restaurant Opening Hours.
Monday - Closed
Tuesday - Thursday 10am - 4pm
Friday - Saturday 10am - 12.30am
Sunday 10am - 4pm

- This voucher offer entitles you to 2 meals for £10
- See voucher for terms and conditions

miss peapod's kitchen cafe is an award winning small independent cafe based amongst all the art and craft workshops at Jubilee wharf (www.jubileewharf.co.uk), **in Penryn.**

We have been built using pioneering techniques of eco-development. Which means we have wind turbines, solar panels and a wood chip boiler, to name a few features. We are family orientated and this means children are welcome anytime including the evenings to eat with their families or attend gigs.

We have a play area with a wooden kitchen, and lots of other toys and books. Out on our decking beside our wind turbines, you can go crabbing or watch the boats go by up the river, whilst enjoying one of our fair trade organic coffees. This year we were voted the 'Best cafe' by Cornwalls Tourism awards 2009 and received the Gold award.

This is because we have a mix of family friendly prices and an ethical approach to sourcing our food. Offering an exciting seasonal menu, we give restaurants a run for their money. But perhaps it was swung by our large range of homemade cakes? Come down and decide for yourselves.

kitchen cafe

Quality Homemade Food
Coffee and Cakes
Fully licenced bar for drinks + beers
Open for Sunday lunch

Friday and Saturday open till late with bands film and food

see www.misspeapod.co.uk

Open 10-4pm weekends 10-12.30am Closed Monday

MISS PEAPOD SOURCES ALL FOOD WITH A PRIORITY TO LOCAL, ORGANIC AND FAIRTRADE

miss peapod's kitchen cafe Jubilee Wharf, Penryn, TR10 8FG 01326 374424

We source with a priority to local, organic and fairtrade. Also we do a lot of live music, check the website to see the latest bands playing.
www.misspeapod.co.uk

Welcome to the Lugger hotel, Penzance

Located on the only promenade in Cornwall and an ideal setting for your holiday. The Lugger Hotel, is a comfortable family run hotel with its own Wheelhouse Restaurant and centrally located for the town's facilities - the Hotel occupies an ideal position overlooking Mounts Bay. It has full central heating throughout and has an informal and convivial atmosphere. We have our own private car park with easy access and ample space at the front of the hotel. With the recent completion of our refurbishment we are now able to offer facilities for conferences, meetings and special celebrations including weddings.

The Lugger Hotel
Wheelhouse Restaurant

5 Amazing offers

The Lugger Hotel

The Promenade, Penzance,
Cornwall TR18 4DL

T 01736 363236
www.theluggerhotel.co.uk

Opening Hours.
Normal pub hours

Please ring in advance for exact times

- This voucher offer entitles you to 5 amazing savings
- See voucher for terms and conditions

he Wheelhouse Restaurant is proud f its reputation for excellent cuisine.

e busy restaurant and terrace make a worthy setting for enjoying our good me cooked English food, prepared and served with care and imagination. e can also offer a selection of wines with which to complement any meal.

erlooking the promenade and with a fine view of the Bay; r comfortable, well-stocked bar lounge is the perfect spot for ›leasant and relaxing evening.

THE WHITE HART & The Turks Head

£5 OFF your bill

The White Hart Ludgvan, one of the oldest pubs in Cornwall. A great place to eat...

Allow your imagination to wander as you decide what to do. Enjoy the relaxing atmosphere in the comfort of the bar area. Ponder over the selection of the finest food in the area from our extensive menu or simply enjoy the ambience of a local friendly pub.
Our restaurant serves the freshest, finest local produce. Our food has been recognised by numerous awards. All you need to do is sit back and enjoy.

The White Hart

Ludgvan, Nr Penzance, Cornwall
TR20 8EY

T 01736 740574
www.whitehartludgvan.co.uk

The Turks Head

Chapel Street, Penzance,
Cornwall, TR18 4AF

T 01736 363093
www.turksheadpenzance.co.uk

Restaurant Opening Hours.
Monday - Sunday
12pm - 2.30pm &
6pm - 9.30pm

- This voucher offer entitles you to £5 off your bill.
- See vouchers for terms and conditions.

Experience the unique atmosphere of a place in history that is steeped in intrigue and mystery

Imagine yourself taking a drink in the same place that Pirates and Smugglers once used some 750 years ago. This is one of the oldest pubs in Cornwall. An underground tunnel leading from the harbour was used to secretly transport their bounty just before their evenings rest at the Public Bar. A warm and friendly welcome awaits you in the restaurant, presented in authentic, traditional surroundings.

An impressive range of fish dishes such as mussels, sea bass, John Dory, lemon sole and tandoori monkfish are typically available as well as sumptuous meat dishes including pan-fried venison, chicken stir-fry, pork tenderloin, mixed grill and steaks. Our Specials Boards are frequently changed to reflect the season and ensure we offer the best available local produce. Whether you choose to enjoy your meal in the sunny flower-filled garden or in the cosy wood panelled restaurant or bar, your hosts Helen and Jonathan look forward to seeing you.

F6

'hether eating alone with friends · meeting colleagues the Blue Bay afe provides the ideal location, rving a delicious selection of coffee, as, breakfasts, sandwiches, snacks, ght bites, and home made cakes, gether with many local wines nd beers.

'herever possible we source our oduct ingredients locally, this all akes for the ideal place to meet with friends, or just sit and read hile enjoying a glass of wine at our leisure, or how about that usiness breakfast/lunch meeting vay from the office, with use of our free WI-FI internet access. If alfresco is your preference, we have an outside seating area where you can just sit and watch the world go by, whilst enjoying and nice cup of coffee with that homemade cake. Everything is made fresh to order we can also supply takeaway sandwiches, baguettes, jacket potatoes, toasted sandwiches, paninis , salads, crisps, cakes, hot & cold soft drinks. This family business run and managed by daughter Angie together with friendly staff all barista trained for that perfect coffee is here to welcome both locals and visitors to the Blue Bay Cafe.

blue bay
• C • A • F • É •

Second glass of wine FREE

Blue Bay Cafe

Unit 15, Wharfside Shopping Centre, Market Jew Street, Penzance TR18 2GB

T 01736 350483
www.webaddresshere.co.uk

Opening Hours.
Summer: Mon - Sat from 8.00am
Sun from 8.00am
Winter: Mon - Sat from 8.30am
Sun from 9.00am

- This voucher offer entitles you to a second glass of wine **FREE**.
- See voucher for terms and conditions.

F12

e Clubhouse Bistro is open members and non members day everyday for breakfasts, nches and dinners, it is a special perience, with a relaxing dining mosphere in a unique setting th views overlooking England's ly Cape.

ur chefs have earned a high putation for their superb homemade od-using ingredients farmed a one's throw away, which are freshly oked to order. We specialise in fresh asonal Cornish produce and this is lected through our carefully selected enu choices and ever-changing ily specials.

Relax by the log fire and sample the delights of our homemade cakes or enjoy a Cape seafood platter overlooking the unique views of the Cape. Join us every Sunday in our cosy Clubhouse for our chef's signature Sunday Roast made from the finest local produce, then top it off with a freshly made indulgent dessert.

Our young and friendly team will ensure you are provided with excellent service and a warm welcome. You can be sure you will be looked after well throughout your time at Cape Cornwall, making your trip one you won't forget, come and visit us to see for yourself.

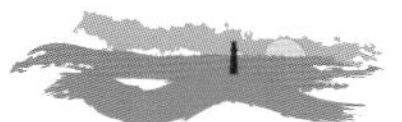

CAPE CORNWALL
Golf and Leisure Resort

10% OFF your final bill

Cape Cornwall
Golf and Leisure Resort

St. Just, Penzance, Cornwall, TR19 7NL
T 01736 788611
www.capecornwall.com
enquiries@capecornwall.com

Opening Hours.
Open all day
Breakfast 8am - 12pm
Lunch 12pm - 2.30pm
Dinner 6.30pm - 9pm

- This voucher offer entitles you to 10% off your bill.
- See voucher for terms and conditions.

THE TAVERN

FREE Bottle of house wine

The Treninnick Tavern is just a short walk from the heart of bustling Newquay

Dating back to the 16th century, it is only since 1965 that this wonderful old building has been an inn and, for many years, it was a farmhouse. To the front is a beautiful cottage garden and patio area - an ideal place to soak up the sun - and the mass of colourful flowers in the borders, window box's and hanging baskets puts most other gardens to shame.

Inside, the inn is equally charming, the olde worlde character of the building is blended perfectly with the new. Managed by local man, Steve Simmons, this inn is a popular place with locals, both young and old, and visitors are given a warm friendly welcome. Just the place to come for those who enjoy a good pint of beer - there are always three real ales on tap.

The Tavern Inn

The Tavern Inn, Mellanvrane Lane, Newquay, Cornwall
TR7 2LQ

T 01637 873564
www.taverninn.co.uk

Opening Hours
Monday - Sunday 11am - 11.30pm
Food served
12pm - 2pm & 6.30pm - 9pm

- This voucher offer entitles you to a **FREE** bottle of house wine.
- See voucher for terms and conditions.

KEEP IT FOOD

We cover restaurants, pubs, cafes, bistros and much more. So if you're looking for a romantic meal for two in the cobbled streets of St Ives, a welcoming pub for all the family, or just a quick bite to eat for lunch, then look no further because we have it all!

Don't forget to check out our website for more information...

www.keepitcornish.co.uk

5 DEGREES WEST

KEEP IT CORNISH — F1

Situated between Falmouth's bustling centre and the Events square, 5 Degrees West is an ideal venue for relaxed drinking or eating at any time of the day. The décor is spacious and modern with open fire places, leather sofas and a great atmosphere.

See reverse for more information

Valid from 01.01.10 to 31.12.10

FREE GLASS OF WINE

TR11 4AU
Tel: 01326 311288

7even

KEEP IT CORNISH — F2

7even has a contemporary, modern and friendly feel and is an established restaurant within the St Ives Culinary scene. We have created a relaxed, cosy and intimate atmosphere.

See reverse for more information

Valid from 01.01.10 to 31.12.10

SAVE 2 PIZZAS FOR £10

Cornwall, TR26 1RR
Tel: 01736 791988

7even

KEEP IT CORNISH — F3

7even has a contemporary, modern and friendly feel and is an established restaurant within the St Ives Culinary scene. We have created a relaxed, cosy and intimate atmosphere.

See reverse for more information

Valid from 01.01.10 to 31.12.10

FREE BOTTLE OF HOUSE WINE

Cornwall, TR26 1RR
Tel: 01736 791988

ASTONS

KEEP IT CORNISH — F4

We are a small privately run restaurant situated opposite the lovely gardens of Boscawen Park. Away from the hustle and bustle of Truro town centre we offer plenty of free parking, and a chance to sit outside whilst enjoying a light lunch or afternoon tea, or Dinner.

See reverse for more information

Valid from 01.01.10 to 31.12.10

SAVE CREDIT CRUNCH LUNCH

Tel: 01872 272121

THE BEACH RESTAURANT

KEEP IT CORNISH — F5

With fabulous panoramic views, child friendly and situated in the heart of beautiful St Ives you will find the beach restaurant. Owned and managed by the same local family since 1957 the restaurant offers first class local fish, seafood's, poultry, meat and game.

See reverse for more information

Valid from 01.01.10 to 31.12.10

SAVE 10% OFF

Tel: 01736 798798

Terms & Conditions

1. Only one voucher per transaction
2. Defaced, torn or photocopied vouchers will not be accepted
3. Not to be used in conjunction with any other offer
4. Not exchangeable for cash
5. Present this voucher to the business to accept the offer
6. **FREE** glass of house wine with every meal purchased over £5

5 DEGREES WEST

Our friendly and helpful staff are always on hand to ensure you have a pleasurable visit. When the sun comes out there is extensive outside seating making this one always a winner! Children and dogs welcome.

5 Degrees West
7 Grove Place, Falmouth, Cornwall
TR11 4AU
Tel: 01326 311288

Terms & Conditions

1. Only one voucher per transaction
2. Defaced, torn or photocopied vouchers will not be accepted
3. Not to be used in conjunction with any other offer
4. Not exchangeable for cash
5. Present this voucher to the business to accept the offer
6. 2 pizzas for £10 for upto 4 people
7. Valid evenings only

7even

Our menu is built around local farm produce and locally sourced fish and is largely influenced by Italian flavours. Why not come and try one of our handmade 11 inch stonebaked pizzas?!

7even
7 High Street, St Ives
Cornwall, TR26 1RR
Tel: 01736 791988

Terms & Conditions

1. Only one voucher per transaction
2. Defaced, torn or photocopied vouchers will not be accepted
3. Not to be used in conjunction with any other offer
4. Not exchangeable for cash
5. Present this voucher to the business to accept the offer
6. **FREE** bottle of house wine with a booking for 4 people dining in the restaurant

7even

Our menu is built around local farm produce and locally sourced fish and is largely influenced by Italian flavours. Why not come and try one of our handmade 11 inch stonebaked pizzas?!

7even
7 High Street, St Ives
Cornwall, TR26 1RR
Tel: 01736 791988

Terms & Conditions

1. Only one voucher per transaction
2. Defaced, torn or photocopied vouchers will not be accepted
3. Not to be used in conjunction with any other offer
4. Not exchangeable for cash
5. Present this voucher to the business to accept the offer
6. CREDIT CRUNCH LUNCH - Haddock, french fries and tartare sauce with a standard tea or coffee for £5.95
7. Valid weekday lunch times only 12p.m. to 3p.m.

We are a small privately run restaurant situated opposite the lovely gardens of Boscawen Park. Away from the hustle and bustle of Truro town centre we offer plenty of free parking, and a chance to sit outside whilst enjoying a light lunch or afternoon tea, or Dinner.

Astons Restaurant
Malpas Road, Truro, Cornwall
TR1 1SG
Tel: 01872 272121

Terms & Conditions

1. Only one voucher per transaction
2. Defaced, torn or photocopied vouchers will not be accepted
3. Not to be used in conjunction with any other offer
4. Not exchangeable for cash
5. Present this voucher to the business to accept the offer
6. 10% OFF final bill
7. Must purchase a starter, main and dessert

With fabulous panoramic views, child friendly and situated in the heart of beautiful St Ives you will find the beach restaurant. Owned and managed by the same local family since 1957 the restaurant offers first class local fish, seafood's, poultry, meat and game.

The Beach Restaurant
The Wharf, St.Ives, Cornwall
TR26 1LG
Tel: 01736 798798

7even
7even
Astons Restaurant
The Beach Restaurant

blue bay
C•A•F•É

F6

Licensed cafe open every day of the week serving home cooked locally sourced food, homemade cakes, daily specials, sandwiches, baguettes, paninis, snacks, and light bites. We also offer a wide selection of hot & cold drinks including speciality teas & coffees, wines and bottled beers.

See reverse for more information

Valid from 01.01.10 to 31.12.10

FREE SECOND GLASS

F7

The Blue Snappa Cafe/Bar is Penzance's premium coffee, food, wine and cocktail bar situated in the heart of Penzance. A fresh lively cosmopolitan venue to enjoy your day or evening till late.

See reverse for more information

Valid from 01.01.10 to 31.12.10

SAVE 2 TAPAS & WINE £15

BUTCHER'S BISTRO
Licensed Cornish Steak & Seafood Restaurant

F8

The Butchers Bistro offers delicious English food, specializing in steak and seafood. The menu is varied offering a wide choice. The local owners pride themselves in using Cornish ingredients. All dishes are homemade and prepared freshly to order, and can be accompanied by a variety of local wines and ales.

See reverse for more information

Valid from 01.01.10 to 31.12.10

SAVE 10% OFF

BUTCHER'S BISTRO
Licensed Cornish Steak & Seafood Restaurant

F9

The Butchers Bistro offers delicious English food, specializing in steak and seafood. The menu is varied offering a wide choice. The local owners pride themselves in using Cornish ingredients. All dishes are homemade and prepared freshly to order, and can be accompanied by a variety of local wines and ales.

See reverse for more information

Valid from 01.01.10 to 31.12.10

SAVE

Buzios award winning club, bar, restaurant and pool hall combines three venues in one. The ground floor is a café bar by day and steak house grill & bar during the evening.

See reverse for more information

Valid from 01.01.10 to 31.12.10

SAVE 10% OFF

Blue Bay Cafe
Unit 15 Wharfside Shopping Centre
Penzance, TR18 2GB
Tel: 01736 350483

Terms & Conditions

1. Only one voucher per transaction
2. Defaced, torn or photocopied vouchers will not be accepted
3. Not to be used in conjunction with any other offer
4. Not exchangeable for cash
5. Present this voucher to the business to accept the offer
6. Second glass of wine FREE when you buy one glass of wine with a meal

blue bay
C A F É

Outside relaxed seating area, and friendly atmosphere. Free WI-FI access, small private functions also catered for.

Blue Snappa
35 market place, Penzance, Cornwall
TR18 2JF
Tel: 01736 363352

Terms & Conditions

1. Only one voucher per transaction
2. Defaced, torn or photocopied vouchers will not be accepted
3. Not to be used in conjunction with any other offer
4. Not exchangeable for cash
5. Present this voucher to the business to accept the offer
6. Get any 2 tapas and a bottle of wine for just £15

The food is sourced locally and is cooked in a open theatre style kitchen.

Blue Snappa
www.bluesnappa.com

Butcher's Bistro
26, Cliff Road, Newquay, Cornwall
TR7 2ND
Tel: 01637 874470

Terms & Conditions

1. Only one voucher per transaction
2. Defaced, torn or photocopied vouchers will not be accepted
3. Not to be used in conjunction with any other offer
4. Not exchangeable for cash
5. Present this voucher to the business to accept the offer
6. Saturday night, steak night, 10% off all main course steak dishes, excluding the £8.50 steak special

BUTCHER'S BISTRO
Licensed Cornish Steak & Seafood Restaurant

The Butchers Bistro offers delicious English food, specializing in steak and seafood. The menu is varied offering a wide choice. The local owners pride themselves in using Cornish ingredients. All dishes are homemade and prepared freshly to order, and can be accompanied by a variety of local wines and ales.

Butcher's Bistro

Butcher's Bistro
26, Cliff Road, Newquay, Cornwall
TR7 2ND
Tel: 01637 874470

Terms & Conditions

1. Only one voucher per transaction
2. Defaced, torn or photocopied vouchers will not be accepted
3. Not to be used in conjunction with any other offer
4. Not exchangeable for cash
5. Present this voucher to the business to accept the offer
6. Friday night, fish night, 10% off all main course fish dishes

BUTCHER'S BISTRO
Licensed Cornish Steak & Seafood Restaurant

The Butchers Bistro offers delicious English food, specializing in steak and seafood. The menu is varied offering a wide choice. The local owners pride themselves in using Cornish ingredients. All dishes are homemade and prepared freshly to order, and can be accompanied by a variety of local wines and ales.

Butcher's Bistro

Buzios
54-56 East Street, Newquay
TR7 1BE
Tel: 01637 870300

Terms & Conditions

1. Only one voucher per transaction
2. Defaced, torn or photocopied vouchers will not be accepted
3. Not to be used in conjunction with any other offer
4. Not exchangeable for cash
5. Present this voucher to the business to accept the offer
6. 10% OFF food, excluding drink, subject to availability
7. Not valid during July and August or any Bank Holiday

The middle floor club style bar is open late with DJ's and live entertainment, while the top floor has a contemporary pool hall. Buzios can be found opposite Senor dick's Mexican restaurant.

Opening times: 11am - late

Buzios

cafe irie

F11

Cafe Irie is located above Newquay's working harbour. We are in one of Newquay's oldest buildings and are classed as the town's only real alternative spot. Enjoy our wholesome, healthy, home cooked food. Brilliant coffees, teas and smoothies.

See reverse for more information

Valid from 01.01.10 to 31.12.10

SAVE 10% OFF

Tel: 01637 859200

F12

The food used in our restaurant is fresh, local and scrumptious! Wherever possible we source our food from local suppliers. We have a bay window, which overlooks the Cape, and with stunning sunsets most nights it is definitely worth a visit.

See reverse for more information

Valid from 01.01.10 to 31.12.10

SAVE 10% OFF

Tel: 01736 788611

F13

The Chy Bar and Kitchen boasts undoubtedly one of the best views in Newquay. Overlooking Towan beach, we offer friendly service, fresh seafood specials, steaks, our famous ribs and vegetarian dishes.

See reverse for more information

Valid from 01.01.10 to 31.12.10

FREE BOTTLE OF WINE

Tel: 01637 873415

F14

Whether you require a Canapé party, Buffet, a Barbecue, Garden Party or sit-down Wedding Breakfast, CK Catering pride themselves on their ability to provide ever changing menus to suit each client's unique needs.

See reverse for more information

Valid from 01.01.10 to 31.12.10

SAVE 5% OFF

Tel: 01326 574950/ 07976596557

F15

The Corner Deli specialises in fine food, wines and wood fired pizzas to take away. Party catering, corporate sandwich platters and gift hampers also available.

See reverse for more information

Valid from 01.01.10 to 31.12.10

SAVE 10% OFF

Tel: 01326 565554

Cafe Irie
38, Fore street, Newquay,
Cornwall, TR71LP
Tel: 01637 859200

Terms & Conditions

1. Only one voucher per transaction
2. Defaced, torn or photocopied vouchers will not be accepted
3. Not to be used in conjunction with any other offer
4. Not exchangeable for cash
5. Present this voucher to the business to accept the offer
6. 10% OFF final bill with every £10 spent

Exciting, forever changing artwork on the walls and great tunes. The only place to relax, eat and enjoy in Newquay.

Cafe Irie

Cape Cornwall Golf and Leisure Resort
St. Just, Penzance, Cornwall,
TR19 7NL
Tel: 01736 788611

Terms & Conditions

1. Only one voucher per transaction
2. Defaced, torn or photocopied vouchers will not be accepted
3. Not to be used in conjunction with any other offer
4. Not exchangeable for cash
5. Present this voucher to the business to accept the offer
6. This does not include Friday Freasts or Sunday lunch

We have a wide range of food on our menu and we have daily changing specials. We are open daily from 8am for breakfast and close when the last person leaves.

Cape Cornwall Golf and Leisure Resort

Chy Bar & Kitchen
12 Beach Road, Newquay,
Cornwall, TR7 1ES
Tel: 01637 873415

Terms & Conditions

1. Only one voucher per transaction
2. Defaced, torn or photocopied vouchers will not be accepted
3. Not to be used in conjunction with any other offer
4. Not exchangeable for cash
5. Present this voucher to the business to accept the offer
6. **FREE** bottle of house wine with every 4 diners ordering a starter and main

The balcony offers additional alfresco dining. Open all day serving freshly ground Italian coffees, relaxed lunches and delicious evening meals. Available for private functions, weddings and parties.

Chy Bar & Kitchen

CK Catering
1 Gwendrona Way, Helston
Cornwall, TR13 8GW
Tel: 01326 574950/ 07976596557

Terms & Conditions

1. Only one voucher per transaction
2. Defaced, torn or photocopied vouchers will not be accepted
3. Not to be used in conjunction with any other offer
4. Not exchangeable for cash
5. Present this voucher to the business to accept the offer
6. 5% OFF any function booking

CK Catering

We can even provide a licensed bar to help you really get the party started!

Quality catering for any event.......

It's not just about the food...... but it's a great place to start!

CK Catering

The Corner Deli
12 Fore Street, Porthleven
Cornwall, TR13 9HJ
Tel: 01326 565554

Terms & Conditions

1. Only one voucher per transaction
2. Defaced, torn or photocopied vouchers will not be accepted
3. Not to be used in conjunction with any other offer
4. Not exchangeable for cash
5. Present this voucher to the business to accept the offer
6. 10% OFF your takeaway wood fired pizza with this voucher

The Corner Deli specialises in fine food, wines and wood fired pizzas to take away. Party catering, corporate sandwich platters and gift hampers also available.

The Corner Deli

The Cornish Deli

The Cornish Deli exists to bring the best quality Cornish and regional produce to its customers. It offers fantastic quality local meats, cheeses, seafood, gourmet hampers, beach picnics and regional specialities.

See reverse for more information

Valid from 01.01.10 to 31.12.10

F16

KEEP IT CORNISH

SAVE 10% OFF

Tel: 01736 795100

de Wynn's

Named after one of Falmouth's earliest entrepreneurs, de Wynn's is housed in a historic Grade II listed building that was once a hotel. The interior of the Tea & Coffee House is furnished and decorated in period style and offers a comfortable and welcoming atmosphere.

See reverse for more information

Valid from 01.01.10 to 31.12.10

F17

KEEP IT CORNISH

SAVE 15% OFF

Tel: 01326 319259

exchange

Whether it's a working lunch, a catch up with friends or a family visit, you'll find something to suit all tastes at The Exchange Cafe. Enjoy a light lunch of scrambled eggs and smoked salmon on toast with a glass of wine, our delicious soups or a slice of cake alongside the best coffee in town.

See reverse for more information

Valid from 01.01.10 to 31.12.10

F18

KEEP IT CORNISH

SAVE 10% OFF

Tel: 01736 363715

The ideal rest stop when out shopping in Truro. Situated on the ground floor of the award winning Lemon Street Market. Freshly prepared meals for all ages and tastes, from nachos to chilli, burgers to jackets, coffees to smoothies.

See reverse for more information

Valid from 01.01.10 to 31.12.10

F19

KEEP IT CORNISH

SAVE 2 FOR 1 ON MEALS

Tel: 01872 222 251

Enjoy a meal inside the award winning Lemon Street Market, situated on the first floor. The Gallery Café combines seasonal, freshly prepared dishes with a relaxed and friendly dining experience.

See reverse for more information

Valid from 01.01.10 to 31.12.10

F20

KEEP IT CORNISH

SAVE 2 FOR 1 ON MEALS

The Cornish Deli
3 Chapel Street, St. Ives, Cornwall
TR26 2LR.
Tel: 01736 795100

Terms & Conditions

1. Only one voucher per transaction
2. Defaced, torn or photocopied vouchers will not be accepted
3. Not to be used in conjunction with any other offer
4. Not exchangeable for cash
5. Present this voucher to the business to accept the offer
6. 10% OFF brunch and lunch menu (eat in meals only)
7. Offers cover all food items from the menu but excludes drinks

Incorporated within the Cornish Deli is the Deli Café, offering hot and cold drinks, brunches, lunches, afternoon tea, and Evening Meals.

The Cornish Deli

De Wynns
55 Church Street, Falmouth
Cornwall, TR11 3DS
Tel: 01326 319259

Terms & Conditions

1. Only one voucher per transaction
2. Defaced, torn or photocopied vouchers will not be accepted
3. Not to be used in conjunction with any other offer
4. Not exchangeable for cash
5. Present this voucher to the business to accept the offer
6. 15% OFF purchases over £5

The Eddy family promote local produce wherever possible and serve (among other local treats) Cornish crab, Cornish blue cheese, Davidstow Cheddar, St Endillion Brie, local clotted cream, strawberry jam made from local berries, and tea grown on nearby Tregothnan Estate.

De Wynns

The Exchange
Princes Street, Penzance
Cornwall, TR18 2NL
Tel: 01736 363715

Terms & Conditions

1. Only one voucher per transaction
2. Defaced, torn or photocopied vouchers will not be accepted
3. Not to be used in conjunction with any other offer
4. Not exchangeable for cash
5. Present this voucher to the business to accept the offer

the exchange

Group bookings are available. We are fully accessible for wheelchair users and have high chairs for the little ones. Self-service coffee facilities are available at Newlyn Art Gallery along with biscuits and cake.

Explorers Cafe
Lemon Street Market, Truro
Cornwall, TR1 2PN
Tel: 01872 222 251

Terms & Conditions

1. Only one voucher per transaction
2. Defaced, torn or photocopied vouchers will not be accepted
3. Not to be used in conjunction with any other offer
4. Not exchangeable for cash
5. Present this voucher to the business to accept the offer
6. Buy one meal get one FREE. Lowest item free. Does not include drinks or cakes

The ideal rest stop when out shopping in Truro. Situated on the ground floor of the award winning Lemon Street Market. Freshly prepared meals for all ages and tastes, from nachos to chilli, burgers to jackets, coffees to smoothies.

The Gallery Café
Lemon Street Market, Truro
Cornwall, TR1 2LQ
Tel: 01872 271 733

Terms & Conditions

1. Only one voucher per transaction
2. Defaced, torn or photocopied vouchers will not be accepted
3. Not to be used in conjunction with any other offer
4. Not exchangeable for cash
5. Present this voucher to the business to accept the offer
6. Buy one meal get one FREE. Lowest item free. Does not include drinks or cakes

the Gallery café

Adjacent to the cafe we have contemporary and classic fine art. There is the Lander Gallery which offers a selection of Contemporary, Modern British and Classic Fine Art from four centuries with a rich Cornish flavour.

HARVEY'S WHARF

F21

Harvey's Wharf is Falmouth's waterfront bar and brasserie. Boasting not only stunning views of the town's beautiful marina but also Falmouth's best fresh fish, shellfish and steaks. Why not try our new deli counter selection for lunch or antipasi.

See reverse for more information

Valid from 01.01.10 to 31.12.10

FREE BOTTLE OF WINE

Tel: 01326 314351

THE HONEY POT

COFFEE CAKE & COMPANY

F22

The Honey Pot is a top-quality and unique establishment in the middle of Penzance, opposite the Acorn Theatre. We serve the best coffees, teas, home-made cakes and sweet delights, as well as a huge range of gourmet sandwiches, soups and light lunches.

See reverse for more information

Valid from 01.01.10 to 31.12.10

FREE COFFEE & CAKE

Tel: 01736 368686

johnny's café

F23

Situated along Penpol Terrace at the Foundry end of Hayle, johnny's is a unique cafe, wholefood shop, gifts & complementary therapy centre. The cafe has an individual style where you can relax on comfy sofas or sit at recycled tables & chairs.

See reverse for more information

Valid from 01.01.10 to 31.12.10

FREE CAKE

Tel: 01736 755928

la bevanda @ CASA FINA

TRURO CORNWALL

F24

A fully licensed coffee shop and restaurant in beautiful surroundings above one of Truro's finest stores – Casa Fina Interiors. We offer a delicious selection of continental style ciabattas & paninis, salads, pastas and daily specials.

See reverse for more information

Valid from 01.01.10 to 31.12.10

FREE DRINK

Tel: 01872 270818

The Lamb & Flag Inn

F25

We firmly believe that in Cornwall, we have some of the very best produce available anywhere. Wherever possible we buy Cornish produce from local producers. Seasonal aspects mean that some items have to be sourced from further afield and some ingredients may not be available locally.

See reverse for more information

Valid from 01.01.10 to 31.12.10

FREE DESSERT

KEEP IT... FOOD

www.keepitcornish.co.uk

Harveys Wharf
Event Square, Discovery Quay
Falmouth, Cornwall, TR11 3XA
Tel: 01326 314351

Terms & Conditions

1. Only one voucher per transaction
2. Defaced, torn or photocopied vouchers will not be accepted
3. Not to be used in conjunction with any other offer
4. Not exchangeable for cash
5. Present this voucher to the business to accept the offer
6. Only available Monday - Thursday
7. **FREE** bottle of house wine with every two main meals purchased.

Harvey's Wharf is Falmouth's waterfront bar and brasserie. Boasting not only stunning views of the town's beautiful marina but also Falmouth's best fresh fish, shellfish and steaks. Why not try our new deli counter selection for lunch or antipasi.

Harveys Wharf

The Honey Pot
5 Parade Street, Penzance, Cornwall
TR18 4BU
Tel: 01736 368686

Terms & Conditions

1. Only one voucher per transaction
2. Defaced, torn or photocopied vouchers will not be accepted
3. Not to be used in conjunction with any other offer
4. Not exchangeable for cash
5. Present this voucher to the business to accept the offer
6. **FREE** coffee and cake, when two people order main course lunches from our specials board
7. Not available on Saturdays during school holidays

Our daily specials are made, as far as possible, with local and seasonal ingredients, featuring the ever-popular café favourites as well as various dishes from around the world.

Johnny's Cafe
50-51 Penpol Terrace, Hayle
Cornwall, TR27 4BQ
Tel: 01736 755928

Terms & Conditions

1. Only one voucher per transaction
2. Defaced, torn or photocopied vouchers will not be accepted
3. Not to be used in conjunction with any other offer
4. Not exchangeable for cash
5. Present this voucher to the business to accept the offer
6. **FREE** cake when you spend £10 or over.

johnny's café

We offer fresh vegan & vegetarian homemade breakfasts, lunches, cakes & evening meals (Saturday nights), which are prepared using locally sourced produce where possible, takeaways & picnics can also be catered for.

La Bevanda at Casa Fina
29 River Street, Truro, Cornwall
TR1 2SJ
Tel: 01872 270818

Terms & Conditions

1. Only one voucher per transaction
2. Defaced, torn or photocopied vouchers will not be accepted
3. Not to be used in conjunction with any other offer
4. Not exchangeable for cash
5. Present this voucher to the business to accept the offer
6. Free drink with every main course ordered

la bevanda @ CASA FINA
TRURO. CORNWALL

In addition we have a separate ice cream dessert menu and lots of yummy gateaux and pastries.

La Bevanda at Casa Fina

The Lamb & Flag Inn
Canonstown, Hayle, Cornwall
TR27 6LU
Tel: 01736 753289

Terms & Conditions

1. Only one voucher per transaction
2. Defaced, torn or photocopied vouchers will not be accepted
3. Not to be used in conjunction with any other offer
4. Not exchangeable for cash
5. Present this voucher to the business to accept the offer
6. **FREE** dessert when you order a starter and main course. Excludes set price menus
7. Excludes evenings in July and August

However, we regularly change our menus to incorporate local produce as it comes into season. To promote animal welfare and to help reduce the amount of food miles covered, we use Cornish meats from local butchers. We hope you enjoy your dining experience and look forward to seeing you soon!

F26

Healthy, Seasonal and Fresh! The Larder Delicatessen is found in the award winning Lemon Street Market. We offer a great range of freshly prepared salads and sandwiches to takeaway, alongside an excellent range of olives, fresh produce, meats and cheeses.

See reverse for more information

Valid from 01.01.10 to 31.12.10

SAVE 2 FOR 1 ON MEALS

Tel: 01872 275218

The Little Barn

F27

The Little Barn Cafe & Gallery situated at Trevescan Sennen, just off the A30 before Lands End. A unique barn converted into a cafe and gallery, with large garden and plenty of parking. Open for breakfasts, lunches and afternoon tea plus some evenings from Easter to end of October.

See reverse for more information

Valid from 01.01.10 to 31.12.10

Tel: 01736 871803

The Lugger Hotel

F28

The Lugger Hotel, is a comfortable family run hotel with its own Wheelhouse Restaurant and centrally located for the town's facilities. The hotel occupies an ideal position overlooking Mounts Bay. The Wheelhouse Restaurant is proud of its reputation for excellent cuisine.

See reverse for more information

Valid from 01.01.10 to 31.12.10

FREE CHEAPEST MEAL

Tel: 01736 363236

The Lugger Hotel

F29

The Lugger Hotel, is a comfortable family run hotel with its own Wheelhouse Restaurant and centrally located for the town's facilities. The hotel occupies an ideal position overlooking Mounts Bay. The Wheelhouse Restaurant is proud of its reputation for excellent cuisine.

See reverse for more information

Valid from 01.01.10 to 31.12.10

FREE KIDS EAT

Tel: 01736 363236

The Lugger Hotel

F30

The Lugger Hotel, is a comfortable family run hotel with its own Wheelhouse Restaurant and centrally located for the town's facilities. The hotel occupies an ideal position overlooking Mounts Bay. The Wheelhouse Restaurant is proud of its reputation for excellent cuisine.

See reverse for more information

Valid from 01.01.10 to 31.12.10

Tel: 01736 363236

The Larder Deli
Lemon Street Market, Truro
Cornwall, TR1 2PN
Tel: 01872 275218

Terms & Conditions

1. Only one voucher per transaction
2. Defaced, torn or photocopied vouchers will not be accepted
3. Not to be used in conjunction with any other offer
4. Not exchangeable for cash
5. Present this voucher to the business to accept the offer
6. Buy one meal get one **FREE**. Lowest item free. Does not include drinks or cakes

Not forgetting our specialist grocery and off licence ranges. Come and have a browse.

The Little Barn
Trevescan, Sennen, Landsend
TR19 7AQ
Tel: 01736 871803

Terms & Conditions

1. Only one voucher per transaction
2. Defaced, torn or photocopied vouchers will not be accepted
3. Not to be used in conjunction with any other offer
4. Not exchangeable for cash
5. Present this voucher to the business to accept the offer
6. **FREE** tea or coffee when you purchase a breakfast or lunch

The Little Barn

The Little Barn Cafe & Gallery situated at Trevescan Sennen, just off the A30 before Lands End. A unique barn converted into a cafe and gallery, with large garden and plenty of parking. Open for breakfasts, lunches and afternoon tea plus some evenings from Easter to end of October.

The Lugger Hotel
The Promenade, Penzance, Cornwall
TR18 4DL
Tel: 01736 363236

Terms & Conditions

1. Only one voucher per transaction
2. Defaced, torn or photocopied vouchers will not be accepted
3. Not to be used in conjunction with any other offer
4. Not exchangeable for cash
5. Present this voucher to the business to accept the offer
6. Cheapest meal **FREE** when a table of 4 have 2 courses or more from the al a carte menu

The busy restaurant and terrace make a worthy setting for enjoying our good home cooked English food, prepared and served with care and imagination. We can also offer a selection of wines with which to complement any meal. Overlooking the promenade and with a fine view of the Bay; our comfortable, well-stocked bar lounge is the perfect spot for a pleasant and relaxing evening.

The Lugger Hotel
The Promenade, Penzance, Cornwall
TR18 4DL
Tel: 01736 363236

Terms & Conditions

1. Only one voucher per transaction
2. Defaced, torn or photocopied vouchers will not be accepted
3. Not to be used in conjunction with any other offer
4. Not exchangeable for cash
5. Present this voucher to the business to accept the offer
6. Kids eat **FREE** - a child eats **FREE** with every adult ordering 2 courses or more from the al a carte menu

The busy restaurant and terrace make a worthy setting for enjoying our good home cooked English food, prepared and served with care and imagination. We can also offer a selection of wines with which to complement any meal. Overlooking the promenade and with a fine view of the Bay; our comfortable, well-stocked bar lounge is the perfect spot for a pleasant and relaxing evening.

The Lugger Hotel
The Promenade, Penzance, Cornwall
TR18 4DL
Tel: 01736 363236

Terms & Conditions

1. Only one voucher per transaction
2. Defaced, torn or photocopied vouchers will not be accepted
3. Not to be used in conjunction with any other offer
4. Not exchangeable for cash
5. Present this voucher to the business to accept the offer
6. **FREE** bottle of wine when a table of 2 has 2 courses or more from the al a carte menu

The busy restaurant and terrace make a worthy setting for enjoying our good home cooked English food, prepared and served with care and imagination. We can also offer a selection of wines with which to complement any meal. Overlooking the promenade and with a fine view of the Bay; our comfortable, well-stocked bar lounge is the perfect spot for a pleasant and relaxing evening.

Tel: 01736 363236

F31

The Lugger Hotel, is a comfortable family run hotel with its own Wheelhouse Restaurant and centrally located for the town's facilities. The hotel occupies an ideal position overlooking Mounts Bay. The Wheelhouse Restaurant is proud of its reputation for excellent cuisine.

FREE

10% OFF

See reverse for more information

Valid from 01.01.10 to 31.12.10

Tel: 01736 363236

F32

The Lugger Hotel, is a comfortable family run hotel with its own Wheelhouse Restaurant and centrally located for the town's facilities. The hotel occupies an ideal position overlooking Mounts Bay. The Wheelhouse Restaurant is proud of its reputation for excellent cuisine.

FREE

10% OFF

See reverse for more information

Valid from 01.01.10 to 31.12.10

Tel: 01872 247900

F33

One of Truro's most popular places to eat, meet and drink. From the lightest snacks to cosmopolitan cuisine; we change our menu to reflect the best of what's seasonal and local. In our bar you'll find the very latest cocktails, cool crisp international beers and an extensive and varied range of wines.

FREE

STARTER

OR **DESSERT**

See reverse for more information

Valid from 01.01.10 to 31.12.10

Tel: 01326 313481

Marine Bar & Resturant

F34

The Marine Bar & Restaurant is located at Falmouth Yacht Marina, over- looking Penryn River & country-side, with stunning scenic views! The Marine Bar has a spacious restaurant with a modern cosy bar lounge and a unique relaxing atmosphere.

SAVE

10% OFF

See reverse for more information

Valid from 01.01.10 to 31.12.10

Tel: 01872 277214

FINE ALES, WINES & SPIRITS

F35

The MI Bar can be found on lemon quay with the biggest outdoor heated and covered area in Truro. We open everyday 10am till late. Serving teas, coffees, draught and bottled beers, ales and a wide selection of wines & spirits.

FREE

CHILDREN

EAT

See reverse for more information

Valid from 01.01.10 to 31.12.10

The Lugger Hotel
The Promenade, Penzance, Cornwall
TR18 4DL
Tel: 01736 363236

Terms & Conditions

1. Only one voucher per transaction
2. Defaced, torn or photocopied vouchers will not be accepted
3. Not to be used in conjunction with any other offer
4. Not exchangeable for cash
5. Present this voucher to the business to accept the offer
6. 10% OFF final bill when a table of 4 have 2 courses or more from the al a carte menu

The busy restaurant and terrace make a worthy setting for enjoying our good home cooked English food, prepared and served with care and imagination. We can also offer a selection of wines with which to complement any meal. Overlooking the promenade and with a fine view of the Bay; our comfortable, well-stocked bar lounge is the perfect spot for a pleasant and relaxing evening.

The Lugger Hotel

The Lugger Hotel
The Promenade, Penzance, Cornwall
TR18 4DL
Tel: 01736 363236

Terms & Conditions

1. Only one voucher per transaction
2. Defaced, torn or photocopied vouchers will not be accepted
3. Not to be used in conjunction with any other offer
4. Not exchangeable for cash
5. Present this voucher to the business to accept the offer
6. 10% OFF final bill when you book to stay in a front room ensuite

The busy restaurant and terrace make a worthy setting for enjoying our good home cooked English food, prepared and served with care and imagination. We can also offer a selection of wines with which to complement any meal. Overlooking the promenade and with a fine view of the Bay; our comfortable, well-stocked bar lounge is the perfect spot for a pleasant and relaxing evening.

The Lugger Hotel

Mannings
Lemon Street, Truro, Cornwall
TR1 2QB
Tel: 01872 247900

Terms & Conditions

1. Only one voucher per transaction
2. Defaced, torn or photocopied vouchers will not be accepted
3. Not to be used in conjunction with any other offer
4. Not exchangeable for cash
5. Present this voucher to the business to accept the offer
6. **FREE** starter or dessert up to the value of £7 when purchasing any main meal from £10.95 upwards (subject to availability)

One of Truro's most popular places to eat, meet and drink. From the lightest snacks to cosmopolitan cuisine; we change our menu to reflect the best of what's seasonal and local. In our bar you'll find the very latest cocktails, cool crisp international beers and an extensive and varied range of wines.

Marine Bar and Restaurant
Falmouth Yacht Marina, Falmouth
TR11 2TD
Tel: 01326 313481

Terms & Conditions

1. Only one voucher per transaction
2. Defaced, torn or photocopied vouchers will not be accepted
3. Not to be used in conjunction with any other offer
4. Not exchangeable for cash
5. Present this voucher to the business to accept the offer
6. 10% OFF food bill. Does not include drinks

Marine Bar & Resturant

We offer an array of daily specials, local Seafood, Mediterranean, traditional English, (v), tapas, Sunday roast and more… All are welcome at the Marine bar! A fantastic venue for small/large parties, weddings etc…

LAST FRIDAY OF EVERY MONTH IS GREEK FOOD NIGHT £17.50 P.P INCL BOTTLE OF WINE PER COUPLE.

Open @ 10am - Late - BAR OPEN ALL DAY.

The MI Bar
Back Quay, Truro, Cornwall
R1 2LL
Tel: 01872 277214

Terms & Conditions

1. Only one voucher per transaction
2. Defaced, torn or photocopied vouchers will not be accepted
3. Not to be used in conjunction with any other offer
4. Not exchangeable for cash
5. Present this voucher to the business to accept the offer
6. For every adults main meal ordered, get a children's meal for **FREE**

We serve food from 12noon till 3pm daily (depending on time of year).

F36

KEEP IT CORNISH

We have been built using pioneering techniques of eco-development. We have wind turbines, solar panels and super insulation. This means our walls are at least 2 foot thick which is useful for when we have D.J's and bands in the evenings!

See reverse for more information

Valid from 01.01.10 to 31.12.10

2 MEALS FOR £10

Tel: 01326 374424

F37

The Olive Farm has been serving delicious deli food with a southern flavour at Wharfside since 2000. But now, in an ambitious and exciting new move, they have expanded into the unit next door with a wonderful menu of traditional Mediterranean food.

See reverse for more information

Valid from 01.01.10 to 31.12.10

SAVE

10% OFF

Tel: 01736 359009

F38

Pea Souk is the only Vegetarian Café in Falmouth and also produces the most interesting food in Falmouth! Pea Souk is run by Cordon Vert graduate Nicola Willis and specializes in Middle Eastern and Moroccan Cuisine as well as baking the best cakes.

See reverse for more information

Valid from 01.01.10 to 31.12.10

SAVE

ONE PERSON EATS HALF PRICE

Tel: 01326 317583

F39

Pea Souk is the only Vegetarian Café in Falmouth and also produces the most interesting food in Falmouth! Pea Souk is run by Cordon Vert graduate Nicola Willis and specializes in Middle Eastern and Moroccan Cuisine as well as baking the best cakes.

See reverse for more information

Valid from 01.01.10 to 31.12.10

SAVE

15% OFF

Tel: 01326 317583

Phoenix Cafe/Bar

F40

Located in the Phoenix Cinema Falmouth, the Phoenix Cafe /Bar is a perfect place to enjoy a bite to eat. Whether watching a film or having a relaxing evening meal, everyone is welcome. Our screens are even licensed!

See reverse for more information

Valid from 01.01.10 to 31.12.10

SAVE

25% OFF

Tel: 01326 313072

Miss Peapod's Kitchen Cafe
Jubilee Wharf, Penryn, Cornwall
TR10 8FG
Tel: 01326 374424

Terms & Conditions

1. Only one voucher per transaction
2. Defaced, torn or photocopied vouchers will not be accepted
3. Not to be used in conjunction with any other offer
4. Not exchangeable for cash
5. Present this voucher to the business to accept the offer
6. 2 meals for £10 based on 2 people sharing
7. Excludes Sundays

We are family orientated and this means children are welcome anytime to eat with their families (including in the evenings).Out on our decking (built from sustainable f.s.c timber) you can watch the boats go by up the river, whilst enjoying one of our fair trade organic coffees from a local family. How right on is that?!

Miss Peapod's Kitchen Cafe

The Olive Farm Restaurant
Units 17/18, Wharfside Shopping Centre
Penzance, Cornwall, TR18 2GB
Tel: 01736 359009

Terms & Conditions

1. Only one voucher per transaction
2. Defaced, torn or photocopied vouchers will not be accepted
3. Not to be used in conjunction with any other offer
4. Not exchangeable for cash
5. Present this voucher to the business to accept the offer
6. 10% OFF when having a 3 course meal

If you like fresh and flavorsome food The Olive Farm is a must!

The Olive Farm Restaurant

Pea Souk Cafe
19c Well Lane, Church Street
Falmouth. TR11 3EG
Tel: 01326 317583

Terms & Conditions

1. Only one voucher per transaction
2. Defaced, torn or photocopied vouchers will not be accepted
3. Not to be used in conjunction with any other offer
4. Not exchangeable for cash
5. Present this voucher to the business to accept the offer
6. If 3 people have 3 course's in the evening then the 4th can eat half price - bookings only

Some of which are now famous in Falmouth, such as the Green and Black's Brownie with chocolate fudge icing and the carrot, beetroot and orange cake. The café has the highest standards of food integrity and uses mainly organic produce from small, local suppliers and recycles nearly everything.

Pea Souk Cafe
19c Well Lane, Church Street
Falmouth. TR11 3EG
Tel: 01326 317583

Terms & Conditions

1. Only one voucher per transaction
2. Defaced, torn or photocopied vouchers will not be accepted
3. Not to be used in conjunction with any other offer
4. Not exchangeable for cash
5. Present this voucher to the business to accept the offer
6. 15% of your total bill after 2.30pm Mon - Fri. Not including alcohol

Some of which are now famous in Falmouth, such as the Green and Black's Brownie with chocolate fudge icing and the carrot, beetroot and orange cake. The café has the highest standards of food integrity and uses mainly organic produce from small, local suppliers and recycles nearly everything.

The Phoenix Cinema
11 Berkeley Vale, Falmouth, Cornwall
TR11 3PL
Tel: 01326 313072

Terms & Conditions

1. Only one voucher per transaction
2. Defaced, torn or photocopied vouchers will not be accepted
3. Not to be used in conjunction with any other offer
4. Not exchangeable for cash
5. Present this voucher to the business to accept the offer
6. 25% OFF your food bill. Does not include drinks

Phoenix Cafe/Bar

Our menu ranges from delicious deep filled pancakes and pasta dishes, to burgers and a mouthwatering choice of daily specials. We look forward to seeing you soon......

Regal Restaurant & Bar

Located in the Regal Cinema Redruth, the Regal Restaurant & Bar is a perfect place to enjoy a bite to eat. Whether watching a film or having a relaxing evening meal, everyone is welcome.

See reverse for more information

Valid from 01.01.10 to 31.12.10

SAVE 25% OFF

Tel: 01209 216278

Renaissance Café • Bar

Come down to the Renaissance & relax as our staff take care of your every need. We offer a large range of excellently prepared food and drinks, our menu has a fresh Mediterranean vibe featuring our signature oven baked pizzas.

See reverse for more information

Valid from 01.01.10 to 31.12.10

SAVE 10% OFF

Tel: 01736 366277

Roseland Inn

Deep in the heart of the Roseland Peninsula nestles a truly traditional rural Cornish pub. The Roseland Inn is a mere stones throw away from the famous King Harry Ferry, in a truly unspoilt rural setting, which is easily accessible from Falmouth, Truro and St Austell.

See reverse for more information

See reverse for details

SAVE 10% OFF

Tel: 01872 580254

sandbar praa sands

the beach at your feet

Sandbar is a relaxed beach bar set right on the bay at Praa Sands. Every seat has a sea view! Open all year round, serving good food all day from breakfasts through to supper. Excellent lunchtime carvery every Sunday with live music.

See reverse for more information

Valid from 01.01.10 to 31.12.10

FREE BOTTLE OF WINE

Tel: 01736 763516

Savoy Restaurant & Bar

Located in the Savoy Cinema Penzance, the Savoy Restaurant & Bar is a perfect place to enjoy a bite to eat. Whether watching a film or having a relaxing evening meal, everyone is welcome.

See reverse for more information

Valid from 01.01.10 to 31.12.10

SAVE 25% OFF

Tel: 01736 363330

The Regal Cinema
Regal Cinema, Fore St, Redruth
Cornwall, TR15 2AZ
Tel: 01209 216278

Terms & Conditions

1. Only one voucher per transaction
2. Defaced, torn or photocopied vouchers will not be accepted
3. Not to be used in conjunction with any other offer
4. Not exchangeable for cash
5. Present this voucher to the business to accept the offer
6. 25% OFF your food bill. Does not include drinks

Regal Restaurant & Bar

Our menu ranges from delicious home baked pizzas, to burgers and a mouthwatering choice of daily specials. We look forward to seeing you soon......

The Regal Cinema

Renaissance Café & Bar
6 Wharfside, Shopping Centre
Penzance, TR18 2GB
Tel: 01736 366277

Terms & Conditions

1. Only one voucher per transaction
2. Defaced, torn or photocopied vouchers will not be accepted
3. Not to be used in conjunction with any other offer
4. Not exchangeable for cash
5. Present this voucher to the business to accept the offer
6. 10% OFF your final bill

Renaissance Café • Bar

Come down to the Renaissance & relax as our staff take care of your every need. We offer a large range of excellently prepared food and drinks, our menu has a fresh Mediterranean vibe featuring our signature oven baked pizzas.

Roseland Inn
Roseland Inn, Philleigh-in-Roseland
Truro, TR2 5NB
Tel: 01872 580254

Terms & Conditions

1. Only one voucher per transaction
2. Defaced, torn or photocopied vouchers will not be accepted
3. Not to be used in conjunction with any other offer
4. Not exchangeable for cash
5. Present this voucher to the business to accept the offer
6. 10% OFF total bill (not including drinks)
7. Valid from 01.01.10 - 10.02.10 and 25.02.10 - 31.03.10

Roseland Inn

Phil & Debbie Heslip pride themselves on the quality of their freshly cooked foods. Whether you want to sit by the fire with a paper and a coffee, meet friends for a drink or enjoy a leisurely meal, the Roseland Inn has exactly the right kind of ambience.

Sandbar
Praa Sands, Penzance, Cornwall
TR20 9TQ
Tel: 01736 763516

Terms & Conditions

1. Only one voucher per transaction
2. Defaced, torn or photocopied vouchers will not be accepted
3. Not to be used in conjunction with any other offer
4. Not exchangeable for cash
5. Present this voucher to the business to accept the offer
6. Receive a **FREE** bottle of wine from our house selection when you spend £25 or more on a meal for 2 people
7. Strictly over 18's

Our 'Beachside Lounge' is an ideal venue for parties & weddings.

Sandbar

The Savoy Cinema
Savoy Cinema Penzance, Causewayhead
Penzance, Cornwall, TR18 2SN
Tel: 01736 363330

Terms & Conditions

1. Only one voucher per transaction
2. Defaced, torn or photocopied vouchers will not be accepted
3. Not to be used in conjunction with any other offer
4. Not exchangeable for cash
5. Present this voucher to the business to accept the offer
6. 25% OFF your food bill. Does not include drinks

Savoy Restaurant & Bar

Our menu ranges from delicious home baked pizzas, to burgers and a mouthwatering choice of daily specials. We look forward to seeing you soon......

Tel: 01637 870350

Discover the authentic taste of Mexico in this stunning theme bar and restaurant. Families welcome with children's menu. Not all Mexican food is spicy and vegetarian dishes and English meals also available.

See reverse for more information

Valid from 01.01.10 to 31.12.10

SAVE 10% OFF

Tel: 01872 260828

Shanghai Lounge

Ying as she is known by her regular guests and friends has a wealth of experience working in catering for fifteen years in China. Now bringing this wealth of talent to Truro, Ying delights customers with her delicious menu and licenced restaurant.

See reverse for more information

Valid from 01.01.10 to 31.12.10

SAVE 10% OFF

Tel: 01637 830205

St Pirans Inn

St Pirans Inn public house, Holywell Bay this wonderful pub is situated just 5 miles from Newquay and is located on the beach of Holywell. Holywell bay has just been voted the 4th best view in England and also came No.1 for the best beach in England by the National trust.

See reverse for more information

Valid from 01.01.10 to 31.12.10

FREE BOTTLE OF HOUSE WINE

Tel: 01637 873564

THE TAVERN

The Treninnick Tavern is just a short walk from the heart of bustling Newquay. Inside, the inn is equally charming, the olde worlde character of the building is blended perfectly with the new.

See reverse for more information

Valid from 01.01.10 to 31.12.10

FREE BOTTLE OF HOUSE WINE

The Falmouth Townhouse

We use the finest ingredients to create a regularly changing, seasonal modern British menu. Our team creates everything from scratch, from the gravy to the pasta. Our fresh produce comes from local boats, farms and herds. Come and sample the finest flavours in Cornwall in a stylish, relaxed setting.

See reverse for more information

Valid from 01.01.10 to 31.12.10

SAVE 20% OFF

Senor Dicks
East St, Newquay, Cornwall,
TR7 1DB
Tel: 01637 870350

Terms & Conditions

1. Only one voucher per transaction
2. Defaced, torn or photocopied vouchers will not be accepted
3. Not to be used in conjunction with any other offer
4. Not exchangeable for cash
5. Present this voucher to the business to accept the offer
6. 10% OFF food, excluding drink, subject to availability
7. Not valid during July and August or any Bank Holiday

Enjoy one of our selections of exotic cocktails in the Fiesta bar. This is one of Newquay's favorite restaurants so reservations are advisable.

Opening times: 5pm - 11pm

Senor Dicks

Shanghai Lounge
Unit 3 Highshore House
New Bridge Street, Truro, TR1 2AA
Tel: 01872 260828

Terms & Conditions

1. Only one voucher per transaction
2. Defaced, torn or photocopied vouchers will not be accepted
3. Not to be used in conjunction with any other offer
4. Not exchangeable for cash
5. Present this voucher to the business to accept the offer
6. 10% OFF food bill does not include drinks

Shanghai Lounge

Ying as she is known by her regular guests and friends has a wealth of experience working in catering for fifteen years in China. Now bringing this wealth of talent to Truro, Ying delights customers with her delicious menu and licenced restaurant. Both restaurant and takeaway menus are available.

St. Pirans Inn
Holywell Bay, Nr. Newquay
Cornwall TR8 5PP
Tel: 01637 830205

Terms & Conditions

1. Only one voucher per transaction
2. Defaced, torn or photocopied vouchers will not be accepted
3. Not to be used in conjunction with any other offer
4. Not exchangeable for cash
5. Present this voucher to the business to accept the offer
6. **FREE** bottle of house wine when 4 people have 2 or more courses

St Pirans Inn

We are now under new management with a renowned chef offering some of the best food and real ales in Cornwall.

St. Pirans Inn

The Tavern Inn
Mellanvrane Lane, Newquay
Cornwall, TR7 2LQ
Tel: 01637 873564

Terms & Conditions

1. Only one voucher per transaction
2. Defaced, torn or photocopied vouchers will not be accepted
3. Not to be used in conjunction with any other offer
4. Not exchangeable for cash
5. Present this voucher to the business to accept the offer
6. **FREE** bottle of house wine with every table booking of four

THE TAVERN

To the front is a beautiful cottage garden and patio area - an ideal place to soak up the sun - and the mass of colourful flowers in the borders, window box's and hanging baskets puts most other gardens to shame.

The Falmouth Townhouse
3 Grove Place, Falmouth
Cornwall, TR11 4AL
Tel: 01326 312009

Terms & Conditions

1. Only one voucher per transaction
2. Defaced, torn or photocopied vouchers will not be accepted
3. Not to be used in conjunction with any other offer
4. Not exchangeable for cash
5. Present this voucher to the business to accept the offer
6. 20% OFF food bill. Does not include drinks

The Falmouth Townhouse

We serve breakfast from 7.30am (8am at weekends) til 10.30am; lunch until 3pm and tapas and full menu from 6pm until 9pm. Sunday Roast (or barbeque in summer) from 12-6pm.

Tel: 01872 245011

F51

KEEP IT CORNISH

The busy Truro Cathedral Coffee Shop and Restaurant offers delicious freshly cooked food throughout the day; from breakfasts in the morning and a full lunchtime menu to cream teas in the afternoon.

See reverse for more information

Valid from 01.01.10 to 31.12.10

Tel: 01872 245011

F52

The busy Truro Cathedral Coffee Shop and Restaurant offers delicious freshly cooked food throughout the day; from breakfasts in the morning and a full lunchtime menu to cream teas in the afternoon.

See reverse for more information

Valid from 01.01.10 to 31.12.10

SAVE UPTO £4

Tel: 01736 363093

The Turks Head

F53

Experience the unique atmosphere of a place in history that is steeped in intrigue and mystery. Imagine yourself taking a drink in the same place that Pirates and Smugglers once used some 750 years ago.

See reverse for more information

Valid from 01.01.10 to 31.12.10

SAVE £5

Tel: 01736 363093

The Turks Head

F54

Experience the unique atmosphere of a place in history that is steeped in intrigue and mystery. Imagine yourself taking a drink in the same place that Pirates and Smugglers once used some 750 years ago.

See reverse for more information

Valid from 01.01.10 to 31.12.10

SAVE £5

Tel: 01736 363093

The Turks Head

F55

KEEP IT CORNISH

Experience the unique atmosphere of a place in history that is steeped in intrigue and mystery. Imagine yourself taking a drink in the same place that Pirates and Smugglers once used some 750 years ago.

See reverse for more information

Valid from 01.01.10 to 31.12.10

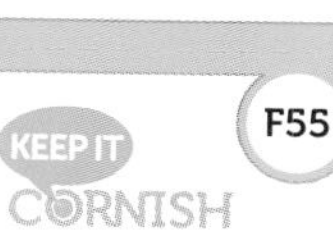

Truro Cathedral Restaurant
High Cross, Truro, Cornwall
TR1 2AF
Tel: 01872 245011

Terms & Conditions

1. Only one voucher per transaction
2. Defaced, torn or photocopied vouchers will not be accepted
3. Not to be used in conjunction with any other offer
4. Not exchangeable for cash
5. Present this voucher to the business to accept the offer
6. Voucher valid for up to 4 people per voucher (price quoted per person)
7. Seasonal Special - 2 course meal £5.95. Usually £6.95
8. Served from 12p.m. until 2.30p.m. - Monday to Friday

Contact the Restaurant Manager if you have an event you would like her to cater for. We are also fully licenced.

Open Monday to Firday 8.30am to 4pm, Saturday 9:30am - 4pm

Truro Cathedral Restaurant
High Cross, Truro, Cornwall
TR1 2AF
Tel: 01872 245011

Terms & Conditions

1. Only one voucher per transaction
2. Defaced, torn or photocopied vouchers will not be accepted
3. Not to be used in conjunction with any other offer
4. Not exchangeable for cash
5. Present this voucher to the business to accept the offer
6. Voucher valid for up to 4 people per voucher (price quoted per person)
7. Available from 10a.m – 4p.m - Monday to Saturday
8. Cornish Cream Tea £2.95, usually £3.95

Contact the Restaurant Manager if you have an event you would like her to cater for. We are also fully licenced.

Open Monday to Friday 8.30am to 4pm, Saturday 9:30am - 4pm

The Turks Head
Chapel Street, Penzance, Cornwall
TR18 4AF
Tel: 01736 363093

Terms & Conditions

1. Only one voucher per transaction
2. Defaced, torn or photocopied vouchers will not be accepted
3. Not to be used in conjunction with any other offer
4. Not exchangeable for cash
5. Present this voucher to the business to accept the offer
6. £5 OFF a meal per table at either the Turks Head or the White Heart
7. Bookings only and can be used in the evenings only

The Turks Head

This is one of of the oldest pubs in Cornwall. An underground tunnel leading from the harbour was used to secretly transport their bounty just before their evenings rest at the Public Bar. Our restaurant serves the freshest, finest local produce. Our food has been recognised by numerous awards. All you need to do is sit back and enjoy. Why not take in the Cornish sun while eating your meal Al Fresco in our covered seating area.

The Turks Head

The Turks Head
Chapel Street, Penzance, Cornwall
TR18 4AF
Tel: 01736 363093

Terms & Conditions

1. Only one voucher per transaction
2. Defaced, torn or photocopied vouchers will not be accepted
3. Not to be used in conjunction with any other offer
4. Not exchangeable for cash
5. Present this voucher to the business to accept the offer
6. £5 OFF a meal per table at either the Turks Head or the White Heart
7. Bookings only and can be used in the evenings only

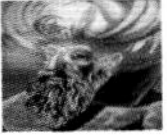

The Turks Head

This is one of of the oldest pubs in Cornwall. An underground tunnel leading from the harbour was used to secretly transport their bounty just before their evenings rest at the Public Bar. Our restaurant serves the freshest, finest local produce. Our food has been recognised by numerous awards. All you need to do is sit back and enjoy. Why not take in the Cornish sun while eating your meal Al Fresco in our covered seating area.

The Turks Head

The Turks Head
Chapel Street, Penzance, Cornwall
TR18 4AF
Tel: 01736 363093

Terms & Conditions

1. Only one voucher per transaction
2. Defaced, torn or photocopied vouchers will not be accepted
3. Not to be used in conjunction with any other offer
4. Not exchangeable for cash
5. Present this voucher to the business to accept the offer
6. £5 OFF a meal per table at either the Turks Head or the White Heart
7. Bookings only and can be used in the evenings only

The Turks Head

This is one of of the oldest pubs in Cornwall. An underground tunnel leading from the harbour was used to secretly transport their bounty just before their evenings rest at the Public Bar. Our restaurant serves the freshest, finest local produce. Our food has been recognised by numerous awards. All you need to do is sit back and enjoy. Why not take in the Cornish sun while eating your meal Al Fresco in our covered seating area.

THE WHITE HART

F56

The White Hart Ludgvan, one of the oldest pubs in Cornwall. A great place to eat...... Allow your imagination to wander as you decide what to do. Enjoy the relaxing atmosphere in the comfort of the bar area.

SAVE £5

See reverse for more information

Valid from 01.01.10 to 31.12.10

THE WHITE HART

F57

The White Hart Ludgvan, one of the oldest pubs in Cornwall. A great place to eat...... Allow your imagination to wander as you decide what to do. Enjoy the relaxing atmosphere in the comfort of the bar area.

See reverse for more information

Valid from 01.01.10 to 31.12.10

F58

Tyacks Hotel, a charming eighteenth century coaching inn nestled in the heart of Cornwall's mining heritage area. Tyacks Hotel has an array of luxurious, en-suite rooms to offer. From standard singles to honeymoon and family suites.

See reverse for more information

Valid from 01.01.10 to 31.12.10

F59

Set in the beautiful Cornish countryside opposite the famous National Trust landmark of Bowl Rock, The Tyringham Arms Inn and restaurant is a converted Victorian School building.

See reverse for more information

Valid from 01.01.10 to 31.12.10

The Victory Inn
ST MAWES CORNWALL

KEEP IT CORNISH

F60

The Victory Inn is the only traditional pub in St Mawes, Cornwall enjoyed by both locals and visitors alike. Serving lunches and dinners seven days a week, the menu contains something for everyone including fresh local seafood dishes, steaks, pasta and vegetarian options.

SAVE 10% OFF

See reverse for more information

Valid from (see reverse for details)

The White Hart
Ludgvan, Nr Penzance, Cornwall
TR20 8EY
Tel: 01736 740574

Terms & Conditions

1. Only one voucher per transaction
2. Defaced, torn or photocopied vouchers will not be accepted
3. Not to be used in conjunction with any other offer
4. Not exchangeable for cash
5. Present this voucher to the business to accept the offer
6. £5 OFF a meal per table at either the Turks Head or the White Heart
7. Bookings only and can be used in the evenings only

THE WHITE HART

Ponder over the selection of the finest food in the area from our extensive menu or simply enjoy the ambience of a local friendly pub.
Our restaurant serves the freshest, finest local produce. Our food has been recognised by numerous awards. All you need to do is sit back and enjoy.

The White Heart

The White Hart
Ludgvan, Nr Penzance, Cornwall
TR20 8EY
Tel: 01736 740574

Terms & Conditions

1. Only one voucher per transaction
2. Defaced, torn or photocopied vouchers will not be accepted
3. Not to be used in conjunction with any other offer
4. Not exchangeable for cash
5. Present this voucher to the business to accept the offer
6. £5 OFF a meal per table at either the Turks Head or the White Heart
7. Bookings only and can be used in the evenings only

THE WHITE HART

Ponder over the selection of the finest food in the area from our extensive menu or simply enjoy the ambience of a local friendly pub.
Our restaurant serves the freshest, finest local produce. Our food has been recognised by numerous awards. All you need to do is sit back and enjoy.

The White Heart

Tyacks Hotel
27 Commercial Street, Camborne
Cornwall, TR14 8LD
Tel: 01209 612424

Terms & Conditions

1. Only one voucher per transaction
2. Defaced, torn or photocopied vouchers will not be accepted
3. Not to be used in conjunction with any other offer
4. Not exchangeable for cash
5. Present this voucher to the business to accept the offer
6. Order 4 meals recieve the cheapest **FREE**

It's stylish restaurant serves delicious home-made food all day and is able to cater for any function, from a special birthday meal to wedding celebrations.Tyacks also has a West Cornwall Conference Centre close to the A30, ideal location for a small conference, meeting room or private celebration.

Tyacks Hotel

The Tyringham Arms
Old Coach Road, Trevarrack, St Ives
Cornwall, TR26 3EZ
Tel: 01736 740 434

Terms & Conditions

1. Only one voucher per transaction
2. Defaced, torn or photocopied vouchers will not be accepted
3. Not to be used in conjunction with any other offer
4. Not exchangeable for cash
5. Present this voucher to the business to accept the offer
6. 10% OFF a la carte menu. Does not include drinks

Close to the well known town of St Ives yet far enough away to relax and enjoy bustle free during the busy summer season, and our ample car park means parking is never a problem. With large gardens and children's play area sunny days can be enjoyed by all at The Tryingham Arms.

The Tyringham Arms

Victory Inn
Victory strps, St Mawes, Cornwall
TR2 5BQ
Tel: 01326 270324

Terms & Conditions

1. Only one voucher per transaction
2. Defaced, torn or photocopied vouchers will not be accepted
3. Not to be used in conjunction with any other offer
4. Not exchangeable for cash
5. Present this voucher to the business to accept the offer
6. 10% OFF total bill (not including drinks)
7. Valid from 01.01.10 - 10.02.10 and 25.02.10 - 31.03.10

Childrens menu also available. Upstairs is an elegant but informal restaurant serving the same excellent menu as well as outside seating with beautiful harbour views.

Victory Inn

The Watermill

The Watermill nestles on the old coach road in extensive mature gardens with a stunning panorama across open countryside. The garden is crossed by the mill stream which feeds the original working waterwheel.

See reverse for more information

Valid from 01.01.10 to 31.12.10

SAVE 10% OFF

Tel: 01736 757912

Whitesands restaurant serves a vast selection of food from 8.30am - 9.30pm and a wide selection of beverages up to 11.00pm. You can start your day with a full English breakfast menu which is available up till 11.30am.

See reverse for more information

Valid from 01.01.10 to 31.12.10

FREE CUP OF TEA OR COFFEE

Tel: 01736 871776

zafiros

Opened in November 2005 by Mandy, Roger, Darren, Scott and Lauren Hoare this is very much a family run establishment and our service and environment portrays this. Whether it's a light lunch or an early evening Mediterranean platter, a quiz night or live music night, Zafiros has something for everyone.

See reverse for more information

Valid from 01.01.10 to 31.12.10

FREE HOT DRINK

Tel: 01872 223163

We cover restaurants, pubs, cafes, bistros and much more.

So if you're looking for a romantic meal for two in the cobbled streets of St Ives, a welcoming pub for all the family, or just a quick bite to eat for lunch, then look no further because we have it all!

Don't forget to check out our website for more information...

www.keepitcornish.co.uk

The Watermill
Old Coach Road Lelant St-Ives
Cornwall, TR27 6LQ
Tel: 01736 757912

Terms & Conditions

1. Only one voucher per transaction
2. Defaced, torn or photocopied vouchers will not be accepted
3. Not to be used in conjunction with any other offer
4. Not exchangeable for cash
5. Present this voucher to the business to accept the offer
6. 10% OFF all food orders over £15
7. Not available during Easter holidays or throughout July and August

The Watermill

This pub and restaurant serves fine Cornish ales and an extensive bar menu of excellent, affordable meals offering a mixture of traditional and contemporary dishes. A children's menu is available and Cream Teas are served on summer afternoons.

The Watermill
www.watermillincornwall.co.uk

Whitesands Hotel Seafood Restaurant & Grill
Sennen, Nr. Land's End, TR19 7AR
Tel: 01736 871776

Terms & Conditions

1. Only one voucher per transaction
2. Defaced, torn or photocopied vouchers will not be accepted
3. Not to be used in conjunction with any other offer
4. Not exchangeable for cash
5. Present this voucher to the business to accept the offer
6. **FREE** cup of tea or coffee with each full English breakfast

White Sands hotel, b&b & restaurant

Including some of the best produce from our area, free range eggs from the farm along with oak smoked salmon from the fishmongers plus award winning sausages from our local butcher are some of what's on offer along with a varied selection of vegetarian options.

Whitesands Hotel Seafood Restaurant & Grill

Zafiros
3 New Bridge Street, Truro
Cornwall, TR1 2AA
Tel: 01872 223163

Terms & Conditions

1. Only one voucher per transaction
2. Defaced, torn or photocopied vouchers will not be accepted
3. Not to be used in conjunction with any other offer
4. Not exchangeable for cash
5. Present this voucher to the business to accept the offer
6. **FREE** hot drink with a purchase of a meal

zafiros

So come in.......sample the family atmosphere, kick your heels back and relax.

Zafiros

We cover restaurants, pubs, cafes, bistros and much more.

So if you're looking for a romantic meal for two in the cobbled streets of St Ives, a welcoming pub for all the family, or just a quick bite to eat for lunch, then look no further because we have it all

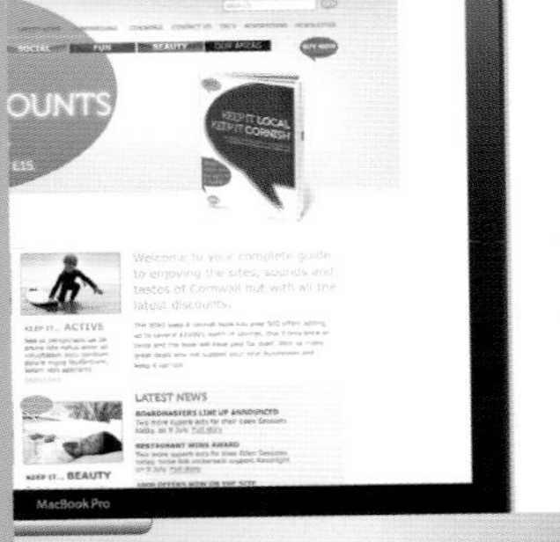

Don't forget to check out our website for more information...

www.keepitcornish.co.uk

FOOD

Fine Dining

Penzance

Bakehouse	D2-3
Boatshed	D4
Chapel Street Brasserie	D8
Cornish Range	D12
Crown	D14-15
Pizza Patio	D29

Hayle

Pizza Patio	D28
Rosewarne Manor	D33-34

St Ives

Alfresco	D1
Loft Restaurant	D23
Onshore	D27
Pizza Patio	D30
Slipways	D35
Wave Restaurant	D39

Newquay

Fistral Blu	D17
La Rochelle	D22
Rock Island Bistro	D32
Smugglers Den Inn	D36
Sugar Bar & Bistro	D37
Viners Bar & Restaurant	D38

Truro

Bustophers	D5
Chantek	D9
Falmouth Bay Seafood Cafe	D16
Mannings	D24
One Eyed Cat	D26

Falmouth

Captain's Table	D6-7
Clarks	D10
Cribbs	D13
Hut	D20
Meudon Hotel	D25
Ratho Wine Bar & Restaurant	D31
Weigela	D40-42

Porthlevan

Kota	D21

Sennen

Whitesands Hotel Seafood Restaurant & Grill	D43

Liskeard

Colliford Tavern	D11

Redruth

Golden Lion Inn	D18

Lizard

Housel Bay	D19

Welcome to the home of good food in West Cornwall. The Chapel Street Brasserie and Wine Bar in the heart of historic Penzance offers a new style of restaurant and dining to the far south west!

wine & dine

We are proud to be a member of Cornish Accredited Restaurants and of Les Routiers, a renowned and widely respected guide with an extensive collection of quality UK establishments.

In a modern, relaxed and comfortable setting you can enjoy modern, simple but delicious food with a French twist made with only the best Cornish ingredients, many sourced within a radius of about 30 miles. We are passionate about the quality of everything we offer our customers and pride ourselves on our knowledge of food and wine and we want you to find our food, atmosphere and service the best in town.

Live Music every Sunday night from 19:15 with a full dinner menu and our usual superb choice of wines and champagne. Based on the traditional French Brasserie we operate a fixed price menu system based on one, two or three courses.

ONE PERSON EATS FREE

Chapel Street Brasserie

12/13 Chapel Street, Penzance, Cornwall, TR18 4AW

T 01736 350222

www.chapelstbrasserie.com
res@chapelstbrasserie.com

Terms and conditions

- This voucher offer entitles you to one person eats FREE
- See voucher for terms and conditions

We're a smart and friendly 3* Georgian townhouse right in the centre of Truro. Thoughtfully unpretentious, the feel is stylish and contemporary but laid back and friendly.

Our Bar & Restaurant is one of Truro's largest most popular places to eat, meet and drink. The atmosphere's informal and relaxed and when we say all budgets are catered for, we mean it.

Our menu's always eclectic, and we change it to reflect the best of what's seasonal and local. We also provide a number of daily specials, running alongside our normal menu.

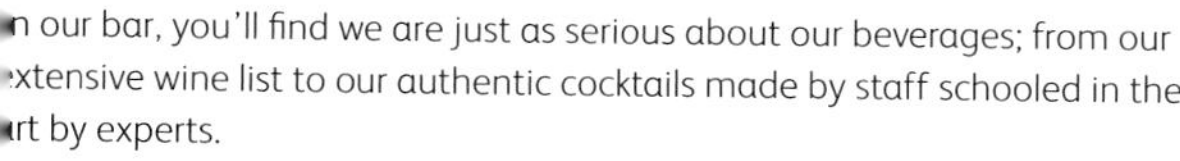

In our bar, you'll find we are just as serious about our beverages; from our extensive wine list to our authentic cocktails made by staff schooled in the art by experts.

We are open morning, afternoon and evening. So whether it's a business breakfast, leisurely lunch, pre-theatre dinner, birthday or anniversary, we have the perfect table for you. For those of you who like things a little more personal we also offer private dining..

We have the ambiance, the know how and the personable team to make your stay a special one.

Our Hotel rooms are stylish, bright and airy with a sense of having been cleverly designed with all your needs in mind. All rooms have a personality of their own, some have baths, some have walk in rain showers, some have air con, some have iPod stations, some have CD stereos, some have big beds..... one thing they all retain is the emphasis on comfort, simplicity and quality. All rooms have flat screen TV's with Sky, hairdryers, work space, free Wi-Fi, hospitality tray, iron & ironing board and toiletries.

Our Apartments are modern, fully equipped and right next door to the hotel. Their bedrooms have oversized beds, duck down duvets, fluffy pillows and en suite power showers; their fully fitted galley kitchens bristle with the most modern appliances; their well-lit workspaces have ISDN lines, free Wi-Fi, CD players and Sky TV as well as all the basics that our hotel rooms offer.

'From the moment you check in you'll notice that it's our individuality that makes us stand out from the rest..'

FREE starter or dessert

Mannings

Mannings Hotel, Lemon Street,
Truro, Cornwall. TR1 2QB

Restaurant
T 01872 247900
Hotel
T 01872 270345

reception@manningshotels.co.uk
www.manningshotels.co.uk

Restaurant Opening Hours.
Breakfast
Monday - Friday 7am - 9.30am
Saturday - 7.30am - 9.30am
Sunday - 8.30am - 11am

Lunch and Dinner
Monday - Saturday - 11am - 10pm
Sunday - 6pm - 10pm

- This voucher offer entitles you to a FREE starter or dessert
- See voucher for full terms and conditions.

Based in the Cathedral city of Truro, the multi award winning Bustophers Bar Bistro brings together the best of an upmarket Lemon Street setting and a stylish contemporary interior.

From the innovative wine list with over twenty varieties available by the glass, to the locally sourced seasonal produce found on our modern yet classic British menu, you'll experience great value dining in our friendly and relaxed environment.

We place a great emphasis on seasonal produce here at Bustophers but also a commitment in showcasing the providence of so many fantastic regional producers like Baker Toms, Roskillys, Tregothnan Estate, Camel Valley, Angus Trotters, and more!

Why not drop in for a mid-morning cappuccino with the paper, enjoy a steaming bowl of mussels over lunch with friends, or relax in our alfresco courtyard in the afternoon with a pot of Tregothnan Estate Tea.

Take advantage of our 'Prix Fixe Menu" ideal for a swift early evening supper before the theatre or cinema starts, or enjoy a romantic evening meal with a loved one over a fine bottle of Burgundy – Bustophers meets the needs of the occasion throughout the day.

FREE pudding

Bustophers

62 Lemon Street, Truro, Cornwall
TR1 2PN

T 01872 279029
www.bustophersbarbistro.com

Opening Hours.
11am - 11pm everyday

Food.
12pm - 2.30pm
5.30pm - 9.30pm

- This voucher offer entitles you to a FREE pudding
- See voucher for terms and conditions.

Tucked away in a back lane of the fishing village of Mousehole, between Penzance and Land's End, the Cornish Range has evolved into one of Cornwall's foremost seafood restaurants.

The restaurant's aim is to produce memorable meals in an unstuffy, relaxed atmosphere to suit a mixture of holiday makers and local people who form its clientele. Three contemporary & stylish en-suite guest bedrooms, make the Cornish Range a welcoming base for exploring this beautiful & historic part of the country. Formerly a pilchard-processing factory, pressing & salting pilchards landed by local fishing boats, the Range still hold its roots and is primarily a seafood restaurant. Dishes are created using local ingredients - fresh fish landed & delivered daily from the port of Newlyn, meat from local hill farms, Cornish vegetables & salads and the finest West Country cheeses.

The Cornish Range

10% OFF your final bill

The Cornish Range

Cornish Range, 6 Chapel Street, Mousehole, Cornwall, TR19 6SB

01736 731488
www.cornishrange.co.uk

Restaurant Opening Hours.
Monday - Sunday
10:00am - 2:00pm
6:00pm - 9:00pm

- This voucher offer entitles you to 10% off your bill.
- See voucher for terms and conditions

The Smugglers' Den is the only place to be after a day by the sea...

A 16th Century, thatched inn with family room, beer garden, children's play area and ample parking. Discover for yourself a place that the locals know about, but don't always tell you.

Enjoy a truly delicious lunch or evening meal in our sixteenth century inn, near Cubert and less than a 15 minute drive from Newquay. We use the freshest local ingredients in our kitchen and have developed our enviable reputation for our fabulous daily specials.

The Smugglers' is also renowned for its real ales, fine wines, entertainment and friendly welcome. We are also listed in the CAMRA guide and The AA Good Pub Guide.

10% OFF your final bill

The Smugglers' Den Inn

Trebellan, Cubert, Newquay, Cornwall, TR8 5PY

T 01637 830209
www.thesmugglersden.co.uk

Opening Hours.
11.30am - 3.00pm
6.00pm - 11.00pm
Times vary depending on season so please phone in advance

- This voucher offer entitles you to 10% off your bill.
- See voucher for terms and conditions.

We cover restaurants, pubs, cafes, bistros and much more. So if you're looking for a romantic meal for two in the cobbled streets of St Ives, a welcoming pub for all the family, or just a quick bite to eat for lunch, then look no further because we have it all!

Fine Dining

DON'T FORGET TO CHECK OUT OUR WEBSITE FOR A COMPREHENSIVE LISTING OF PLACES TO SHOP, EAT, DRINK & BE MERRY ALONG WITH SOME EXCELLENT IDEAS FOR DAYS OUT

www.keepitcornish.co.uk

SAVINGS, DISCOUNTS & ADVENTURE

OVER 300 OFFERS FROM ADVENTURE PARKS TO RESTAURANTS

TR26 1LG
Tel: 01736 793737

D1

KEEP IT CORNISH

Located on the picturesque harbourside at St. Ives. Friendly staff welcome you to sample the local seafood with a Mediterranean twist at this open-fronted Continental style restaurant with seating outside.

See reverse for more information

Valid from 01.01.10 to 31.12.10

SAVE **10% OFF**

Penzance, Cornwall, TR18 4AE
Tel: 01736 331331

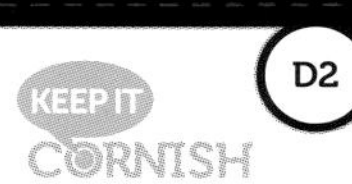

D2

KEEP IT CORNISH

Hidden just off Chapel Street, Penzance in it's own beautiful courtyard you will find The Bakehouse Restaurant. For Six Years Andy and Rachel Carr have been delighting their customers with the quality of the food and service at the Bakehouse.

See reverse for more information

Valid from 01.01.10 to 31.12.10

SAVE **10% OFF**

Penzance, Cornwall, TR18 4AE
Tel: 01736 331331

D3

KEEP IT CORNISH

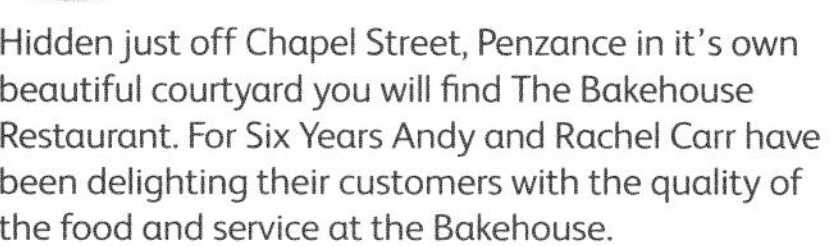

Hidden just off Chapel Street, Penzance in it's own beautiful courtyard you will find The Bakehouse Restaurant. For Six Years Andy and Rachel Carr have been delighting their customers with the quality of the food and service at the Bakehouse.

See reverse for more information

Valid from 01.01.10 to 31.12.10

FREE BOTTLE OF **HOUSE WINE**

TR18 4AS
Tel: 01736 368845

boatshed cafe-bar

D4

KEEP IT CORNISH

The Boatshed Cafe-Bar has fresh local sea food, succulent cornish steaks, chefs daily specials, inspirational vegetarian dishes. Dine beneath old ships timbers in this historic harbourside building.

See reverse for more information

Valid from 01.01.10 to 31.12.10

SAVE **10% OFF**

Tel: 01872 279029

D5

KEEP IT CORNISH

Welcome to Bustophers Bar Bistro, Truro - Cornwall's finest dining experience. A lot of fun yet at its own pace. A wine bar and restaurant that offers classic, stylish and great value dining, set in wonderful surroundings.

See reverse for more information

Valid from 01.01.10 to 31.12.10

SAVE **FREE PUDDING**

Alfresco Cafe Bar Restaurant
Wharf Road, St.Ives, Cornwall
TR26 1LG
Tel: 01736 793737

Terms & Conditions

1. Only one voucher per transaction
2. Defaced, torn or photocopied vouchers will not be accepted
3. Not to be used in conjunction with any other offer
4. Not exchangeable for cash
5. Present this voucher to the business to accept the offer
6. 10% OFF final bill
7. Must purchase a starter, main and dessert

A recent visit to Alfresco by the Environmental Health Officer (EHO) resulted in the highest accolade for cleanliness possible: 5 Stars. Alfresco features in the Which? Good Food Guide and is also Michelin recommended. Alfresco has also secured the highest honour possible from Cornwall Healthier Eating And Food Safety - the prestigious Gold Award!

Alfresco Cafe Bar Restaurant

The Bakehouse Restaurnat
Old Bakehouse Lane,, Chapel Street,
Penzance, Cornwall , TR18 4AE
Tel: 01736 331331

Terms & Conditions

1. Only one voucher per transaction
2. Defaced, torn or photocopied vouchers will not be accepted
3. Not to be used in conjunction with any other offer
4. Not exchangeable for cash
5. Present this voucher to the business to accept the offer
6. 10% off week nights only (excluding Early Bird Menu)

Using the Best local produce available, cooked simply to let its flavour and quality shine.

The Bakehouse Restaurnat

The Bakehouse Restaurant
Old Bakehouse Lane, Chapel Street,
Penzance, Cornwall , TR18 4AE
Tel: 01736 331331

Terms & Conditions

1. Only one voucher per transaction
2. Defaced, torn or photocopied vouchers will not be accepted
3. Not to be used in conjunction with any other offer
4. Not exchangeable for cash
5. Present this voucher to the business to accept the offer
6. Bottle of house wine with bookings for a table for four (Week days only, excluding early bird menu)

Using the Best local produce available, cooked simply to let its flavour and quality shine.

The Bakehouse Restaurnat

Boatshed Cafe - Bar
Wharf Road, Penzance ,Cornwall,
TR18 4AS
Tel: 01736 368845

Terms & Conditions

1. Only one voucher per transaction
2. Defaced, torn or photocopied vouchers will not be accepted
3. Not to be used in conjunction with any other offer
4. Not exchangeable for cash
5. Present this voucher to the business to accept the offer

boatshed cafe-bar

The Boatshed Cafe-Bar has fresh local sea food, succulent cornish steaks, chefs daily specials, inspirational vegetarian dishes. Dine beneath old ships timbers in this historic harbourside building.

Boatshed Cafe - Bar

Bustophers
62 Lemon Street, Truro,
Cornwall, TR1 2PN
Tel: 01872 279029

Terms & Conditions

1. Only one voucher per transaction
2. Defaced, torn or photocopied vouchers will not be accepted
3. Not to be used in conjunction with any other offer
4. Not exchangeable for cash
5. Present this voucher to the business to accept the offer
6. The offer entitles customers to a complimentary pudding when a starter & main course are purchased together on Sunday nights only

Bustophers has all the elements of a first rate venue to wine & dine. The wine list is one of the most innovative, balanced and exclusive around. Come and sample Cornwall's finest and most atmospheric dining experience serving modern British cuisine paired with progressive seasonal produce.

Bustophers

CAPTAIN'S Table

The Captains table is a traditional seafood and grill restaurant with a very friendly and warm atmosphere, all of our produce is sourced locally because we believe in doing that little bit more for local businesses.

See reverse for more information

Valid from 01.01.10 to 31.12.10

SAVE

UPTO **£20**

TR11 4AU
Tel: 01326 218999

D7

The Captains table is a traditional seafood and grill restaurant with a very friendly and warm atmosphere, all of our produce is sourced locally because we believe in doing that little bit more for local businesses.

See reverse for more information

Valid from 01.01.10 to 31.12.10

UPTO **£13**

TR11 4AU
Tel: 01326 218999

D8

Based in the heart of historic Penzance, the Chapel Street Brasserie & Wine bar has an excellent reputation for top class food and service along with the best selection of wines in town.

See reverse for more information

Valid from 01.01.10 to 31.12.10

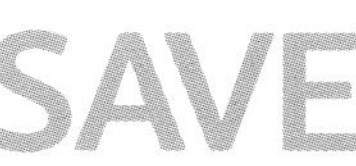

ONE PERSON EATS **FREE**

Cornwall, TR18 4AW
Tel: 01736 350222

Located in the heart of Truro, Chantek offers a exciting menu of authentic Thai and South East Asian cuisine. Beautiful decor, a lively atmosphere buzzing with the drama of an open kitchen and friendly staff combine to ensure that Chantek has established itself as one of Cornwall's top restaurants.

See reverse for more information

Valid from 01.01.10 to 31.12.10

BOTTLE OF BUBBLY

Cornwall, TR1 2AA
Tel: 01872 225071

D10

Situated in a prominent position in Falmouth's Arwenack Street, Clark's Restaurant was established in May 2005 by husband and wife team; Barry and Naomi Clark, aided by talented head chef Mark Horrell.

See reverse for more information

Valid from 01.01.10 to 31.12.10

Tel: 01326 312678

Terms & Conditions

1. Only one voucher per transaction
2. Defaced, torn or photocopied vouchers will not be accepted
3. Not to be used in conjunction with any other offer
4. Not exchangeable for cash
5. Present this voucher to the business to accept the offer
6. One voucher used per table for upto 4 people
7. Offer is valid every night excluding wednesdays
8. Offer is a Rib Eye Steak with all the trimmings and a glass of house wine for £13.50, normal price £18.50

Tel: 01326 218999

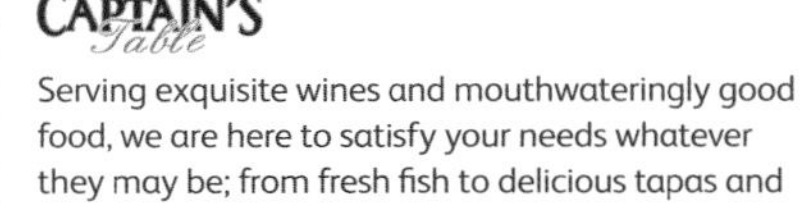

Serving exquisite wines and mouthwateringly good food, we are here to satisfy your needs whatever they may be; from fresh fish to delicious tapas and sumptuous steaks, our menu has everything you could want and more!

Terms & Conditions

1. Only one voucher per transaction
2. Defaced, torn or photocopied vouchers will not be accepted
3. Not to be used in conjunction with any other offer
4. Not exchangeable for cash
5. Present this voucher to the business to accept the offer
6. One voucher used per couple per order
7. Offer is for Paella night, only valid on a wednesday night
8. Receive Paella for two to share for £25, normally £30, as well as a small glass of house wine per person

Tel: 01326 218999

Serving exquisite wines and mouthwateringly good food, we are here to satisfy your needs whatever they may be; from fresh fish to delicious tapas and sumptuous steaks, our menu has everything you could want and more!

Terms & Conditions

1. Only one voucher per transaction
2. Defaced, torn or photocopied vouchers will not be accepted
3. Not to be used in conjunction with any other offer
4. Not exchangeable for cash or gift vouchers
5. Present this voucher to the business to accept the offer
6. One person eats FREE when 4 people dine
7. Valid Monday to Thurdays. Excludes early dining, Christmas and special offer promotional menus.
8. Reservations essential and please quote "**Keep it Cornish**"

Tel: 01736 350222

Chapel Street
Brasserie & Wine Bar

Enjoy lovingly prepared Cornish produce, tantalising desserts and the fantastic atmosphere of the Brasserie. Main menu from

£15 -£20 for 2 courses.

Live music every Sunday night.

Terms & Conditions

1. Only one voucher per transaction
2. Defaced, torn or photocopied vouchers will not be accepted
3. Not to be used in conjunction with any other offer
4. Not exchangeable for cash
5. Present this voucher to the business to accept the offer
6. Booking required for Birthday offer, minimum party of 4
7. Birthday drink is sparkling Cava Portaceli Reserva or similar quality
8. Excludes December and 14th Feb
9. Proof of birth date required

Tel: 01872 225071

Located in the heart of Truro, Chantek offers a exciting menu of authentic Thai and South East Asian cuisine. Beautiful decor, a lively atmosphere buzzing with the drama of an open kitchen and friendly staff combine to ensure that Chantek has established itself as one of Cornwall's top restaurants.

Terms & Conditions

1. Only one voucher per transaction
2. Defaced, torn or photocopied vouchers will not be accepted
3. Not to be used in conjunction with any other offer
4. Not exchangeable for cash
5. Present this voucher to the business to accept the offer
6. 10% OFF al a carte menu

Tel: 01326 312678

Offering an extensive menu of traditional English fayre alongside local seafood dishes, Clarks prides itself on offering delicious, imaginative & value for money dishes. Clark's is open seven days a week, lunchtimes & evenings throughout the year; so whether you're looking for coffee and cake at lunchtime, an early bird special menu, a sumptuous three course meal or a venue for a party then Clark's is the place to try.

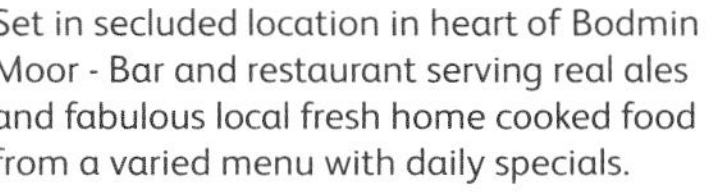

Set in secluded location in heart of Bodmin Moor - Bar and restaurant serving real ales and fabulous local fresh home cooked food from a varied menu with daily specials.

See reverse for more information

Valid from 01.01.10 to 31.12.10

FREE BOTTLE OF WINE

D12

The Cornish Range

Tucked away in a backlane of the fishing village of Mousehole, between Penzance and Land's End, the Cornish Range has evolved into one of Cornwall's foremost seafood restaurants.

See reverse for more information

Valid from 01.01.10 to 31.12.10

SAVE 10% OFF

D13

CRIBBS
Dine & Lounge
-Caribbean Restaurant-
...Falmouth...
Bar-Cafe-Restaurant
01326 210000

Always a popular corner this med-style Bistro has been transformed with the warmth of its owners smile. A fresh vibe in Falmouth a different menu of classic dishes with a Caribbean twist, combined with local produce.

See reverse for more information

Valid from 01.01.10 to 31.12.10

SAVE 10% OFF

D14

THE CROWN

Family run free house presently in the good beer guide serving three real ales including Otter and a Cornish beer. Serving over 60 spirits, a dozen wines and a selection of hot and cold drinks including fresh ground espresso coffee.

See reverse for more information

Valid from 01.01.10 to 31.12.10

SAVE 20% OFF

D15

KEEP IT CORNISH

THE CROWN

Family run free house presently in the good beer guide serving three real ales including Otter and a Cornish beer. Serving over 60 spirits, a dozen wines and a selection of hot and cold drinks including fresh ground espresso coffee.

See reverse for more information

Valid from 01.01.10 to 31.12.10

SAVE BUY ONE PIZZA GET ONE HALF PRICE

Colliford Tavern
Colliford Lake, Nr St. Neot., Liskeard
Cornwall, PL14 6PZ
Tel: 01208 821335

Terms & Conditions

1. Only one voucher per transaction
2. Defaced, torn or photocopied vouchers will not be accepted
3. Not to be used in conjunction with any other offer
4. Not exchangeable for cash
5. Present this voucher to the business to accept the offer
6. **FREE** bottle of wine with 2 people having two courses
7. Present voucher prior to food order

Bed and breakfast available as well as 1st class camping and touring caravan or motorhome facilities. Near to Colliford Lake and Kids Kingdom adventure park - ideal for family day out or walks and fishing on the lake.

Colliford Tavern
www.colliford.com

The Cornish Range
6 Chapel Street, Mousehole
Cornwall, TR19 6SB
Tel: 01736 731488

Terms & Conditions

1. Only one voucher per transaction
2. Defaced, torn or photocopied vouchers will not be accepted
3. Not to be used in conjunction with any other offer
4. Not exchangeable for cash
5. Present this voucher to the business to accept the offer
6. 10% OFF your food bill, does not include drinks

The restaurant's aim is to produce memorable meals in an unstuffy, relaxed atmosphere to suit a mixture of holiday makers and local people who form its clientele.

The Cornish Range
www.cornishrange.co.uk

Cribbs
33 Arwenack Street, Falmouth
Cornwall, TR11 3JE
Tel: 01326 210000

Terms & Conditions

1. Only one voucher per transaction
2. Defaced, torn or photocopied vouchers will not be accepted
3. Not to be used in conjunction with any other offer
4. Not exchangeable for cash
5. Present this voucher to the business to accept the offer
6. This offer excludes our Meal deal and Saturdays
7. 10% OFF our main menu and lunch menu

Open everyday of the week!

The Crown
1 Victoria Square, Penzance,
Cornwall, TR18 2EP
Tel: 01736 351070

Terms & Conditions

1. Only one voucher per transaction
2. Defaced, torn or photocopied vouchers will not be accepted
3. Not to be used in conjunction with any other offer
4. Not exchangeable for cash
5. Present this voucher to the business to accept the offer
6. 20% OFF when you buy a bottle of wine with a meal.

THE CROWN

Home cooked food is served throughout the year including Sunday Roast.

The Crown

The Crown
1 Victoria Square, Penzance,
Cornwall, TR18 2EP
Tel: 01736 351070

Terms & Conditions

1. Only one voucher per transaction
2. Defaced, torn or photocopied vouchers will not be accepted
3. Not to be used in conjunction with any other offer
4. Not exchangeable for cash
5. Present this voucher to the business to accept the offer

THE CROWN

Home cooked food is served throughout the year including Sunday Roast.

The Crown

D16

FALMOUTH BAY Seafood Café

KEEP IT CORNISH

Truro's only dedicated fish restaurant. Come and enjoy a quintessentially British approach to local oysters and shellfish. Fresh fish landed daily as well as daily specials, cooked to order by our chef in our elegant venue on Castle Street, Truro.

£5

See reverse for more information

Valid from 01.01.10 to 31.12.10

Cornwall, TR1 3AF
Tel: 01872 278884

D17

FISTRALBLU bar restaurant

KEEP IT CORNISH

Fistral Blu Restaurant perched on the edge of Fistral beach Newquay offers great food & drink to suit all. Over looking magnificent 180 degree views across the bay, capturing the essence of that chilled out surf vibe.

SAVE **10% OFF**

See reverse for more information

Valid from 01.01.10 to 31.12.10

Newquay, Cornwall TR7 1HY
Tel: 01637 879444

D18

The Golden Lion Inn

KEEP IT CORNISH

Enjoy some of the best food the county has to offer in one of the most beautiful settings in Cornwall. Choose between dining in our traditional Bar beside a real log fire, in our Restaurant overlooking the Lake, or in our award winning Gardens, with full Waitress Service throughout.

FREE **BOTTLE OF HOUSE WINE**

See reverse for more information

Valid from 01.01.10 to 31.12.10

Tel: 01209 860332

D19

KEEP IT CORNISH

Nestled in Housel Cove near the Lizard, Housel Bay Hotel (Established in 1894) is a small, family run business with its own unique character and charm. This Victorian hotel has unspoiled views of the Cornish coastline and across the Atlantic Ocean.

See reverse for more information

Valid from 01.01.10 to 31.12.10

Tel: 01326 290417/917

D20

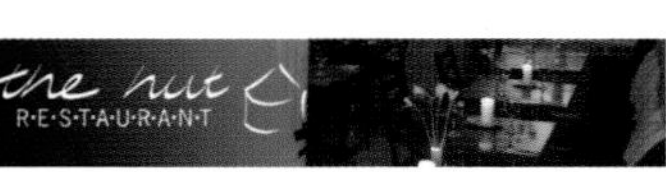

The Hut Restaurant is cosy and intimate with just 32 seats. We serve a mix of fresh local Seafood. Our seafood platter varies depending on the days catch. Mussels, crab, monkfish, smoked haddock, guarnard, pollock and lemon sole all regularly included.

FREE **BOTTLE OF WINE**

See reverse for more information

Valid from 26.01.10 to 31.03.10 & 10.09.10 to 31.12.11

Tel: 01326 318 229

Falmouth Bay Seafood Cafe
Castle Lodge, 10 Castle Street, Truro
Cornwall, TR1 3AF
Tel: 01872 278884

Terms & Conditions

1. Only one voucher per transaction
2. Defaced, torn or photocopied vouchers will not be accepted
3. Not to be used in conjunction with any other offer
4. Not exchangeable for cash
5. Present this voucher to the business to accept the offer
6. Save £5 per party when you spend a minimum of £15.00

With its beautiful South facing garden overlooking Truro River. Wonderful food matched by an easy drinking wine list, local ales and much more…

Falmouth Bay Seafood Cafe
www.falmouthbayseafoodcafe.com

Fistral Blu
Fistral Beach, Headland Road
Newquay, Cornwall TR7 1HY
Tel: 01637 879444

Terms & Conditions

1. Only one voucher per transaction
2. Defaced, torn or photocopied vouchers will not be accepted
3. Not to be used in conjunction with any other offer
4. Not exchangeable for cash
5. Present this voucher to the business to accept the offer
6. Voucher not to be used with other offers, set menus or loyalty cards

Fistral Blu is a perfect venue for any occasion from weddings to birthday celebrations. Guests can enjoy awe-inspiring sunsets from our new beach bar adding a hopelessly romantic backdrop to your evening all suited on Fistral beach Newquay.

Fistral Blu

The Golden Lion Inn
Stithians Lake, Menherion,
Nr. Redruth, TR16 6NW
Tel: 01209 860332

Terms & Conditions

1. Only one voucher per transaction
2. Defaced, torn or photocopied vouchers will not be accepted
3. Not to be used in conjunction with any other offer
4. Not exchangeable for cash
5. Present this voucher to the business to accept the offer
6. The Voucher is valid on Monday to Thursdays only
7. The Voucher cannot be used on the following dates in 2010: April 5 - May 3, July & August, December 27, 28
8. **FREE** bottle of house wine with every booking of 4 or more adults each ordering a main course

The Golden Lion Inn

Enjoy some of the best food the county has to offer in one of the most beautiful settings in Cornwall.

The Golden Lion Inn

Housel Bay
The Lizard, Cornwall
TR12 7PG
Tel: 01326 290417/917

Terms & Conditions

1. Only one voucher per transaction
2. Defaced, torn or photocopied vouchers will not be accepted
3. Not to be used in conjunction with any other offer
4. Not exchangeable for cash
5. Present this voucher to the business to accept the offer
6. 5% OFF your final bill

Relaxed dining in the bar is available for lunch, dinner, morning and afternoon teas. Open to non-residents, the Housel View Restaurant features contemporary, daily changing menus, show casing the best of local, seasonal produce, including organic, free range and also wild ingredients, foraged by our head chef Fiona Were. Our style is classical with modern and international twists.

Housel Bay

The Hut
2 Quay Street, Falmouth
Cornwall, TR11 3HH.
Tel: 01326 318 229

Terms & Conditions

1. Only one voucher per transaction
2. Defaced, torn or photocopied vouchers will not be accepted
3. Not to be used in conjunction with any other offer
4. Not exchangeable for cash
5. Present this voucher to the business to accept the offer
6. **FREE** bottle of red or white wine when 2 people have three courses each

We serve steaks, duck, lamb, chicken and also cater for vegetarians and vegans. All our desserts are homemade. Firm favourites are the creme brulee, cheesecake and apple crumble served with Cornish clotted cream.

The Hut

D21

KEEP IT CORNISH

Kota, meaning 'shellfish' in Maori (chef Jude is from New Zealand) offers fresh exciting food using the best local produce with a slight Asian twist. Named by The Telegraph as one of the Top 50 Summer Restaurants in Britain (Aug 09).

See reverse for more information

Valid from 08.02.10 to 31.12.10

FREE OYSTER TEMPURA

Cornwall TR13 9JA
Tel: 01326 562407

D22

La Rochelle French Restaurant

KEEP IT CORNISH

La Rochelle is open for dinner daily serving superb food, excellent wines with attentive but discreet service.

See reverse for more information

Valid from 01.01.10 to 31.12.10

SAVE 25% OFF

Cornwall, TR7 1DB
Tel: 01637 873455

D23

KEEP IT CORNISH

The Loft is situated in the heart of old St Ives' artists' quarter, overlooking St Ives Bay & Godrevy Lighthouse. Our menu offers mouthwatering dishes prepared by our award winning chef using the best produce our beautiful county has to offer, including fresh fish and seafood.

See reverse for more information

Valid from 01.01.10 to 31.12.10

FREE DESSERT

Tel: 01736 794204

D24

KEEP IT CORNISH

One of Truro's most popular places to eat, meet and drink. From the lightest snacks to cosmopolitan cuisine; we change our menu to reflect the best of what's seasonal and local. In our bar you'll find the very latest cocktails, cool crisp international beers and an extensive and varied range of wines.

See reverse for more information

Valid from 01.01.10 to 31.12.10

FREE STARTER OR DESSERT

Tel: 01872 247900

D25

Meudon Hotel

Meudon's elegant conservatory restaurant offers fabulous cuisine created using only the best local produce. Dine beneath a fruiting vine where every table has a garden view. Daily seafood specialities are sourced straight from the sea by Cornish fishermen.

See reverse for more information

Valid from 01.02.10 to 31.12.10

FREE GLASS OF HOUSE WINE

Tel: 01326 250541

Kota Restaurant with Rooms
Harbour Head, Porthleven,
Cornwall TR13 9JA
Tel: 01326 562407

Terms & Conditions

1. Only one voucher per transaction
2. Defaced, torn or photocopied vouchers will not be accepted
3. Not to be used in conjunction with any other offer
4. Not exchangeable for cash
5. Present this voucher to the business to accept the offer
6. **FREE** Tempura oyster with wasabi tartare when ordering a Kota champagne cocktail

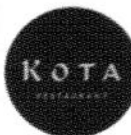

Recognised by all the top guides, Kota is situated on the idyllic quayside of Porthleven. Kota has the added bonus of an extensive wine list and two en-suite double rooms.

La Rochelle Restaurant
Hotel Victoria, East Street, Newquay
Cornwall, TR7 1DB
Tel: 01637 873455

Terms & Conditions

1. Only one voucher per transaction
2. Defaced, torn or photocopied vouchers will not be accepted
3. Not to be used in conjunction with any other offer
4. Not exchangeable for cash
5. Present this voucher to the business to accept the offer
6. 25% OFF food bill when ordering 3 courses per person

La Rochelle is open for dinner daily serving superb food, excellent wines with attentive but discreet service.

The ideal venue for celebrations and life events.

The Loft Restaurant & Terrace
Norway Lane, St Ives, Cornwall
TR26 1LZ
Tel: 01736 794204

Terms & Conditions

1. Only one voucher per transaction
2. Defaced, torn or photocopied vouchers will not be accepted
3. Not to be used in conjunction with any other offer
4. Not exchangeable for cash
5. Present this voucher to the business to accept the offer
6. **FREE** dessert of choice for every customer purchasing both a starter and main course from our regular dinner menu
7. Valid for a maximum group size of 6

However, our carnivorous and vegetarian guests will not be disappointed! Whether you are visiting for a coffee, a glass of chilled wine or a sumptuous meal, we guarantee your experience will be enjoyable. The restaurant, a former sail loft is bursting with charm.

Mannings
Lemon Street, Truro, Cornwall
TR1 2QB
Tel: 01872 247900

Terms & Conditions

1. Only one voucher per transaction
2. Defaced, torn or photocopied vouchers will not be accepted
3. Not to be used in conjunction with any other offer
4. Not exchangeable for cash
5. Present this voucher to the business to accept the offer
6. **FREE** starter or dessert up to the value of £7 when purchasing any main meal from £10.95 upwards (subject to availability)

One of Truro's most popular places to eat, meet and drink. From the lightest snacks to cosmopolitan cuisine; we change our menu to reflect the best of what's seasonal and local. In our bar you'll find the very latest cocktails, cool crisp international beers and an extensive and varied range of wines.

Meudon
Mawnan Smith, Falmouth, South
Cornwall, TR11 5HT
Tel: 01326 250541

Terms & Conditions

1. Only one voucher per transaction
2. Defaced, torn or photocopied vouchers will not be accepted
3. Not to be used in conjunction with any other offer
4. Not exchangeable for cash
5. Present this voucher to the business to accept the offer
6. **FREE** glass of house Chardonnay, house Merlot or soft drink when you dine in Meudon's Conservatory restaurant

Fine wines from the old and new world compliment your evening perfectly.

The One Eyed Cat is a beautifully converted 19th Century Chapel, now operating as a Bar and Brasserie offering a professional, but relaxed and friendly atmosphere.

SAVE 15% OFF

See reverse for more information

Valid from 01.01.10 to 31.12.10

onshore

Onshore is an award winning Meditaranean seafood, pasta and pizza restaurant situated on the delightful harbourside in the bustling Cornish town of St Ives.

SAVE 15% OFF

See reverse for more information

Valid from 01.01.10 to 31.12.10

The Pizza Patio Al Fresco are Hayle, St Ives and Newlyn's premier mediterranean al fresco pizza and pasta restaurants. Eat with us at Hayle and drink in the view that reaches across from Phillack Church down towards the Harbour.

SAVE 10% OFF

See reverse for more information

Valid from 01.01.10 to 31.12.10

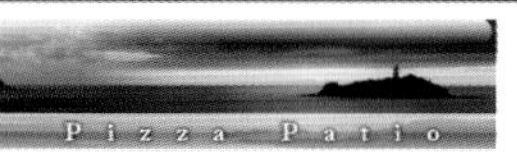

D29

The Pizza Patio Al Fresco are Hayle, St Ives and Newlyn's premier Mediterranean al fresco pizza and pasta restaurants. What about an evening in Mount's Bay? Then try our restaurant at Newlyn!

SAVE 10% OFF

See reverse for more information

Valid from 01.01.10 to 31.12.10

The Pizza Patio Al Fresco are Hayle, St Ives and Newlyn's premier mediterranean al fresco pizza and pasta restaurants. There's our restaurant in St. Ives, overlooking the quaint meandering streets of the legendary fishing town.

SAVE 10% OFF

See reverse for more information

Valid from 01.01.10 to 31.12.10

Tel: 01872 222122

Tel: 01736 753745

Tel: 01736 363446

The One Eyed Cat
The One Eyed Cat, 116 Kenwyn St, Truro, TR1 1DJ
Tel: 01872 222122

Terms & Conditions

1. Only one voucher per transaction
2. Defaced, torn or photocopied vouchers will not be accepted
3. Not to be used in conjunction with any other offer
4. Not exchangeable for cash
5. Present this voucher to the business to accept the offer
6. 15% OFF food and drink bill

Being renowned for our fresh, local produce we welcome families, friends or work colleagues to lunch or dinner, or even just to pop in for a drink. We hope this makes the "purrrrrfect destination" for you.

Onshore
Wharf rd, St Ives, Cornwall, TR26 1LF
Tel: 01736 796000

Terms & Conditions

1. Only one voucher per transaction
2. Defaced, torn or photocopied vouchers will not be accepted
3. Not to be used in conjunction with any other offer
4. Not exchangeable for cash
5. Present this voucher to the business to accept the offer
6. 15% OFF food and drink bill

onshore

The restaurant prides itself on the quality & freshness of its local produce across its breakfast, lunch and evening menus. The ambiance is relaxed and informal, but with 1st class food and service.

Open 364 days of the year from 8.30am in the summer and 9.00am in the winter.

Pizza Patio Al Fresco
35 Commercial Road, Hayle Cornwall, TR27 4DE
Tel: 01736 753745

Terms & Conditions

1. Only one voucher per transaction
2. Defaced, torn or photocopied vouchers will not be accepted
3. Not to be used in conjunction with any other offer
4. Not exchangeable for cash
5. Present this voucher to the business to accept the offer
6. 10% off final bill

The Pizza Patio Al Fresco are Hayle, St Ives and Newlyn's premier mediterranean al fresco pizza and pasta restaurants. Eat with us at Hayle and drink in the view that reaches across from Phillack Church down towards the Harbour.

Pizza Patio Al Fresco
4 New Road, Newlyn, Penzance, Cornwall, TR18 5PZ
Tel: 01736 363446

Terms & Conditions

1. Only one voucher per transaction
2. Defaced, torn or photocopied vouchers will not be accepted
3. Not to be used in conjunction with any other offer
4. Not exchangeable for cash
5. Present this voucher to the business to accept the offer
6. 10% off final bill

The Pizza Patio Al Fresco are Hayle, St Ives and Newlyn's premier Mediterranean al fresco pizza and pasta restaurants. What about an evening in Mount's Bay? Then try our restaurant at Newlyn!

Pizza Patio Al Fresco
31 Fore Street, St. Ives, Cornwall TR26 1HE
Tel: 01736 798235

Terms & Conditions

1. Only one voucher per transaction
2. Defaced, torn or photocopied vouchers will not be accepted
3. Not to be used in conjunction with any other offer
4. Not exchangeable for cash
5. Present this voucher to the business to accept the offer
6. 10% off final bill

The Pizza Patio Al Fresco are Hayle, St Ives and Newlyn's premier mediterranean al fresco pizza and pasta restaurants. There's our restaurant in St. Ives, overlooking the quaint meandering streets of the legendary fishing town.

Tel: 01326 212848

Wine Bar & Resturant

Tucked away above The Falmouth Bookseller, Ratho provides some of the finest dining in the South West, with local seafood, beautiful Cornish meat, game and fine vegetarian options all on a menu that changes almost daily.

See reverse for more information

Valid from 01.01.10 to 31.12.10

SAVE
10% OFF

Tel: 01637 877271

Rock Island Bistro & Tapas Bar

The Rock Island Bistro & Tapas Bar has a perfect riverside location with beach and sunset views. The atmosphere is contemporary, light and very relaxing. The cosy restaurant is family run and has an exciting menu that caters for all tastes.

See reverse for more information

Valid from 01.01.10 to 31.12.10

SAVE
10% OFF

Tel: 01209 610414

Rosewarne MANOR

Rosewarne Manor offers superb dining with a choice of bar menu (at pub prices) and a la carte dining. We also have excellent business meeting facilities, host functions for special occasions and a bar for a leisurely drink or coffee.

See reverse for more information

Valid from 01.01.10 to 31.12.10

Tel: 01209 610414

Rosewarne MANOR

Rosewarne Manor offers superb dining with a choice of bar menu (at pub prices) and a la carte dining. We also have excellent business meeting facilities, host functions for special occasions and a bar for a leisurely drink or coffee.

See reverse for more information

Valid from 01.01.10 to 31.12.10

SAVE
10% OFF

Tel: 01736 799950

Slipways Restaurant

SLIPWAYS RESTAURANT probably the best kept secret in St Ives, Slipways Restaurant is tucked away only 50 meters from the harbour slipway. Fashionably modern with a nautical theme, the restaurant offers a fantastic venue for intimate dinners and parties alike.

See reverse for more information

Valid from 01.01.10 to 31.12.10

SAVE
15% OFF

Ratho Wine Bar & Restaurant
21 Church Street Falmouth, Cornwall
TR11 3EG
Tel: 01326 212848

Terms & Conditions

1. Only one voucher per transaction
2. Defaced, torn or photocopied vouchers will not be accepted
3. Not to be used in conjunction with any other offer
4. Not exchangeable for cash
5. Present this voucher to the business to accept the offer
6. 10% OFF your final bill

Wine Bar & Resturant

The beautiful period dining room, circa 1820, has been restored to its former glory by brothers Aly and Ru Cameron. Ascending the stairs you will be greeted with a relaxed and peaceful space in which to enjoy yourselves, treat friends, or get away from the crowds with a glass of wine. Ratho Wine Bar and Restaurant is a hidden gem in the very heart of Falmouth...
Easy to miss but hard to forget...

Rock Island Bistro & Tapas Bar
Alexandra Road, Porth Beach
Newquay, TR7 3NB
Tel: 01637 877271

Terms & Conditions

1. Only one voucher per transaction
2. Defaced, torn or photocopied vouchers will not be accepted
3. Not to be used in conjunction with any other offer
4. Not exchangeable for cash
5. Present this voucher to the business to accept the offer
6. 10% OFF final bill
7. Valid fo upto 6 poeple

Rock Island Bistro & Tapas Bar

The Rock Island Bistro & Tapas Bar has a perfect riverside location with beach and sunset views. The atmosphere is contemporary, light and very relaxing. The cosy restaurant is family run and has an exciting menu that caters for all tastes.

Rosewarne Manor
Gwinear Road, Connor Downs, Hayle
Cornwall, TR27 5JQ
Tel: 01209 610414

Terms & Conditions

1. Only one voucher per transaction
2. Defaced, torn or photocopied vouchers will not be accepted
3. Not to be used in conjunction with any other offer
4. Not exchangeable for cash
5. Present this voucher to the business to accept the offer
6. **FREE** dessert when you order a starter and main course from the restaurant menu. Excludes set price menus

Rosewarne MANOR

Rosewarne Manor makes an excellent venue for any dining event or special occasion. We are passionate about using local fresh produce. Our menus reflect seasonal availability and do, therefore, change with the seasons. We source Cornish produce where-ever possible, buying direct from local farmers and butchers.

Rosewarne Manor
Gwinear Road, Connor Downs, Hayle
Cornwall, TR27 5JQ
Tel: 01209 610414

Terms & Conditions

1. Only one voucher per transaction
2. Defaced, torn or photocopied vouchers will not be accepted
3. Not to be used in conjunction with any other offer
4. Not exchangeable for cash
5. Present this voucher to the business to accept the offer
6. Book a function (business or private) and save 10% on the food (valid Sunday to Friday)

Rosewarne MANOR

Rosewarne Manor makes an excellent venue for any dining event or special occasion. We are passionate about using local fresh produce. Our menus reflect seasonal availability and do, therefore, change with the seasons. We source Cornish produce where-ever possible, buying direct from local farmers and butchers.

Slipways Restaurant
Fish Street, St.Ives, Cornwall
TR26 1LT
Tel: 01736 799950

Terms & Conditions

1. Only one voucher per transaction
2. Defaced, torn or photocopied vouchers will not be accepted
3. Not to be used in conjunction with any other offer
4. Not exchangeable for cash
5. Present this voucher to the business to accept the offer
6. 15% OFF total bill

Slipways Restaurant

We pride ourselves in serving the finest food from locally sourced produce. Known for our fabulous steaks and fish dishes, and with our superb ribs freshly smoked on the premises, we're sure that Slipways is a secret you'll love to share.

Tel: 01637 830209

D36

KEEP IT CORNISH

A 16th Century, thatched inn with family room, beer garden, children's play area and ample parking. Discover for yourself a place that the locals know about, but don't always tell you …

See reverse for more information

Valid from 01.01.10 to 31.12.10

SAVE **10% OFF**

Tel: 01637 872228

D37

KEEP IT CORNISH

Sugar Bar & Bistro

The Sugar Bar & Bistro is at the heart of the Newquay social scene. Whether a quick lunch or a relaxed dinner, Sugars menu has tempting treats to suit all tastes. It has a cosmopolitan feel which really distinguishes it from other Newquay venues.

See reverse for more information

Valid from 01.01.10 to 31.12.10

SAVE **10% OFF**

Tel: 01872 510 544

Viners bar & restaurant

D38

KEEP IT CORNISH

The ambience at Viners is relaxed and friendly. Using the freshest, seasonal local produce, enjoy fine food in cosy and relaxed surroundings or simply stay for a drink. Seafood as well as vegetarian options are always available.

See reverse for more information

Valid from 01.01.10 to 31.12.10

SAVE **5% OFF**

Tel: 01736 796661

D39

KEEP IT CORNISH

The Wave Restaurant is located in St Andrews Street, in the heart of St Ives, away from the hustle and bustle of the main streets. We have held an AA rosette for 6 consecutive years and as a member of the Cornish Accredited

See reverse for more information

Valid from 01.01.10 to 31.12.10

FREE **GLASS OF WINE**

Tel: 01326 313 983

D40

KEEP IT CORNISH

Bringing European eating to Cornwall Weigela Bistro is all about taking your time to enjoy a great meal. Using local produce where possible we offer delicious freshly made lunches. In the evenings you can relax with one of a variety of fondues.

See reverse for more information

Valid from 01.01.10 to 31.12.10

FREE **CLASSIC CHOCOLATE FONDUE**

The Smugglers' Den Inn
Trebellan, Cubert, Newquay
Cornwall, TR8 5PY
Tel: 01637 830209

Terms & Conditions

1. Only one voucher per transaction
2. Defaced, torn or photocopied vouchers will not be accepted
3. Not to be used in conjunction with any other offer
4. Not exchangeable for cash
5. Present this voucher to the business to accept the offer
6. 10% OFF your final bill when dining

Enjoy a truly delicious lunch or evening meal in our sixteenth century inn, near Cubert and less than a 15 minute drive from Newquay. We use the freshest local ingredients in our kitchen and have developed our enviable reputation for our fabulous daily specials.

Sugar Bar & Bistro
19 Bank St, Newquay, Cornwall,
TR7 1DH
Tel: 01637 872228

Terms & Conditions

1. Only one voucher per transaction
2. Defaced, torn or photocopied vouchers will not be accepted
3. Not to be used in conjunction with any other offer
4. Not exchangeable for cash
5. Present this voucher to the business to accept the offer
6. 10% OFF for evening diners

Sugar Bar & Bistro

All dishes are prepared freshly on the premises using only the finest ingredients. The European influenced menu really does have something for everyone!

Viners
Carvynick, Summercourt, Newquay
Cornwall, TR8 5AF
Tel: 01872 510 544

Terms & Conditions

1. Only one voucher per transaction
2. Defaced, torn or photocopied vouchers will not be accepted
3. Not to be used in conjunction with any other offer
4. Not exchangeable for cash
5. Present this voucher to the business to accept the offer
6. 5% OFF any meal from either our fine dining or brasserie
7. This offer does not extend to drinks at the bar

Viners bar & restaurant

Our offer 5% is off any meal from either our Fine Dining or Brasserie.

The Wave Restaurant
St- Andrews Street, St Ives
Cornwall, TR26 1AH
Tel: 01736 796661

Terms & Conditions

1. Only one voucher per transaction
2. Defaced, torn or photocopied vouchers will not be accepted
3. Not to be used in conjunction with any other offer
4. Not exchangeable for cash
5. Present this voucher to the business to accept the offer
6. One glass of house wine per person with every a la carte meal purchased

The Wave Restaurant

Restaurants. The modern Mediterranean menu and specials board reflect the best in Cornish produce and only St Ives suppliers are used where possible.

Weigela Bistro
27 Arwenack Street, Falmouth
Cornwall, TR11 3JE
Tel: 01326 313 983

Terms & Conditions

1. Only one voucher per transaction
2. Defaced, torn or photocopied vouchers will not be accepted
3. Not to be used in conjunction with any other offer
4. Not exchangeable for cash
5. Present this voucher to the business to accept the offer
6. **FREE** classic chocolate fondue when you share a classic cheese fondue for two

How about meat or fish on hot lava stones? Vegetarian options and gluten or lactose free food also available. Great wines, local beers and German beers.

Bringing European eating to Cornwall Weigela Bistro is all about taking your time to enjoy a great meal. Using local produce where possible we offer delicious freshly made lunches. In the evenings you can relax with one of a variety of fondues.

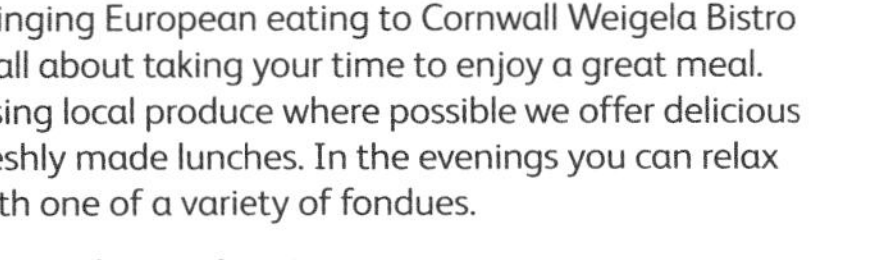

FREE GLASS OF HOUSE WINE

See reverse for more information

Valid from 01.01.10 to 31.12.10

Bringing European eating to Cornwall Weigela Bistro is all about taking your time to enjoy a great meal. Using local produce where possible we offer delicious freshly made lunches. In the evenings you can relax with one of a variety of fondues.

FREE BOTTLE OF HOUSE WINE

See reverse for more information

Valid from 01.01.10 to 31.12.10

Our restaurant menu ranges from a whitesands burger to a thai green curry, pizzas and pastas along with a children's menu and vegetarian options perfect for those of you who don't eat meat or fish. But for those of you who do!

FREE GLASS OF WINE OR BEER

See reverse for more information

Valid from 01.01.10 to 31.12.10

We cover restaurants, pubs, cafes, bistros and much more. So if you're looking for a romantic meal for two in the cobbled streets of St Ives, a welcoming pub for all the family, or just a quick bite to eat for lunch, then look no further because we have it all!

Weigela Bistro
27 Arwenack Street, Falmouth
Cornwall, TR11 3JE
Tel: 01326 313 983

Terms & Conditions

1. Only one voucher per transaction
2. Defaced, torn or photocopied vouchers will not be accepted
3. Not to be used in conjunction with any other offer
4. Not exchangeable for cash
5. Present this voucher to the business to accept the offer
6. **FREE** glass of house wine with every meat on a stone

How about meat or fish on hot lava stones? Vegetarian options and gluten or lactose free food also available. Great wines, local beers and German beers.

Weigela Bistro

Weigela Bistro
27 Arwenack Street, Falmouth
Cornwall, TR11 3JE
Tel: 01326 313 983

Terms & Conditions

1. Only one voucher per transaction
2. Defaced, torn or photocopied vouchers will not be accepted
3. Not to be used in conjunction with any other offer
4. Not exchangeable for cash
5. Present this voucher to the business to accept the offer
6. **FREE** bottle of house wine with a meal on your **NEXT** visit when you spend £25 per person

How about meat or fish on hot lava stones? Vegetarian options and gluten or lactose free food also available. Great wines, local beers and German beers.

Weigela Bistro

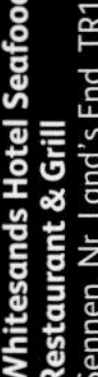

Whitesands Hotel Seafood Restaurant & Grill
Sennen, Nr. Land's End, TR19 7AR
Tel: 01736 871776

Terms & Conditions

1. Only one voucher per transaction
2. Defaced, torn or photocopied vouchers will not be accepted
3. Not to be used in conjunction with any other offer
4. Not exchangeable for cash
5. Present this voucher to the business to accept the offer
6. Valid 5.30pm to 8.30pm
7. **FREE** glass of beer or wine with every meal

Savour the delights of fresh lobster from our local harbour (to order) scallops and sea bass or the best cuts of meat for the grill from our award-winning butcher.

WE ARE ALSO OPEN FOR SUNDAY LUNCH FROM 12:30 - 4:30

Whitesands Hotel Seafood

We cover restaurants, pubs, cafes, bistros and much more. So if you're looking for a romantic meal for two in the cobbled streets of St Ives, a welcoming pub for all the family, or just a quick bite to eat for lunch, then look no further because we have it all!

KEEP IT SOCIAL

enzance

oney Pot	SO6
enaissance	SO14
ero Lounge	SO20

ayle

alt Kitchen/Bar	SO15-16

Newquay

Berties	SO1
Minnies Dinky Diner	SO8-11
Pure	SO13

Truro

Bunters Bar	SO2
L2	SO7
Office	SO12

Falmouth

De Wynns	SO4
Falmouth Townhouse	SO19
Great Shakes	SO5
Shake Shop	SO17-18

Camborne

Corn Exchange	SO3

The Honey Pot is a top-quality and unique establishment in the middle of Penzance, opposite the Acorn Theatre. We serve the best coffees, teas, home-made cakes and sweet delights, as well as a huge range of gourmet sandwiches, soups and light lunches.

Our daily specials are made, as far as possible, with local and seasonal ingredients, featuring the ever-popular café favourites as well as various dishes from around the world. We usually have five different chocolate cakes on offer, cheesecakes and slices, as well as gluten-free cakes, soups and specials, plus a wide range of vegetarian and vegan choices. Sit and soak up the atmosphere, or read the papers, surrounded by antique tables and chairs, fabulous and friendly staff, and see why this is the favoured haunt of so many locals....

FREE cake and coffee

The Honey Pot

5 Parade Street, Penzance
TR18 4BU

T 01736 368686

Restaurant Opening Hours.
Mon - Sun. 10am - 6pm
Closed on Bank Holidays

Free Wi-Fi is available to customers having coffee and cake except during lunchtime and at busy periods

- This voucher offer entitles you to a FREE coffee and cake.
- See vouchers for terms and conditions

KEEP IT SOCIAL

Why not catch up with friends over a coffee, enjoy a freshl[y] blended smoothie, or even hit the local bars and clubs tha[t] Cornwall has to offer.

SO1

KEEP IT CORNISH

Cornwall's and Newquay's premier nightclub Berties hosts some of the UK's biggest names and artist including Radio 1 DJ's. Refitted for 2009 with a fresh new look Berties has three clubs under one roof and seven bars when all the clubs are open.

See reverse for more information

Valid from 01.01.10 to 31.12.10

FREE BOTTLE OF BUBBLY

Cornwall, TR7 1DB
Tel: 01637 870369

SO2

KEEP IT CORNISH

Cornwall's best small live music venue & Truro's liveliest bar.

See reverse for more information

Valid from 01.01.10 to 31.12.10

SAVE 3 FOR 2 COCKTAILS

Cornwall, TR1 3DL
Tel: 01872 241220

SO3

KEEP IT CORNISH

Fantastic entertainment venue in West Cornwall spread over 2 rooms with 2 stages of popular music which has hosted amazing award winning acts such as N-Dubz, Chipmunk & Sash.

See reverse for more information

Valid from 01.01.10 to 31.12.10

SAVE HALF PRICE STUDENT ENTRY

Tel: 01209 611966

de Wynn's

SO4

KEEP IT CORNISH

Named after one of Falmouth's earliest entrepreneurs, de Wynn's is housed in a historic Grade II listed building that was once a hotel. The interior of the Tea & Coffee House is furnished and decorated in period style and offers a comfortable and welcoming atmosphere.

See reverse for more information

Valid from 01.01.10 to 31.12.10

SAVE 15% OFF

Tel: 01326 319259

Great Shakes!

SO5

KEEP IT CORNISH

A Greatshake! is a milkshake made with loads of icecream, there are over 70 flavours including: Snickers, Black Jack, Pineapple, Gingernuts, Skittles…After you have tried your free Greatshake! We are sure you will be back for more.

See reverse for more information

Valid from 01.01.10 to 31.12.10

FREE 1 FREE

MILKSHAKE

Tel: 07814 433671

Berties
Berties Club, East St, Newquay
Cornwall, TR7 1DB
Tel: 01637 870369

Terms & Conditions

1. Only one voucher per transaction
2. Defaced, torn or photocopied vouchers will not be accepted
3. Not to be used in conjunction with any other offer
4. Not exchangeable for cash
5. Present this voucher to the business to accept the offer
6. **FREE** bottle of bubbly and **FREE** use of a VIP booth when 6 or more party
7. To book this offer you MUST text BERTIES, YOUR NAME and DATE REQUIRED to 61211
8. Valid Sunday - Thursday during July and August

Luxury VIP Booths are available to hire and look out for flyers holding great entry and drinks deals for the club from Berties Bar and Buzios.

Opening times 10:30 - late

Berties
Email: tony.townsend@bertiesclub.com

Bunters Bar
58 Little Castle Street, Truro
Cornwall, TR1 3DL
Tel: 01872 241220

Terms & Conditions

1. Only one voucher per transaction
2. Defaced, torn or photocopied vouchers will not be accepted
3. Not to be used in conjunction with any other offer
4. Not exchangeable for cash
5. Present this voucher to the business to accept the offer
6. Voucher entitles customer to 3 classic cocktails from Bunters cocktail menu for the price of 2
7. Customers must be 18 or over and ID may be required.
8. Management reserve the right to refuse entry or, to alter or withdraw the promotion at any time

Showing all the popular live sporting events across it's big screens and providing quality weekend entertainment every week. This free-trade establishment offers delightful cocktails and fantastic array of Cornish drinks in a friendly environment and most importantly... all reasonably priced.

Bunters Bar

The Corn Exchange
19 Commercial Street, Camborne
Cornwall, TR14 8JZ
Tel: 01209 611966

Terms & Conditions

1. Only one voucher per transaction
2. Defaced, torn or photocopied vouchers will not be accepted
3. Not to be used in conjunction with any other offer
4. Not exchangeable for cash
5. Present this voucher to the business to accept the offer
6. Voucher entitles student half price entry on Thursdays only
7. Customers must be 18 or over and ID may be required
8. Management reserve the right to refuse entry or, to alter or withdraw the promotion at any time

Thursday Nights host a lively Student Night with plenty of theme nights to go with the great offers and fantastic atmosphere. Keep an eye out for their events listings which see the best acts of commercial dance visiting the South West.

The Corn Exchange

De Wynns
55 Church Street, Falmouth
Cornwall, TR11 3DS
Tel: 01326 319259

Terms & Conditions

1. Only one voucher per transaction
2. Defaced, torn or photocopied vouchers will not be accepted
3. Not to be used in conjunction with any other offer
4. Not exchangeable for cash
5. Present this voucher to the business to accept the offer
6. 15% OFF purchases over £5

de Wynn's

The Eddy family promote local produce wherever possible and serve (among other local treats) Cornish crab, Cornish blue cheese, Davidstow Cheddar, St Endillion Brie, local clotted cream, strawberry jam made from local berries, and tea grown on nearby Tregothnan Estate.

De Wynns

Great Shakes
2a Berkeley Vale, (opposite Argos)
Falmouth, TR11 3XE
Tel: 07814 433671

Terms & Conditions

1. Only one voucher per transaction
2. Defaced, torn or photocopied vouchers will not be accepted
3. Not to be used in conjunction with any other offer
4. Not exchangeable for cash
5. Present this voucher to the business to accept the offer
6. One **FREE** medium milkshake

Great Shakes!

We also sell Fairtrade Coffee, 12 Flavours of Hot Chocolate and 16 Varieties of Tea.

Cornwall, TR18 4BU
Tel: 01736 368686

The Honey Pot is a top-quality and unique establishment in the middle of Penzance, opposite the Acorn Theatre. We serve the best coffees, teas, home-made cakes and sweet delights, as well as a huge range of gourmet

See reverse for more information

Valid from 01.01.10 to 31.12.10

FREE COFFEE AND CAKE

TR1 2SL
Tel: 01872 222023

One of Cornwall's busiest late night entertainment venues with a massive reputation for it's acts and specialist guest DJ's. With 4 bars over 2 floors you get a different atmosphere from each.

See reverse for more information

Valid from 01.01.10 to 31.12.10

SAVE HALF PRICE ENTRY

Tel: 01637 878385

Minnie's ethos is to provide fresh, locally sourced produce in a fun and relaxing atmosphere. With a quirky, 50's American Diner feel, we aim to provide you with great food and drink in a friendly helpful manner.

See reverse for more information

Valid from 01.01.10 to 31.12.10

SAVE £2.50 FOR LARGE COFFEE & CAKE

Tel: 01637 878385

Minnie's ethos is to provide fresh, locally sourced produce in a fun and relaxing atmosphere. With a quirky, 50's American Diner feel, we aim to provide you with great food and drink in a friendly helpful manner.

See reverse for more information

Valid from 01.01.10 to 31.12.10

FREE COOKIE

Tel: 01637 878385

SO10

KEEP IT CORNISH

Minnie's ethos is to provide fresh, locally sourced produce in a fun and relaxing atmosphere. With a quirky, 50's American Diner feel, we aim to provide you with great food and drink in a friendly helpful manner.

See reverse for more information

Valid from 01.01.10 to 31.12.10

SAVE JUICE OR SMOOTHIE £2.50

The Honey Pot
5 Parade Street, Penzance
Cornwall, TR18 4BU
Tel: 01736 368686

Terms & Conditions

1. Only one voucher per transaction
2. Defaced, torn or photocopied vouchers will not be accepted
3. Not to be used in conjunction with any other offer
4. Not exchangeable for cash
5. Present this voucher to the business to accept the offer
6. FREE coffee and cake for one, when four people have coffee and cake
7. Cheapest free. Not valid between 12 and 2.30p.m

sandwiches, soups and light lunches. Our daily specials are made, as far as possible, with local and seasonal ingredients, featuring the ever-popular café favourites as well as various dishes from around the world.

L2 Nightclub
Calenick Street, Truro, Cornwall
TR1 2SL
Tel: 01872 222023

Terms & Conditions

1. Only one voucher per transaction
2. Defaced, torn or photocopied vouchers will not be accepted
3. Not to be used in conjunction with any other offer
4. Not exchangeable for cash
5. Present this voucher to the business to accept the offer
6. Voucher entitles customer to half price entry before 11pm
7. Customers must be 18 or over and ID may be required
8. Management reserve the right to refuse entry or, to alter or withdraw the promotion at any time

Monday Nights is the longest running Student night which makes a great way to extend your weekend. Full listing and line-ups available on www.L2Club.co.uk

L2 Nightclub

Minnies dinky diner
33b Bank Street, Newquay
Cornwall, Tr7 1DJ
Tel: 01637 878385

Terms & Conditions

1. Only one voucher per transaction
2. Defaced, torn or photocopied vouchers will not be accepted
3. Not to be used in conjunction with any other offer
4. Not exchangeable for cash
5. Present this voucher to the business to accept the offer

So if your looking for a funky, healthy alternative in food and drink, then come and join us at Minnie's Dinky Diner.

Minnies dinky diner

Minnies dinky diner
33b Bank Street, Newquay
Cornwall, Tr7 1DJ
Tel: 01637 878385

Terms & Conditions

1. Only one voucher per transaction
2. Defaced, torn or photocopied vouchers will not be accepted
3. Not to be used in conjunction with any other offer
4. Not exchangeable for cash
5. Present this voucher to the business to accept the offer
6. **FREE** cookie when you buy a large coffee

So if your looking for a funky, healthy alternative in food and drink, then come and join us at Minnie's Dinky Diner.

Minnies dinky diner

Minnies dinky diner
33b Bank Street, Newquay
Cornwall, Tr7 1DJ
Tel: 01637 878385

Terms & Conditions

1. Only one voucher per transaction
2. Defaced, torn or photocopied vouchers will not be accepted
3. Not to be used in conjunction with any other offer
4. Not exchangeable for cash
5. Present this voucher to the business to accept the offer
6. Any menu juice or smoothie for £2.50 (excluding Acai, Acerola, Green Meanie, Summer Fruits or Goji)

So if your looking for a funky, healthy alternative in food and drink, then come and join us at Minnie's Dinky Diner.

Minnies dinky diner

KEEP IT CORNISH

SO11

Minnie's ethos is to provide fresh, locally sourced produce in a fun and relaxing atmosphere. With a quirky, 50's American Diner feel, we aim to provide you with great food and drink in a friendly helpful manner.

See reverse for more information

Valid from 01.01.10 to 31.12.10

SAVE
SPECIALITY
MILKSHAKES **£2.20**

the office

SO12

Have you checked out the new office in Truro yet?? Well it's situated just behind Zafiros bar. This is the new trendy end of town with other new bars, all in the same area.

See reverse for more information

Valid from 01.01.10 to 31.12.10

SAVE
HALF PRICE ENTRY

pure

SO13

Pure Newquay has landed with a beat that will resonate out across Cornwall and the South-West… Newquay's only Superclub is offering a fresh, exciting experience to the discerning clubber.

See reverse for more information

Valid from 01.05.10 to 31.12.10

SAVE
2 FOR 1

Renaissance
Café • Bar

SO14

Come down to the Renaissance & relax as our staff take care of your every need. We offer a large range of excellently prepared food and drinks, our menu has a fresh Mediterranean vibe featuring our signature oven baked pizzas.

See reverse for more information

Valid from 01.01.10 to 31.12.10

SAVE
10% OFF

salt*
Kitchen/Bar

SO15

Open from 10am every day Salt serves breakfast till noon. Lunch is served from noon till 3pm and dinner from 6pm till 9pm, although you can get a sandwich at anytime. Use us for a quiet coffee or join us of an evening and try one of our cocktails. We look forward to meeting you.

See reverse for more information

Valid from 01.01.10 to 31.12.10

SAVE
2 FOR 1
COCKTAILS

Cornwall, Tr7 1DJ Tel: 01637 878385

Tel: 01872 223163

Tel: 01637 850313

Tel: 01736 366277

Tel: 01736 755862

Minnies dinky diner
33b Bank Street, Newquay
Cornwall, Tr7 1DJ
Tel: 01637 878385

Terms & Conditions

1. Only one voucher per transaction
2. Defaced, torn or photocopied vouchers will not be accepted
3. Not to be used in conjunction with any other offer
4. Not exchangeable for cash
5. Present this voucher to the business to accept the offer
6. Buy any speciality milkshake for £2.20 (choose from Oreo, Chocoholic, Tropicana, Charlie Brown or Angel's Delight)

So if your looking for a funky, healthy alternative in food and drink, then come and join us at Minnie's Dinky Diner.

Minnies dinky diner

The Office
1 River Walk, Truro, Cornwall
TR1 2AB
Tel: 01872 223163

Terms & Conditions

1. Only one voucher per transaction
2. Defaced, torn or photocopied vouchers will not be accepted
3. Not to be used in conjunction with any other offer
4. Not exchangeable for cash
5. Present this voucher to the business to accept the offer
6. Half price entry – before 11

Our new club in town offers a classy, trendy venue for all to enjoy from students to adults who still want to party. With a 450 capacity it's the perfect size to socialize and still enjoy a great atmosphere. Get that Friday feeling and start the weekend with a night at the office its an alternative night with a host of different DJ's ranging from D&B, reggae and everything in between. Most definitely beat the credit crunch this year by staying in the office.

The Office

Pure Nightclub
52, Tolcarne Road, Newquay
Cornwall, TR7 2NQ
Tel: 01637 850313

Terms & Conditions

1. Only one voucher per transaction
2. Defaced, torn or photocopied vouchers will not be accepted
3. Not to be used in conjunction with any other offer
4. Not exchangeable for cash
5. Present this voucher to the business to accept the offer
6. Valid only on a Pure promoted night- not on a night organised by outside promoters
7. 2 for 1 on entry

Spread across 7 unique spaces over 3 floors, Pure offers something for everyone, from the massive branded club nights in the Main Room, Funktion Room, and Soundshaft to the opulent exclusivity of the Island Bar, and party atmosphere in the Players Lounge.

Pure Nightclub

Renaissance Café & Bar
6 Wharfside, Shopping Centre
Penzance, TR18 2GB
Tel: 01736 366277

Terms & Conditions

1. Only one voucher per transaction
2. Defaced, torn or photocopied vouchers will not be accepted
3. Not to be used in conjunction with any other offer
4. Not exchangeable for cash
5. Present this voucher to the business to accept the offer
6. 10% OFF your final bill

Renaissance Café • Bar

Come down to the Renaissance & relax as our staff take care of your every need. We offer a large range of excellently prepared food and drinks, our menu has a fresh Mediterranean vibe featuring our signature oven baked pizzas.

Salt Kitchen/Bar
25 Foundry Square, Hayle
Cornwall, TR27 4HH
Tel: 01736 755862

Terms & Conditions

1. Only one voucher per transaction
2. Defaced, torn or photocopied vouchers will not be accepted
3. Not to be used in conjunction with any other offer
4. Not exchangeable for cash
5. Present this voucher to the business to accept the offer
6. Buy one cocktail, get another one **FREE** (cheapest free)

Open from 10am every day Salt serves breakfast till noon. Lunch is served from noon till 3pm and dinner from 6pm till 9pm although you can get a sandwich at anytime. Use us for a quiet coffee or join us of an evening and try one of our cocktails. We look forward to meeting you.

Salt Kitchen/Bar

Open from 10am every day Salt serves breakfast till noon. Lunch is served from noon till 3pm and dinner from 6pm till 9pm, although you can get a sandwich at anytime. Use us for a quiet coffee or join us of an evening and try one of our cocktails. We look forward to meeting you.

See reverse for more information

Valid from 01.01.10 to 31.12.10

SO16

SAVE

2 FOR 1
HOT DRINKS

Cornwall, TR27 4HH
Tel: 01736 755862

Our shop is called The Shake Shop, situated at no. 45 Church Street in Falmouth. We offer a range of milkshakes made from your favourite chocolate, sweets, biscuits, and other delights! Mix and match from 100+ options to create the shake of your dreams.

See reverse for more information

Valid from 01.01.10 to 31.12.10

SO17

SAVE

45 Chruch Street, Falmouth
Cornwall, TR11 3EF

Our shop is called The Shake Shop, situated at no. 45 Church Street in Falmouth. We offer a range of milkshakes made from your favourite chocolate, sweets, biscuits, and other delights! Mix and match from 100+ options to create the shake of your dreams.

See reverse for more information

Valid from 01.01.10 to 31.12.10

SO18

TOPPING

45 Chruch Street, Falmouth
Cornwall, TR11 3EF

The Falmouth Townhouse

One of Falmouth's finest bars - relaxed, stylish and friendly with great music and drinks. We have one of Falmouth's best stocked bars, with a great range of unusual draft and bottled beer and cider, real ales, fine wines, spirits and liqueurs, along with expertly mixed cocktails. Tapas served in the bar from 6-9pm.

See reverse for more information

Valid from 01.01.10 to 31.12.10

SO19

SAVE

2 FOR 1
COCKTAILS

Tel: 01326 312 009

The hottest place to be in Penzance! A fabulous bar, great wines and stunning cocktails. Live Bands on Fridays, DJs every Saturday and Open Mic on Thursdays. SkySports and ESPN football events on a 92" HD screen and movies nights on Mondays. **FREE** Entry every night of the week!

See reverse for more information

Valid from 01.01.10 to 31.03.10

SO20

COCKTAILS

Tel: 01736 361220

KEEP IT... SOCIAL

www.keepitcornish.co.uk

Salt Kitchen/Bar
25 Foundry Square, Hayle
Cornwall, TR27 4HH
Tel: 01736 755862

Terms & Conditions

1. Only one voucher per transaction
2. Defaced, torn or photocopied vouchers will not be accepted
3. Not to be used in conjunction with any other offer
4. Not exchangeable for cash
5. Present this voucher to the business to accept the offer
6. Buy one hot drink, get another **FREE** (cheapest free)

Open from 10am every day Salt serves breakfast till noon. Lunch is served from noon till 3pm and dinner from 6pm till 9pm although you can get a sandwich at anytime. Use us for a quiet coffee or join us of an evening and try one of our cocktails. We look forward to meeting you.

Salt Kitchen/Bar
info@salt-hayle.co.uk

The Shake Shop
45 Chruch Street, Falmouth
Cornwall, TR11 3EF

Terms & Conditions

1. Only one voucher per transaction
2. Defaced, torn or photocopied vouchers will not be accepted
3. Not to be used in conjunction with any other offer
4. Not exchangeable for cash
5. Present this voucher to the business to accept the offer
6. Any size shake with one flavour - cheapest shake is **FREE**
7. The management reserve the right to withdraw this offer at any time
8. Not valid in June, July, August and September

We also sell American candy (specially imported) and refreshing fruit smoothies.

The Shake Shop
45 Chruch Street, Falmouth
Cornwall, TR11 3EF

Terms & Conditions

1. Only one voucher per transaction
2. Defaced, torn or photocopied vouchers will not be accepted
3. Not to be used in conjunction with any other offer
4. Not exchangeable for cash
5. Present this voucher to the business to accept the offer
6. The management reserve the right to withdraw this offer at any time
7. Not valid in June, July, August and September
8. One **FREE** topping with any shake

We also sell American candy (specially imported) and refreshing fruit smoothies.

The Falmouth Townhouse
3 Grove Place
Falmouth TR11 4AL
Tel: 01326 312 009

Terms & Conditions

1. Only one voucher per transaction
2. Defaced, torn or photocopied vouchers will not be accepted
3. Not to be used in conjunction with any other offer
4. Not exchangeable for cash
5. Present this voucher to the business to accept the offer
6. Buy one cocktail get one **FREE** (cheapest one free)

The Falmouth Townhouse

Chic bar, relaxed seating, great tunes and a wide range of beers including two cask ales and a range of cider, wines, spirits and cocktails. Open from 7.30am for coffee, cakes and food with free wi-fi, papers and magazines. Why not join us in the evening for one of our stunning cocktails……

The Falmouth Townhouse

The Zero Lounge
Regent Basement, Chapel Street
Penzance, TR18 4AE
Tel: 01736 361220

Terms & Conditions

1. Only one voucher per per person per visit
2. Defaced, torn or photocopied vouchers will not be accepted
3. Not to be used in conjunction with any other offer
4. Not exchangeable for cash
5. Present this voucher to the business to accept the offer
6. Buy one cocktail get one **FREE**
7. Valid Sundays, Mondays and Tuesdays

The hottest place to be in Penzance! A fabulous bar, great wines and stunning cocktails. Live Bands on Fridays, DJs every Saturday and Open Mic on Thursdays. SkySports and ESPN football events on a 92" HD screen and movies nights on Mondays. **FREE** Entry every night of the week!

The Zero Lounge

KEEP IT
BEAUTY

DON'T FORGET TO CHECK OUT OUR WEBSITE FOR A COMPREHENSIVE LISTING OF PLACES TO SHOP, EAT, DRINK & BE MERRY ALONG WITH SOME EXCELLENT IDEAS FOR DAYS OUT

www.keepitcornish.co.uk

SAVINGS, DISCOUNTS & ADVENTURE

OVER 300 OFFERS FROM ADVENTURE PARKS TO RESTAURANTS

Beautiful U

B1

In a friendly, professional environment, clients can enjoy a wide range of beauty treatments which include: relaxing and anti aging facials, waxing, manicures, pedicures, acrylic nails, swedish and aromatherapy massage, lash and brow tinting, make up, electrolysis and more…

See reverse for more information

Valid from 01.01.10 to 31.12.10

SAVE **10% OFF**

Chapel terrace, Hayle
Tel: 01736 759377 OR 07980906663

B2

Our beauty section can provide online skincare advice from professional therapist as well as selling specific product brands email mail@bydesign-newquay.com

See reverse for more information

Valid from 01.01.10 to 31.12.10

FREE **DETOX SESSION**

Cornwall, TR7 2NE
Tel: 01637 852777

B3

For a completely different hairdressing experience, why not come to Castle Rooms Hair Boutique, Truro? We pride ourselves on our relaxed and personal approach to all hairdressing services.

See reverse for more information

Valid from 01.01.10 to 31.12.10

SAVE **40% OFF**

Tel: 01872 274452

B4

For a completely different hairdressing experience, why not come to Castle Rooms Hair Boutique, Truro? We pride ourselves on our relaxed and personal approach to all hairdressing services.

See reverse for more information

Valid from 01.01.10 to 31.12.10

SAVE **FREE CUT**

Tel: 01872 274452

KEEP IT CORNISH

B5

For a completely different hairdressing experience, why not come to Castle Rooms Hair Boutique, Truro? We pride ourselves on our relaxed and personal approach to all hairdressing services.

See reverse for more information

Valid from 01.01.10 to 31.12.10

Tel: 01872 274452

Beautiful U
Hayle shopping arcade
Chapel terrace, Hayle
Tel: 01736 759377 OR 07980906663

Terms & Conditions

1. Only one voucher per transaction
2. Defaced, torn or photocopied vouchers will not be accepted
3. Not to be used in conjunction with any other offer
4. Not exchangeable for cash
5. Present this voucher to the business to accept the offer
6. 10% OFF any beauty treatment on your 1st visit

Beautiful U

Packages and gift vouchers available.

By Design
23 Cliff Road, Newquay
Cornwall, TR7 2NE
Tel: 01637 852777

Terms & Conditions

1. Only one voucher per transaction
2. Defaced, torn or photocopied vouchers will not be accepted
3. Not to be used in conjunction with any other offer
4. Not exchangeable for cash
5. Present this voucher to the business to accept the offer
6. Free detox session when you spend £30 on products

Simply precious......Simply beautiful......Simply by design.

By Design

Castle Rooms
Castle Lodge, 10 Castle Street,
Truro, TR1 3AF.
Tel: 01872 274452

Terms & Conditions

1. Only one voucher per transaction
2. Defaced, torn or photocopied vouchers will not be accepted
3. Not to be used in conjunction with any other offer
4. Not exchangeable for cash
5. Present this voucher to the business to accept the offer
6. 40% off a cut and blow dry with Stacey

Situated above designer boutique Bishop Philpott, and the Falmouth Bay Oyster and Champagne Café, we have created the perfect environment to escape the daily hustle and bustle, relax, and leave feeling a million dollars!

Castle Rooms

Castle Rooms
Castle Lodge, 10 Castle Street,
Truro, TR1 3AF.
Tel: 01872 274452

Terms & Conditions

1. Only one voucher per transaction
2. Defaced, torn or photocopied vouchers will not be accepted
3. Not to be used in conjunction with any other offer
4. Not exchangeable for cash
5. Present this voucher to the business to accept the offer
6. FREE cut with any colour service

Situated above designer boutique Bishop Philpott, and the Falmouth Bay Oyster and Champagne Café, we have created the perfect environment to escape the daily hustle and bustle, relax, and leave feeling a million dollars!

Castle Rooms

Castle Rooms
Castle Lodge, 10 Castle Street,
Truro, TR1 3AF.
Tel: 01872 274452

Terms & Conditions

1. Only one voucher per transaction
2. Defaced, torn or photocopied vouchers will not be accepted
3. Not to be used in conjunction with any other offer
4. Not exchangeable for cash
5. Present this voucher to the business to accept the offer
6. Buy one get one FREE on all products

Situated above designer boutique Bishop Philpott, and the Falmouth Bay Oyster and Champagne Café, we have created the perfect environment to escape the daily hustle and bustle, relax, and leave feeling a million dollars!

Castle Rooms

COMPANY salon

B6

Company Salon is a brand new salon situated in the heart of Newquay's town centre comprising of a Fast Tan Studio and Hair & Nail Salon. The salon offers clients an indulgent environment where they can relax in the confidence of our highly trained dedicated team.

See reverse for more information

Valid from 01.01.10 to 31.12.10

SAVE
10% OFF
HAIR & NAILS

Cornwall, TR7 1JF
Tel: 01637 876857

COMPANY salon

B7

Company Salon is a brand new salon situated in the heart of Newquay's town centre comprising of a Fast Tan Studio and Hair & Nail Salon. The salon offers clients an indulgent environment where they can relax in the confidence of our highly trained dedicated team.

See reverse for more information

Valid from 01.01.10 to 31.12.10

SAVE
10% OFF
PRODUCTS

Cornwall, TR7 1JF
Tel: 01637 876857

COMPANY salon

B8

Company Salon is a brand new salon situated in the heart of Newquay's town centre comprising of a Fast Tan Studio and Hair & Nail Salon. The salon offers clients an indulgent environment where they can relax in the confidence of our highly trained dedicated team.

See reverse for more information

Valid from 01.01.10 to 31.12.10

SAVE
TANNING 50p
PER MINUTE

Tel: 01637 876857

greenwood style

B9

Learn how to enjoy the way you look! Develop your style! Looking good and feeling great, just got easy!

See reverse for more information

Valid from 01.01.10 to 31.12.10

SAVE
10% OFF

Tel: 01872 277066/ 07877 654543

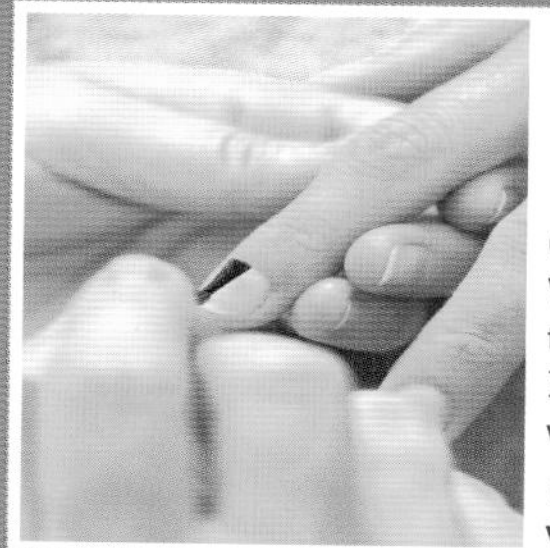

HENDRA *beauty*

KEEP IT CORNISH

B10

Come, relax and be pampered in our central Truro salon. We offer a large range of holistic and maintenance treatments such as; Guinot treatments, hot stones, Indian head and aromatherapy massages, specialist waxing, tinting, tanning, manicures and pedicures.

See reverse for more information

Valid from 01.01.10 to 31.12.10

FREE
MANICURE

Tel: 01872 270090

Company Salon
10a Bank Street, Newquay
Cornwall, TR7 1JF
Tel: 01637 876857

Terms & Conditions

1. Only one voucher per transaction
2. Defaced, torn or photocopied vouchers will not be accepted
3. Not to be used in conjunction with any other offer
4. Not exchangeable for cash
5. Present this voucher to the business to accept the offer
6. 10% OFF hair and nails

COMPANY salon

The salon offers clients an indulgent environment where they can relax in the confidence of our highly trained dedicated team of stylists who are passionate about achieving total client satisfaction. Company salon prides itself on offering a great service and specialising in creative unisex hair offering advice on all aspects of hairdressing. We have on board a dedicated Colour Technician, Nail Technician & a Qualified Racoon Hair Extension specialist.

Company Salon
10a Bank Street, Newquay
Cornwall, TR7 1JF
Tel: 01637 876857

Terms & Conditions

1. Only one voucher per transaction
2. Defaced, torn or photocopied vouchers will not be accepted
3. Not to be used in conjunction with any other offer
4. Not exchangeable for cash
5. Present this voucher to the business to accept the offer
6. 10% OFF products

COMPANY salon

The salon offers clients an indulgent environment where they can relax in the confidence of our highly trained dedicated team of stylists who are passionate about achieving total client satisfaction. Company salon prides itself on offering a great service and specialising in creative unisex hair offering advice on all aspects of hairdressing. We have on board a dedicated Colour Technician, Nail Technician & a Qualified Racoon Hair Extension specialist.

Company Salon
10a Bank Street, Newquay
Cornwall, TR7 1JF
Tel: 01637 876857

Terms & Conditions

1. Only one voucher per transaction
2. Defaced, torn or photocopied vouchers will not be accepted
3. Not to be used in conjunction with any other offer
4. Not exchangeable for cash
5. Present this voucher to the business to accept the offer
6. Pay 50p per minute for one tanning session

COMPANY salon

The salon offers clients an indulgent environment where they can relax in the confidence of our highly trained dedicated team of stylists who are passionate about achieving total client satisfaction. Company salon prides itself on offering a great service and specialising in creative unisex hair offering advice on all aspects of hairdressing. We have on board a dedicated Colour Technician, Nail Technician & a Qualified Racoon Hair Extension specialist.

Greenwood Style
24 Carclew Street, Truro
TR1 2DZ
Tel: 01872 277066/ 07877 654543

Terms & Conditions

1. Only one voucher per transaction
2. Defaced, torn or photocopied vouchers will not be accepted
3. Not to be used in conjunction with any other offer
4. Not exchangeable for cash
5. Present this voucher to the business to accept the offer
6. 10% OFF any full image, style or colour consultation

greenwood style

Capturing the essence of your individuality Clare will enable you to understand your colouring and body image, and to be positive and creative about achieving your goals!

Greenwood Style

Hendra Beauty
6-9 Lemon Street, Truro
Cornwall, TR1 2LQ
Tel: 01872 270090

Terms & Conditions

1. Only one voucher per transaction
2. Defaced, torn or photocopied vouchers will not be accepted
3. Not to be used in conjunction with any other offer
4. Not exchangeable for cash
5. Present this voucher to the business to accept the offer
6. Book an extra relaxing facial and recieve a manicure worth £19 absolutely **FREE**
7. This voucher is not redeemable during December

Face and body treatments. Packages are available for up to 6 people.

Hendra Beauty

Image hair and Beauty

Image is a small and friendly salon and is operated by senior stylist and manager Byron. Byron is a well qualified stylist and colour technician, he is in his tenth year at this salon and has a lengthy client list.

See reverse for more information

Valid from 01.01.10 to 31.12.10

FREE MANICURE

TR1 3DN Tel: 01872 273784

inkfish HAIR DESIGN GROUP

Our highly skilled team are trained to the highest industry standards, providing the very best in hair care for over 15 years. Beauty salon situated on the top floor, offering a wide range of treatments from Nails to Waxing. Making sure you leave our salons looking and feeling fantastic.

See reverse for more information

Valid from 01.01.10 to 31.12.10

SAVE 20% OFF

Cornwall, TR1 2AA Tel: 01872 222468

Jb's hairdressing

Jb's hairdressing salon is a long established small freindly salon with both senior stylists, having had many years experience, plus young junior stylists providing traditional and latest trends in all aspects of hairdressing.

See reverse for more information

Valid from 01.01.10 to 31.12.10

SAVE 25% OFF

Cornwall, TR1 2AA Tel: 01872 272227

Jb's hairdressing

Jb's hairdressing salon is a long established small freindly salon with both senior stylists, having had many years experience, plus young junior stylists providing traditional and latest trends in all aspects of hairdressing.

See reverse for more information

Valid from 01.01.10 to 31.12.10

SAVE 10% OFF

Tel: 01872 272227

Kerry Prynn

B15

Kerry Prynn is a friendly, professional and creative hair salon based in Falmouth, Cornwall. We offer a first class service at a surprisingly affordable price, to help our clients maintain beautiful, luscious and most of all healthy hair.

See reverse for more information

Valid from 01.01.10 to 01.12.10

SAVE 15% OFF

Tel: 01326 312412

KEEP IT... BEAUTY

Image Hair and Beauty
13, Frances ST. Truro, Cornwall
TR1 3DN
Tel: 01872 273784

Terms & Conditions

1. Only one voucher per transaction
2. Defaced, torn or photocopied vouchers will not be accepted
3. Not to be used in conjunction with any other offer
4. Not exchangeable for cash
5. Present this voucher to the business to accept the offer
6. **FREE** manicure when purchasing a full head of highlights

Image hair and Beauty

Rose is the junior stylist and is also the owner. We have two beauty rooms and the therapists are Wendy and Rachel, they are qualified in many beauty treatments including electrolysis, waxing. massage, facials, manicures/pedicures and non-surgical face-lifts. Appointments are recommended but not always necessary.

Inkfish
10 New Bridge Street, Truro,
Cornwall, TR1 2AA
Tel: 01872 222468

Terms & Conditions

1. Only one voucher per transaction
2. Defaced, torn or photocopied vouchers will not be accepted
3. Not to be used in conjunction with any other offer
4. Not exchangeable for cash
5. Present this voucher to the business to accept the offer
6. 20% OFF any service
7. Not to be used for any retail products

inkfish
HAIR DESIGN GROUP

Our highly skilled team are trained to the highest industry standards, providing the very best in hair care for over 15 years. Beauty salon situated on the top floor, offering a wide range of treatments from Nails to Waxing. Making sure you leave our salons looking and feeling fantastic.

Inkfish

Jb's hairdressing
New Bridge Street, Truro,
Cornwall, TR1 2AA
Tel: 01872 272227

Terms & Conditions

1. Only one voucher per transaction
2. Defaced, torn or photocopied vouchers will not be accepted
3. Not to be used in conjunction with any other offer
4. Not exchangeable for cash
5. Present this voucher to the business to accept the offer
6. 10% OFF with junior stylist

Jb's hairdressing

Easy access from carpark, top quality products used, organic colours and perms as well as the well known brands.

Jb's hairdressing
New Bridge Street, Truro,
Cornwall, TR1 2AA
Tel: 01872 272227

Terms & Conditions

1. Only one voucher per transaction
2. Defaced, torn or photocopied vouchers will not be accepted
3. Not to be used in conjunction with any other offer
4. Not exchangeable for cash
5. Present this voucher to the business to accept the offer
6. 10% OFF with senior stylist

Jb's hairdressing

Easy access from carpark, top quality products used, organic colours and perms as well as the well known brands.

Kerry Prynn
36 High Street, Falmouth, Cornwall
TR11 2AF
Tel: 01326 312412

Terms & Conditions

1. Only one voucher per transaction
2. Defaced, torn or photocopied vouchers will not be accepted
3. Not to be used in conjunction with any other offer
4. Not exchangeable for cash
5. Present this voucher to the business to accept the offer
6. 15% OFF to new clients
7. Speak to staff for terms

We also offer a fantastic bridal service, that can accommodate any brides need.

Tel: 01736 754698

B16

Situated in the town of Hayle, Living Canvas Tattoo & Body Piercing is a fully liscensed, friendly and clean studio offering full custom design. Allow us to help you achieve your dream tattoo!

See reverse for more information

Valid from 01.01.10 to 31.12.10

SAVE 10% OFF

Tel: 01326 313116

B17

NV Hairdressing

Located just off the high street, enjoy the unique salon experience that is NV Hairdressing including a relaxed atmosphere, amazing harbour views and of course great haircuts from top stylists.

See reverse for more information

Valid from 01.01.10 to 31.12.10

SAVE HALF PRICE CUT & STYLE

Tel: 01326 561005

B18

Welcome to Revive Natural Living. Revive Natural Living is a spa therapy salon based in Helston, south west Cornwall. We are dedicated to improving your general feeling of well-being through the use of holistic treatments and natural products.

See reverse for more information

Valid from 01.01.10 to 31.12.10

FREE FACE MAPPING

Tel: 01326 561005

B19

Welcome to Revive Natural Living. Revive Natural Living is a spa therapy salon based in Helston, south west Cornwall. We are dedicated to improving your general feeling of well-being through the use of holistic treatments and natural products.

See reverse for more information

Valid from 01.01.10 to 31.12.10

SAVE 10% OFF

Tel. 01872 260800

B20

KEEP IT CORNISH

Created some 8 years ago with an experienced group of gifted professionals, we are ready to advise and recommend, to pamper and please your every wish. Whether you seek advise on Hair, Beauty or your Wedding.

See reverse for more information

Valid from 01.01.10 to 31.12.10

SAVE 20% OFF

Living Canvas
75 Fore Street, Hayle,, Cornwall
TR27 4DX
Tel: 01736 754698

Terms & Conditions

1. Only one voucher per transaction
2. Defaced, torn or photocopied vouchers will not be accepted
3. Not to be used in conjunction with any other offer
4. Not exchangeable for cash
5. Present this voucher to the business to accept the offer
6. 10% OFF a tattoo or piercing

Find our group on Facebook - Living Canvas Tattoo & Body Piercing.

NV Hairdressing
38 Malins Hall, Middle Floor
High Street, Falmouth
Tel: 01326 313116

Terms & Conditions

1. Only one voucher per transaction
2. Defaced, torn or photocopied vouchers will not be accepted
3. Not to be used in conjunction with any other offer
4. Not exchangeable for cash
5. Present this voucher to the business to accept the offer
6. Half price cut and style with stylist
7. You must state that you are using this voucher when booking

NV Hairdressing

Located just off the high street, enjoy the unique salon experience that is NV Hairdressing including a relaxed atmosphere, amazing harbour views and of course great haircuts from top stylists.

NV Hairdressing

Revive
5 Coinage Ope, Helston, Cornwall,
TR13 8EB
Tel: 01326 561005

Terms & Conditions

1. Only one voucher per transaction
2. Defaced, torn or photocopied vouchers will not be accepted
3. Not to be used in conjunction with any other offer
4. Not exchangeable for cash
5. Present this voucher to the business to accept the offer
6. FREE Dermalogica face mapping session

If you are in Helston, please come and browse in our store. We stock a wide range of natural bath, beauty & body products, crystals and gifts.

Revive

Revive
5 Coinage Ope, Helston, Cornwall,
TR13 8EB
Tel: 01326 561005

Terms & Conditions

1. Only one voucher per transaction
2. Defaced, torn or photocopied vouchers will not be accepted
3. Not to be used in conjunction with any other offer
4. Not exchangeable for cash
5. Present this voucher to the business to accept the offer
6. 10% OFF Dermalogica products when you have a 1 hour Dermalogica facial treatment

If you are in Helston, please come and browse in our store. We stock a wide range of natural bath, beauty & body products, crystals and gifts.

Revive

Sarah Louise Hair and Beauty Ltd
5 Frances Street, Truro, Cornwall,
TR1 3DN
Tel. 01872 260800

Terms & Conditions

1. Only one voucher per transaction
2. Defaced, torn or photocopied vouchers will not be accepted
3. Not to be used in conjunction with any other offer
4. Not exchangeable for cash
5. Present this voucher to the business to accept the offer
6. 20% OFF one hair or beauty treatment

Created some 8 years ago with an experienced group of gifted professionals, we are ready to advise and recommend, to pamper and please your every wish. Whether you seek advise on Hair, Beauty or your Wedding.

Sarah Louise Hair and Beauty Ltd

TR18 2JL
Tel: 01736 367269 or 07841339196

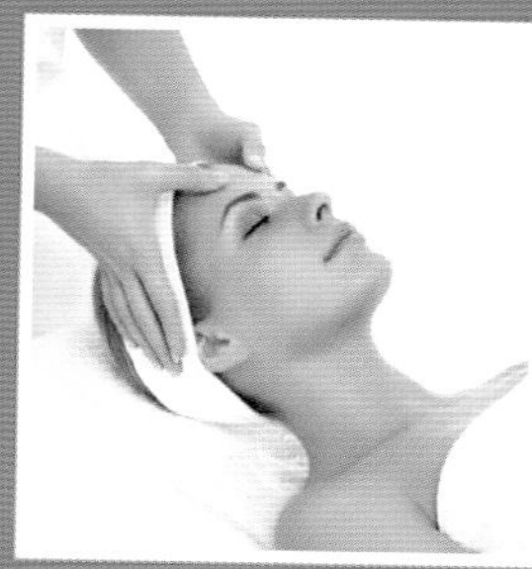

B21

KEEP IT CORNISH

Sorcha Cubitt is a qualified Beauty Therapist and Lecturer with over 15 years experience, specialising in IPL hair removal for the last 9 years.

See reverse for more information

Valid from 01.01.10 to 31.12.10

SAVE 50% OFF

Cornwall, TR18 2HT
Tel: 01736 360622

B22

KEEP IT CORNISH

SHB is a modern, award winning Hair and Beauty Salon. SHB has a 5 star accolade in the Good Salon Guide which reflects the extremely professional level of service.

See reverse for more information

Valid from 01.01.10 to 31.12.10

SAVE 10% OFF

Cornwall, TR18 2HT
Tel: 01736 360622

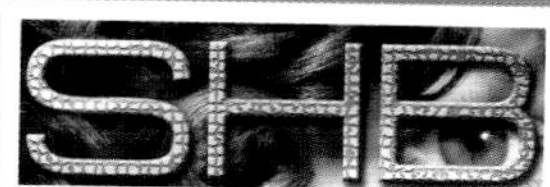

B23

KEEP IT CORNISH

SHB is a modern, award winning Hair and Beauty Salon. SHB has a 5 star accolade in the Good Salon Guide which reflects the extremely professional level of service.

See reverse for more information

Valid from 01.01.10 to 31.12.10

SAVE 10% OFF

Tel: 01736 757000

B24

KEEP IT CORNISH

TJ's BARBER SHOP

TJ's is a funky and fresh barbers shop cutting hair of both the old and the young. Tina and the team are always on hand whether it's a quick trim you need or a whole new restyle!

See reverse for more information

Valid from 01.01.10 to 31.12.10

SAVE 10% OFF

Tel: 01736 360022

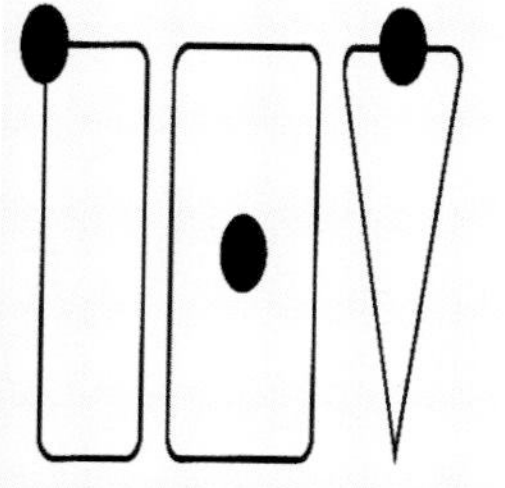

B25

KEEP IT CORNISH

Tswei Hunter Walsh

Tswei Hunter Walsh is situated in the beautiful and historic Chapel Street in Penzance. The salon is full of charm and character. The owners Daniel Tswei, Nadine Hunter and Vivienne Walsh opened their doors seven years ago and since then have become leaders in their field.

See reverse for more information

Valid from 01.01.10 to 31.12.10

SAVE 20% OFF

see reverse for details

Sorcha Cubitt Beauty Therapist
Shop 2 13/14 Market Place Penzance
TR18 2JL
Tel: 01736 367269 or 07841339196

Terms & Conditions

1. Only one voucher per transaction
2. Defaced, torn or photocopied vouchers will not be accepted
3. Not to be used in conjunction with any other offer
4. Not exchangeable for cash
5. Present this voucher to the business to accept the offer
6. 50% OFF Sothys Hydroptimale Facial

Sorcha also offers other advanced treatments, such as Micro-dermabrasion, Specialised Electrolysis for the removal of thread veins, skin tags, warts and milia, as well as non-surgical face and body lift.

Sorcha Cubitt Beauty Therapist
www.sorchacubitt.com

SHB (Stuarts Hair and Beauty)
33 Market Jew Street, Penzance,
Cornwall, TR18 2HT
Tel: 01736 360622

Terms & Conditions

1. Only one voucher per transaction
2. Defaced, torn or photocopied vouchers will not be accepted
3. Not to be used in conjunction with any other offer
4. Not exchangeable for cash
5. Present this voucher to the business to accept the offer
6. 10% OFF all retail products. Does not apply to any electrical items

SHB are the major stockists of Dermalogica, TIGI, KMS and GHDs in Penzance.

SHB (Stuarts Hair and Beauty)

SHB (Stuarts Hair and Beauty)
33 Market Jew Street, Penzance,
Cornwall, TR18 2HT
Tel: 01736 360622

Terms & Conditions

1. Only one voucher per transaction
2. Defaced, torn or photocopied vouchers will not be accepted
3. Not to be used in conjunction with any other offer
4. Not exchangeable for cash
5. Present this voucher to the business to accept the offer
6. 10% OFF dermalogica facial treatments

SHB are the major stockists of Dermalogica, TIGI, KMS and GHDs in Penzance.

SHB (Stuarts Hair and Beauty)

T.J's Barber Shop
2 Market Square, Hayle, Cornwall
TR27 4EA
Tel: 01736 757000

Terms & Conditions

1. Only one voucher per transaction
2. Defaced, torn or photocopied vouchers will not be accepted
3. Not to be used in conjunction with any other offer
4. Not exchangeable for cash
5. Present this voucher to the business to accept the offer

TJ's BARBER SHOP

Just pop in or if you don't want to wait why not book an appointment.

Tswei Hunter Walsh
55 Chapel Street, Penzance,
Cornwall, TR18 4AE
Tel: 01736 360022

Terms & Conditions

1. Only one voucher per transaction
2. Defaced, torn or photocopied vouchers will not be accepted
3. Not to be used in conjunction with any other offer
4. Not exchangeable for cash
5. Present this voucher to the business to accept the offer
6. 20% OFF any products when you purchase two or more. Quote **TSW002** when booking your appointment

Tswei Hunter Walsh

Employing the very best hairdressers in colour, cutting, bridal styling and correction work they have built a reputation that is second to none. The atmosphere is friendly and welcoming, they pride themselves on their relaxed but professional approach and treat each client as an individual.

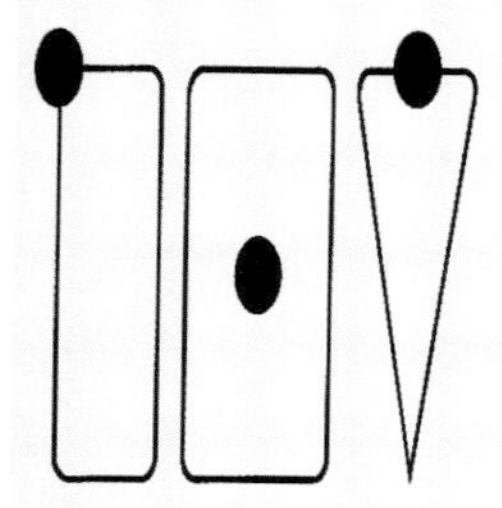

Tswei Hunter Walsh

B26

KEEP IT CORNISH

SAVE 20% OFF

see reverse for details

Tswei Hunter Walsh is situated in the beautiful and historic Chapel Street in Penzance. The salon is full of charm and character. The owners Daniel Tswei, Nadine Hunter and Vivienne Walsh opened their doors seven years ago and since then have become leaders in their field.

See reverse for more information

Valid from 01.01.10 to 31.12.10

Tel: 01736 360022

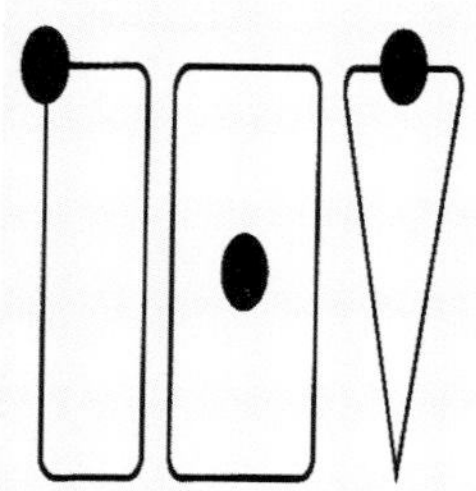

Tswei Hunter Walsh

B27

KEEP IT CORNISH

FREE TREATMENT

see reverse for details

Tswei Hunter Walsh is situated in the beautiful and historic Chapel Street in Penzance. The salon is full of charm and character. The owners Daniel Tswei, Nadine Hunter and Vivienne Walsh opened their doors seven years ago and since then have become leaders in their field.

See reverse for more information

Valid from 01.01.10 to 31.12.10

Tel: 01736 360022

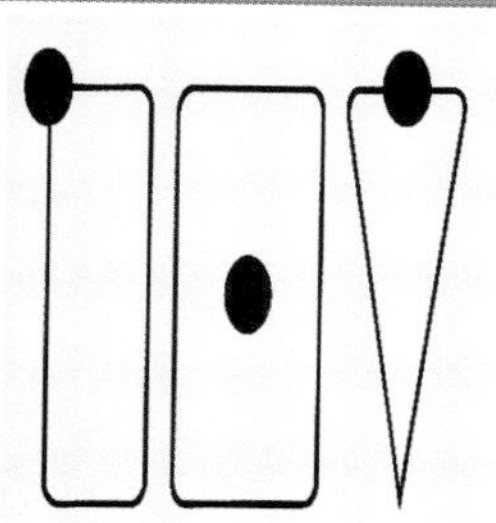

Tswei Hunter Walsh

B28

KEEP IT CORNISH

FREE SHINE TREATMENT

see reverse for details

Tswei Hunter Walsh is situated in the beautiful and historic Chapel Street in Penzance. The salon is full of charm and character. The owners Daniel Tswei, Nadine Hunter and Vivienne Walsh opened their doors seven years ago and since then have become leaders in their field.

See reverse for more information

Valid from 01.01.10 to 31.12.10

Tel: 01736 360022

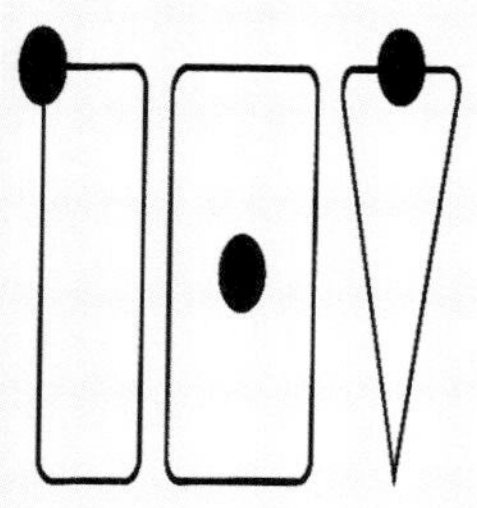

Tswei Hunter Walsh

B29

KEEP IT CORNISH

SAVE 20% OFF

see reverse for details

Tswei Hunter Walsh is situated in the beautiful and historic Chapel Street in Penzance. The salon is full of charm and character. The owners Daniel Tswei, Nadine Hunter and Vivienne Walsh opened their doors seven years ago and since then have become leaders in their field.

See reverse for more information

Valid from 01.01.10 to 31.12.10

Tel: 01736 360022

Waves

B30

KEEP IT CORNISH

SAVE 25% OFF

Waves hairdressing is one Falmouth most established hair salons, specialising in hair colouring. With over 50 years of combined experience all our stylists have attended Wella courses to keep up to date with the latest techniques and trends.

See reverse for more information

Valid from 01.01.10 to 31.12.10

Tswei Hunter Walsh
55 Chapel Street, Penzance,
Cornwall, TR18 4AE
Tel: 01736 360022

Terms & Conditions

1. Only one voucher per transaction
2. Defaced, torn or photocopied vouchers will not be accepted
3. Not to be used in conjunction with any other offer
4. Not exchangeable for cash
5. Present this voucher to the business to accept the offer
6. 20% OFF a semi-permanent or permanent colour with a graduate style. Quote **TSW003** when booking your appointment

Tswei Hunter Walsh

Employing the very best hairdressers in colour, cutting, bridal styling and correction work they have built a reputation that is second to none. The atmosphere is friendly and welcoming, they pride themselves on their relaxed but professional approach and treat each client as an individual.

Tswei Hunter Walsh
55 Chapel Street, Penzance,
Cornwall, TR18 4AE
Tel: 01736 360022

Terms & Conditions

1. Only one voucher per transaction
2. Defaced, torn or photocopied vouchers will not be accepted
3. Not to be used in conjunction with any other offer
4. Not exchangeable for cash
5. Present this voucher to the business to accept the offer
6. One FREE conditioning treatment with a cut and finish. Quote **TSW004** when booking your appointment

Tswei Hunter Walsh

Employing the very best hairdressers in colour, cutting, bridal styling and correction work they have built a reputation that is second to none. The atmosphere is friendly and welcoming, they pride themselves on their relaxed but professional approach and treat each client as an individual.

Tswei Hunter Walsh
55 Chapel Street, Penzance,
Cornwall, TR18 4AE
Tel: 01736 360022

Terms & Conditions

1. Only one voucher per transaction
2. Defaced, torn or photocopied vouchers will not be accepted
3. Not to be used in conjunction with any other offer
4. Not exchangeable for cash
5. Present this voucher to the business to accept the offer
6. One FREE shine treatment with a cut and finish. Quote **TSW005** when booking your appointment

Tswei Hunter Walsh

Employing the very best hairdressers in colour, cutting, bridal styling and correction work they have built a reputation that is second to none. The atmosphere is friendly and welcoming, they pride themselves on their relaxed but professional approach and treat each client as an individual.

Tswei Hunter Walsh
55 Chapel Street, Penzance,
Cornwall, TR18 4AE
Tel: 01736 360022

Terms & Conditions

1. Only one voucher per transaction
2. Defaced, torn or photocopied vouchers will not be accepted
3. Not to be used in conjunction with any other offer
4. Not exchangeable for cash
5. Present this voucher to the business to accept the offer
6. 20% OFF when you spend over £100. Quote **TSW001** when booking your appointment

Tswei Hunter Walsh

Employing the very best hairdressers in colour, cutting, bridal styling and correction work they have built a reputation that is second to none. The atmosphere is friendly and welcoming, they pride themselves on their relaxed but professional approach and treat each client as an individual.

Waves Hairdressing
4 Arwenack Street, Falmouth,
Cornwall, TR11 3HZ
Tel: 01326 319120

Terms & Conditions

1. Only one voucher per transaction
2. Defaced, torn or photocopied vouchers will not be accepted
3. Not to be used in conjunction with any other offer
4. Not exchangeable for cash
5. Present this voucher to the business to accept the offer
6. 25% OFF you final bill

Waves

We are stockists of the full ghd range and Paul Mitchell products.

Opening hours 9 to 4.30 Mon to Fri and Sat 9 till 3

KEEP IT ACTIVE

Cape Cornwall Golf and Leisure Resort is situated on the cliff tops above Cape Cornwall where the oceans meet. It is England's first and last 18-hole course, offering a challenging and unbelievably scenic experience for golfers of all levels aand abilities. The course was designed in 1980 by Bob Hamilton who later became the first club professional. Our current P.G.A Professional is Cornishman Scott Richards who specialises in golf coaching for all ages and abilities as well as having a very well stocked Pro Shop packed with golfing equipment for all standards of golfer.

Features of the course are the Cornish hedges (walls), which surround many holes and cut across some fairways, which can be formidable hazards, but they replace the usual golfing challenges such as lakes and trees. Adding to the difficulty is the capricious wind sometimes a gentle breeze at other times a force eight gale but rarely absent.

Without doubt Cape Cornwall should be on every golfers lifetime itinerary. But once ticked-off you'll want to come back again and again. If you are up for the challenge, please call us to book a tee time.

2 FOR 1
on green fees

Cape Cornwall
Golf and Leisure Resort

St. Just, Penzance, Cornwall, TR19 7NL

T 01736 788611
www.capecornwall.com
golf@capecornwall.com

Opening Hours.
Dawn till dusk

- This voucher offer entitles you to 2 for 1 on green fees.
- See voucher for terms and conditions.

KEEP IT ACTIVE

We have activities for everyone from surfing for the whole family to coasteering around the beautiful Cornish coastline. For those adrenaline junkies why not take to the skies and jump from a plane at 10,000 feet!

Arvor offers sea kayaking and sit on top sessions, courses and guided trips. We are registered with the Adventure Activities Licensing Agency.

See reverse for more information

Valid from 01.01.10 to 31.12.10

A1

KEEP IT CORNISH

SAVE 10% OFF

Arvor Mountain biking based at Bissoe near Falmouth, offer guided Mountain Biking with half and full days rides for beginners or experienced riders.

See reverse for more information

Valid from 01.01.10 to 31.12.10

A2

SAVE 10% OFF

Let us show you just how exhilarating surfing can be in a safe environment. There's much more space to learn and enjoy surfing on the beaches around St Agnes, far away from the crowded 'surf city' surf schools further up the coast.

See reverse for more information

Valid from 01.01.10 to 31.12.10

A3

KEEP IT CORNISH

SAVE BRING A FRIEND FREE

Cape Cornwall Golf and Leisure Resort is situated on the cliff tops above Cape Cornwall. It is England's first and last golf course, offering a challenging and scenic golfing experience for golfers of all levels and abilities.

See reverse for more information

Valid from 01.01.10 to 31.12.10

A4

SAVE 2 FOR 1

COASTLINE COASTEER

Newquay has some of the best coastlines in the UK and the best way to explore it is not only from the land but from the sea; inside caves, ducking through coves, negotiating rock jumps, plunge pools and whirl pools.

See reverse for more information

Valid from 01.01.10 to 31.12.10

A5

SAVE £8 OFF

Arvor Sea Kayaking
www.arvorseakayakingcornwall.co.uk
Tel: 07990 515263

Terms & Conditions

1. Only one voucher per transaction
2. Defaced, torn or photocopied vouchers will not be accepted
3. Not to be used in conjunction with any other offer
4. Not exchangeable for cash
5. Present this voucher to the business to accept the offer
6. 10% OFF with voucher (individuals or groups)

We primarily operate off Maenporth beach, but also use the sheltered waters of the Falmouth estuary, if conditions dictate. We cater for: BCU star awards, families and corporate groups. All equipment supplied!

Arvor Sea Kayaking

Arvor Mountain Biking
www.arvormoutainbikingcornwall.co.uk
Tel: 07990 515263

Terms & Conditions

1. Only one voucher per transaction
2. Defaced, torn or photocopied vouchers will not be accepted
3. Not to be used in conjunction with any other offer
4. Not exchangeable for cash
5. Present this voucher to the business to accept the offer
6. 10% OFF with a coupon (individuals or groups)

Led by a level 4 coach you can experience the easy going disused railway lines to the more hard – core steep descending single tracks, there's a trail for all levels. All equipment supplied!

Arvor Mountain Biking

Breakers Surf School
www.surf-lessons.co.uk.
Tel: 07725842196

Terms & Conditions

1. Only one voucher per transaction
2. Defaced, torn or photocopied vouchers will not be accepted
3. Not to be used in conjunction with any other offer
4. Not exchangeable for cash
5. Present this voucher to the business to accept the offer

Check us out at www.surf-lessons.co.uk or call 07725842196.

Breakers Surf School

Cape Cornwall Golf and Leisure Resort
St. Just, Penzance, Cornwall,
TR19 7NL
Tel: 01736 788611

Terms & Conditions

1. Only one voucher per transaction
2. Defaced, torn or photocopied vouchers will not be accepted
3. Not to be used in conjunction with any other offer
4. Not exchangeable for cash
5. Present this voucher to the business to accept the offer
6. 2 for 1 on a round of golf

Cape Cornwall Golf and Leisure Resort is situated on the cliff tops above Cape Cornwall. It is England's first and last golf course, offering a challenging and scenic golfing experience for golfers of all levels and abilities.

Cape Cornwall Golf and Leisure Resort

Coastline Coasteer
www.coastlinecoasteering.com
Tel: 01637 879571

Terms & Conditions

1. Only one voucher per transaction
2. Defaced, torn or photocopied vouchers will not be accepted
3. Not to be used in conjunction with any other offer
4. Not exchangeable for cash
5. Present this voucher to the business to accept the offer
6. £8 OFF a coasteering session
7. Voucher can only be used with pre-bookings

COASTLINE COASTEER

We specialise in family groups, stags, hens, schools, colleges and military groups. Please ask about our awesome group discounts.

Coastline Coasteer

A6

KEEP IT CORNISH

Located in the heart of Falmouth, The Core provides a friendly and comfortable atmosphere for attaining and maintaining your fitness goals.

See reverse for more information

Valid from 01.01.10 to 31.12.10

VIP PASS

Tel: 01326 310760

A7

The Cornish Parachute Club is based at Perranporth Airfield. Tandem Skydive, in our opinion is the ultimate high speed experience of a life time. After only 30 minutes briefing, you will be harnessed to your instructor.

See reverse for more information

Valid from 01.01.10 to 31.12.10

SAVE

£45 OFF

Tel: 07790439653

Curves

A8

Curves is not your typical gym. It's a unique place designed just for women. Even the machines are designed just for you. At every Curves, you'll find friendly instructors to help you reach your goals.

See reverse for more information

Valid from 01.01.10 to 31.12.10

FREE

ONE MONTH

Tel: 0800 130 0544

A9

Rip Curl English Surfing Federation Surf School. We have the equipment, expertise and enthusiasm to ensure that you achieve your goals and leave with a smile on your face.

See reverse for more information

Valid from 01.01.10 to 31.12.10

SAVE

15% OFF

falmouth& porthtowan surfschool
01326 212144

A10

We provide the experience, expertise and enthusiasm to ensure that you and your family have the time of your lives, safe in the knowledge that our fully qualified and expert staff will get you cruising on clean Atlantic waves and feeling the rush that only surfing can bring!

See reverse for more information

Valid from 01.01.10 to 31.07.10

SAVE

UPTO £30

The Core
2nd Floor, Post Office Buildings, The Moor, Falmouth TR11 3QA
Tel: 01326 310760

Terms & Conditions

1. Only one voucher per transaction
2. Defaced, torn or photocopied vouchers will not be accepted
3. Not to be used in conjunction with any other offer
4. Not exchangeable for cash
5. Present this voucher to the business to accept the offer
6. Receive a complimentary VIP pass to try one of our studio classes

We offer a range of fun studio classes to keep you in the mood for fitness as well as a dedicated personal training facility and a state-of-the-art Vibrogym.

The Core

Cornish Parachute Club Ltd
Perranporth Airfield, Higher Trevellas St Agnes, Cornwall, TR5 0XS
Tel: 07790439653

Terms & Conditions

1. Only one voucher per transaction
2. Defaced, torn or photocopied vouchers will not be accepted
3. Not to be used in conjunction with any other offer
4. Not exchangeable for cash
5. Present this voucher to the business to accept the offer
6. Save £45. Skydive for £190, normal price £235

You will exit the aircraft at 10,000ft and experience the thrill and exhilaration this sport can offer. With the parachute open take 5 minutes to enjoy the spectacular views, as you float back to the earth.

Cornish Parachute Club Ltd

Curves
Truro, Newquay, Penryn St Austell and Launceston
Tel: 0800 130 0544

Terms & Conditions

1. Only one voucher per transaction
2. Defaced, torn or photocopied vouchers will not be accepted
3. Not to be used in conjunction with any other offer
4. Not exchangeable for cash
5. Present this voucher to the business to accept the offer
6. 1 month free at any participating venue

Curves

At Curves we offer commonsense weight loss and a motivating workout that anyone can do. Best of all, Curves really works.

Curves

English Surfing Federation
www.englishsurfschool.com
Tel: 01637 879571

Terms & Conditions

1. Only one voucher per transaction
2. Defaced, torn or photocopied vouchers will not be accepted
3. Not to be used in conjunction with any other offer
4. Not exchangeable for cash
5. Present this voucher to the business to accept the offer
6. 15% OFF your first surfing lesson

We also offer amazing group discounts, family surf packages, specialist one to one coaching and equipment hire. We will not be beaten on price or service.

English Surfing Federation

Falmouth Surf School
www.falmouthsurfschool.co.uk
Tel: 01326 212144

Terms & Conditions

1. Only one voucher per transaction
2. Defaced, torn or photocopied vouchers will not be accepted
3. Not to be used in conjunction with any other offer
4. Not exchangeable for cash
5. Present this voucher to the business to accept the offer
6. Save £10 per person
7. Valid for advance bookings for 3 or more people between April and June 2010
8. All terms and conditions refer to their website under 'booking form'

At Falmouth / Porthtowan Surf School, we provide transport to wherever the best waves are and all equipment including wetsuits and boards. Your first surf can change your life forever. It's hard to believe anything this fun can be healthy!

We provide the experience, expertise and enthusiasm to ensure that you and your family have the time of your lives, safe in the knowledge that our fully qualified and expert staff will get you cruising on clean Atlantic waves and feeling the rush that only surfing can bring!

See reverse for more information

Valid from 01.01.10 to 31.07.10

SAVE 10% OFF

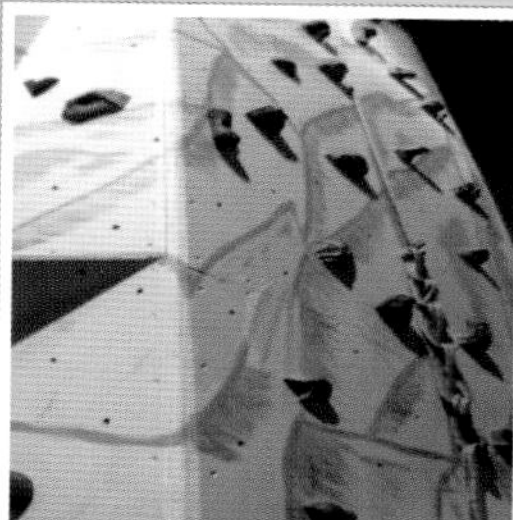

Granite Planet Climbing Centre

The Only Dedicated Climbing Centre in Cornwall. A new indoor climbing facility, ideal location to improve your skills or to learn how to climb.

The centre is open from 10am - 10pm Monday to Saturday, and 10am - 5pm Sundays.

See reverse for more information

Valid from 01.01.10 to 31.12.10

SAVE £12.50

Gwithian Academy of Surfing

Learn the basics or fine tune your surfing with a lesson at the Gwithian Academy of Surfing. A lesson at our surf school can help you achieve your surfing goals.

See reverse for more information

SAVE 20% OFF

HOTROCK CLIMBS

Hotrockclimbs is a Newquay based adventure activities company. We offer a broad variety of outdoor activities throughout the year.

See reverse for more information

Valid from 01.01.10 to 31.12.10

SAVE 10% OFF

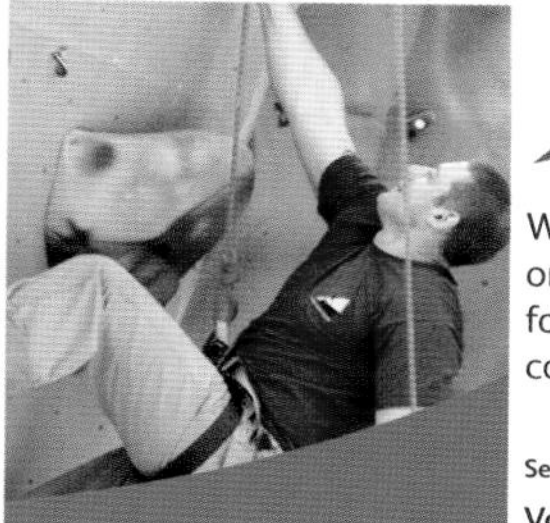

A15 KEEP IT CORNISH

Weather you're an experienced climber or a novice, our indoor climbing wall caters for casual climbing and a variety of climbing courses and sessions.

See reverse for more information

Valid from 01.01.10 to 31.12.10

SAVE £2.90

Tel: 01326 376633

Tel: 01637 878743 or 07729091380

KEEP IT... ACTIVE

Falmouth Surf School
www.falmouthsurfschool.co.uk
Tel: 01326 212144

Terms & Conditions

1. Only one voucher per transaction
2. Defaced, torn or photocopied vouchers will not be accepted
3. Not to be used in conjunction with any other offer
4. Not exchangeable for cash
5. Present this voucher to the business to accept the offer
6. 10% discount on all full priced lessons booked in advance untill August 2010
7. All terms and conditions refer to their website under 'booking form'

At Falmouth / Porthtowan Surf School, we provide transport to wherever the best waves are and all equipment including wetsuits and boards. Your first surf can change your life forever. It's hard to believe anything this fun can be healthy!

Granite Planet Climbing Centre
Parkengue, Kernick Industrial Estate,
Penryn, TR10 9EP
Tel: 01326 376633

Terms & Conditions

1. Only one voucher per transaction
2. Defaced, torn or photocopied vouchers will not be accepted
3. Not to be used in conjunction with any other offer
4. Not exchangeable for cash
5. Present this voucher to the business to accept the offer
6. Must be pre-booked
7. Taster session for up to 6 people for one and a half hours is £25, which is the normal price for 4 so saving £12.50

Granite Planet Climbing Centre

Ideal opportunity for Schools, youth groups to undertake an adventurous activity in a controlled environment. Corporate training, birthday parties please phone for details.

The centre is open from 10am - 10pm Monday to Saturday, and 10am - 5pm Sundays.

Gwithian Academy of Surfing
www.surfacademy.co.uk
Tel: 01736 757579

Terms & Conditions

1. Only one voucher per transaction
2. Defaced, torn or photocopied vouchers will not be accepted
3. Not to be used in conjunction with any other offer
4. Not exchangeable for cash
5. Present this voucher to the business to accept the offer
6. 20% OFF in April, May and June 2010

The Gwithian Academy of Surfing is a British Surfing Association Approved Level 4 (the highest possible approval rating) surf school that operates from Gwithian in St Ives Bay.

Hotrockclimbs
15b Tolcarne Road, Newquay,
Cornwall, TR7 2NQ
Tel: 01637878743 or 07729091380

Terms & Conditions

1. Only one voucher per transaction
2. Defaced, torn or photocopied vouchers will not be accepted
3. Not to be used in conjunction with any other offer
4. Not exchangeable for cash
5. Present this voucher to the business to accept the offer
6. 10% OFF to all new customers

Our outdoor adventure activities include rock climbing courses in Newquay, surfing on the world famous Fistral beach, coasteering in Newquay at the Gazzle and rock climbing courses on the Cornish Moors (Dartmoor, Bodmin Moor). We take great pride ensuring that all our adventure activities are tailored to the groups or clients age, abilities and needs. We also provide a unique mobile adventure activities service for the UK.

Newquay Sports Centre
Tretherras Road, Yeoman Way,
Newquay, TR7 2SL
Tel: 01637 875533

Terms & Conditions

1. Only one voucher per transaction
2. Defaced, torn or photocopied vouchers will not be accepted
3. Not to be used in conjunction with any other offer
4. Not exchangeable for cash
5. Present this voucher to the business to accept the offer
6. FREE registration to become a climbing wall user (value of £2.90)

The 120m squared wall includes a basic selection, a challenging Cristalithe and a Freefrom area all boasting features such as ledges and hand jams; all in all a perfect alternative to traditional methods of keeping fit. It is these essential elements that produces our walls appeal and attracts experienced climbers and beginners, providing an exciting and exhilarating experience that even the whole family can enjoy.

A16

KEEP IT CORNISH

Kitesurfing is the fastest growing water sport in the world. Ocean High Kiteboarding provides lessons from taster days to full courses with professional IKO/BKSA instructors.

See reverse for more information

Valid from 01.01.10 to 31.12.10

SAVE 15% OFF

OceanHigh KITEBOARDING

A17

Kitesurfing is the fastest growing water sport in the world. Ocean High Kiteboarding provides lessons from taster days to full courses with professional IKO/BKSA instructors.

See reverse for more information

Valid from 01.01.10 to 31.12.10

SAVE 10% OFF

A18

The Oxygen Health Club is a unique one-stop Health Centre, which is located in the heart of Penzance. Our aim is to help you improve your life!

See reverse for more information

Valid from 01.01.10 to 31.12.10

SAVE 1 MONTH FREE

A19

Penzance Leisure Centre, now 4 years old comprises a 25-metre 6-lane competition standard main swimming pool, learner pool, flume, sports hall, fitness gym & health suite, dance/exercise studio, ancillary club & meeting rooms, crèche and café bar.

See reverse for more information

Valid from 01.01.10 to 31.12.10

SAVE £20

A20

Based in Newquay, RBBS are the only bodyboarding school in the UK. We coach complete novices, top level competitors and everyone in between. We are open for business 7 days a week, 12 months a year.

See reverse for more information

Valid from 01.01.10 to 31.12.10

SAVE 15% OFF

Ocean High
www.oceanhigh.co.uk
Tel: 01736 390 001

Terms & Conditions

1. Only one voucher per transaction
2. Defaced, torn or photocopied vouchers will not be accepted
3. Not to be used in conjunction with any other offer
4. Not exchangeable for cash
5. Present this voucher to the business to accept the offer
6. 15% OFF a course per person if 2 people book to come on the course together

Friendly, safe tuition, 7 Days per week from March to November. Based in Marazion, West Cornwall.

Ocean High

Ocean High
www.oceanhigh.co.uk
Tel: 01736 390 001

Terms & Conditions

1. Only one voucher per transaction
2. Defaced, torn or photocopied vouchers will not be accepted
3. Not to be used in conjunction with any other offer
4. Not exchangeable for cash
5. Present this voucher to the business to accept the offer
6. 10% OFF a 2 or 3 day kite surf course for one person

Friendly, safe tuition, 7 Days per week from March to November. Based in Marazion, West Cornwall.

Ocean High

Oxygen Health Club
1st floor, 4 Market Jew Street, Penzance, Cornwall, TR18 2HN
Tel: 01736 333831

Terms & Conditions

1. Only one voucher per transaction
2. Defaced, torn or photocopied vouchers will not be accepted
3. Not to be used in conjunction with any other offer
4. Not exchangeable for cash
5. Present this voucher to the business to accept the offer
6. 1 Month FREE Membership for new members ONLY
7. Valid for 50 Keep it Cornish customers on a first come, first served basis

We offer the following services: State-of-the-art Gymnasium, Massage, Pilates, Yoga, Chiropractic Clinic, Kinesiology Clinic, Homoeopathy, Traditional and Infra-Red Saunas.

Oxygen Health Club

Penzance Leisure Centre
St Clare, Penzance, Cornwall, TR18 3QW
Tel: 01736 874744

Terms & Conditions

1. Only one voucher per transaction
2. Defaced, torn or photocopied vouchers will not be accepted
3. Not to be used in conjunction with any other offer
4. Not exchangeable for cash
5. Present this voucher to the business to accept the offer
6. Pay no joining fee, saving £20, monthly subscription applies
7. Membership includes use of the pool, the gym, all group work out classes, use of the steam room, sauna & spa

For detailed programmes & prices please visit our website www.leisurecentre.com or call reception on 01736 874744.

Penzance Leisure Centre

Rob Barbers Bodyboarding School
www.robbarber.com
Tel: 01637 879571

Terms & Conditions

1. Only one voucher per transaction
2. Defaced, torn or photocopied vouchers will not be accepted
3. Not to be used in conjunction with any other offer
4. Not exchangeable for cash
5. Present this voucher to the business to accept the offer
6. 15% OFF first bodyboard lesson
7. Voucher can only be used with pre-bookings

Our instructors are BSA approved, fully qualified beach lifeguards and members of the National Coaching Federation so you can have confidence that you are in safe, qualified hands. We also offer amazing group discounts, family packages, specialist one to one coaching and equipment hire.

Rob Barbers Bodyboarding School

A21

KEEP IT CORNISH

SAVE

2 FOR 1

Sal Diving Company is a PADI 5* Center & a BSAC Premier Center. We offer a full range of dive courses from beginner to Instructor level and run an active dive club. We have a well stocked shop & also offer a full range of equipment servicing.

See reverse for more information

Valid from 01.01.10 to 31.12.10

Cornwall, PL26 6BU
Tel: 01726 844640

Ships & Castles
CLL

A22

SAVE

FREE DAY GYM PASS

Superb fitness facilities to help make you the person you want to be; fitter, slimmer, healthier. Fully equipped gym + fitness classes + swimming pool. No joining fees or long commitments. Please ask about special joining offers.

See reverse for more information

Valid from 01.01.10 to 31.12.10

Tel: 01326 212129

A23

SAVE

HALF PRICE LESSON

Run by locals in Sennen Cove. Our surf school emphasises on maximum water time and less time talking on the beach as learning to surf is all about being in the water learning the techniques.

See reverse for more information

Valid from 01.01.10 to 31.12.10

Mobile: 07590 043419

Truro Leisure Centre
CLL

A24

SAVE

FREE DAY GYM PASS

Superb fitness facilities to help make you the person you want to be; fitter, slimmer, healthier. Fully equipped gym + fitness classes + swimming pool. No joining fees or long commitments. Please ask about special joining offers.

See reverse for more information

Valid from 01.01.10 to 31.12.10

Tel: 01872 261628

SAVING YOU HUNDREDS OF POUNDS ON GOING OUT IN YOUR LOCAL AREA

Sal diving
Old Pump House, Pentewan, St Austell
Cornwall, PL26 6BU
Tel: 01726 844640

Terms & Conditions

1. Only one voucher per transaction
2. Defaced, torn or photocopied vouchers will not be accepted
3. Not to be used in conjunction with any other offer
4. Not exchangeable for cash
5. Present this voucher to the business to accept the offer
6. 2 for 1 discover scuba diving , normally £25pp for an introductory session in the pool, one person pays, one person goes free

All divers must be medically fit & will be required to complete a medical form and must be aged 10 years +

Sal diving

Ships & Castles Leisure Centre
Castle Drive, Falmouth
TR11 4NG
Tel: 01326 212129

Terms & Conditions

1. Only one voucher per person
2. Photocopied vouchers will not be accepted
3. Not to be used in conjunction with any other offer
4. Not exchangeable for cash
5. Present this voucher to the business to accept the offer
6. Health questionnaire + mini induction required
7. Call to book a day. Spaces subject to availability

Ships & Castles
CLL

Superb fitness facilities to help make you the person you want to be; fitter, slimmer, healthier. Fully equipped gym + fitness classes + swimming pool. No joining fees or long commitments. Please ask about special joining offers.

Ships & Castles Leisure Centre

Smart Surf School
Sennen Cove
Tel: 01736 871817
Mobile: 07590 043419

Terms & Conditions

1. Only one voucher per transaction
2. Defaced, torn or photocopied vouchers will not be accepted
3. Not to be used in conjunction with any other offer
4. Not exchangeable for cash
5. Present this voucher to the business to accept the offer
6. Buy one surf lesson get one half price

We have the cheapest prices around and all of our instructors are sponsored surfers with years of beach lifeguard experience, what more do you want!

Smart Surf School

Truro Leisure Centre
College Road, Truro.
TR1 3GA
Tel: 01872 261628

Terms & Conditions

1. Only one voucher per person
2. Photocopied vouchers will not be accepted
3. Not to be used in conjunction with any other offer
4. Not exchangeable for cash
5. Present this voucher to the business to accept the offer
6. Health questionnaire + mini induction required
7. Call to book a day. Spaces subject to availability

Truro Leisure Centre
CLL

Superb fitness facilities to help make you the person you want to be; fitter, slimmer, healthier. Fully equipped gym + fitness classes + swimming pool. No joining fees or long commitments. Please ask about special joining offers.

Truro Leisure Centre

KEEP IT FUN

Maritime Museum Cornwall

china clay
COUNTRY PARK
MINING & HERITAGE CENTRE
A DAY OF
DISCOVERY &
ADVENTURE
IN THE HEART OF
CORNWALL
What's on
OFFER
• 26 acres of woodland
• Cycle / walking trail to St Austell & Eden Project (Part of the Clay Trails Project)
• Indoor interactive displays
• Nature Trails & woodland walks
• Cornwall's largest working water wheel
• Preserved Victorian china clay works, machinery & equipment exhibitions
• Vintage commercial vehicles & locomotive
• Children's Challenge Trail
• Visitor platform overlooking a working China Clay Pit
• Licensed cafe with outside terrace
• Gift shop
www.chinaclaycountry.co.uk
tel: 01726 850362 · email: info@chinaclaycountry.co.uk
2 miles north of St Austell on the B3274 - China Clay Country Park
Wheal Martyn · Carthew · St Austell PL26 8XG

FREE entry for under 16's

China CLay Country Park

Wheal Martyn, Carthew,
St Austell, Cornwall, PL26 8XG

T 01726 850362
www.chinaclaycountry.co.uk
info@chinaclaycountry.co.uk

Opening Hours.
Varies, please check with attraction.

Terms and Conditions

- This voucher offer entitles you to FREE child entry
- See voucher for terms and conditions

Discover yourself at China Clay Country Park

Discover for yourself how Cornwall's china clay industry literally shaped the environment and communities of the heart of Cornwall at this preserved Victorian clay-works set in 26 acres of woodland. The modern industry is revealed with a view of a massive working pit.

Set in 26 acres of woodland, nestling in the historic Ruddle Valley on the outskirts of St Austell, the China Clay Country Park provides a fascinating day out for all the family. The Park, now part of the Cornish Mining World Heritage Site, is set in the grounds of two former working china clay pits and provides visitors with a fascinating insight into china clay - how it was mined, what is was used for and what it meant for the families who lived in the area.

Whether you want to find out more about Cornwall's rich China Clay heritage in the interactive visitor centre, fancy exploring the nature trails complete with children's woodland play area and adventure course, or want a unique view of a modern China Clay pit at work with monitor jets and giant machinery, the China Clay Country Park has something for everyone.

FN11

FREE entrance for up to 6

see voucher for terms and conditions

ountry Skittles a great fun xperience whether r a family get gether or a night ut with friends.

as everything you need to have ally good time. There are 4 omated skittle alleys, a restaurant n delicious home cooked food ging from generous griddled steaks l the ever-popular Skittles Grillstones everal vegetarian dishes.

There are lots of great games, a shooting gallery, crazy golf, pool and video games, and last but not least a well-stocked bar to quench your thirst after all your activity! The special Christmas menu is always something to look out for. Highly recommended.

Country Skittles

Country Skittles, Townshend,
Hayle TR27 6ER

01736 850209
www.countryskittles.com

During school holidays
2pm - 11pm Mon-Sat
12pm - 10:30 Sundays

All other times
6 pm - 11pm Mon - Fri
2pm - 11pm Saturday
12pm - 10:30pm Sundays

FN26

10% OFF full admission price

cently voted the South West's itor Attraction of the Year, this ard winning Museum offers nething for everyone.

up your sleeves with fun filled ivities to suit all ages, take in the breathtaking views from the 29 metre tower, marvel at one of only three natural underwater viewing windows in the world and explore the amazing interactive hands-on exhibits.

There's ever changing exhibitions, hands-on family activities, talks, lectures, displays, events and the opportunity to get out on the water and see marine and bird life.

National Maritime Museum Cornwall is a new generation of Museum offering a lot more than you might expect.

National Maritime Museum Cornwall

National Maritime Museum
Cornwall, Discovery Quay
Falmouth, Cornwall, TR11 3QY

T 01326 313388
www.nnmc.co.uk

Opening Hours.
10am - 5pm everyday of the year
(except Christmas day & boxing day)

- This voucher offer entitles you to 10% off your admission.
- See voucher for terms and conditions

TR4 8HJ
Tel: 01872 560753

FN1

When you arrive & ride at the ATV Centre you will be quad biking on the UK's largest and best outdoor ATV track.

See reverse for more information

Valid from 01.01.10 to 31.12.10

SAVE 10% OFF

PL33 9EU
Tel: 01840 211 460

BIG DUNK'S Paintball

FN2

At Big Dunk's play paintball or Outdoor Digital Laser Tag on a purpose built UKPSF accredited site with 9 game zones set in 20 acres. Full instruction and organised games from £10 per player, twilight and night games also available.

See reverse for more information

Valid from 01.01.10 to 31.12.10

SAVE UPTO £10

Tel: 01637 878134

FN3

Take the ultimate undersea safari at the award-winning Blue Reef Aquarium in Newquay where there's a world of underwater adventure just waiting to be discovered. Over 40 living displays reveal the sheer variety of life in the deep.

See reverse for more information

Valid from 01.01.10 to 31.12.10

SAVE 15% OFF

Tel: 01872 573126

Callestick Farm
Cornish Dairy Ice Cream

FN4

Superb ice creams made on our Cornish farm with fresh whole milk, rich Cornish cream and the finest confectionery or fruits. Also offering an excellent range of sorbets made with our own spring water.

See reverse for more information

Valid from 01.01.10 to 31.12.10

SAVE 15% OFF

Tel: 01579 320251

FN5

- Open All Year for tours underground
- 3 Gigantic Caverns with stunning Subterranean Lake
- 6.5 Acres of Woodland Walk & Faery Dell with picnic areas

See reverse for more information

Valid from 01.01.10 to 31.12.10

SAVE 10% OFF

The ATV Centre
Blackwater, Truro, Cornwall
TR4 8HJ
Tel: 01872 560753

Terms & Conditions

1. Only one voucher per transaction
2. Defaced, torn or photocopied vouchers will not be accepted
3. Not to be used in conjunction with any other offer
4. Not exchangeable for cash
5. Present this voucher to the business to accept the offer
6. 10% OFF arrive and ride quad biking sessions
7. **ALL RIDERS MUST WEAR LONG TROUSERS, FULL LENGTH TOPS, NO OPEN SHOES AND OVER THE ANKLE SOCKS**

Whatever your age or experience you will be kitted up in full safety gear (including elbow & knee pads, body armour, helmet, gloves and safety goggles) and then taken to our learner track to be given expert tuition by experienced instructors prior to spending your time on our intermediate 1 and intermediate 2 tracks. Marshalls are positioned around the track to keep you safe while you experience the challenge and thrills of the ATV Centre. (No experience required)

The ATV Centre
Email: atvcentre@yahoo.co.uk

Big Dunk's Paintball
Trevilley Farm, Delabole, Cornwall
PL33 9EU
Tel: 01840 211 460

Terms & Conditions

1. Only one voucher per transaction
2. Defaced, torn or photocopied vouchers will not be accepted
3. Not to be used in conjunction with any other offer
4. Not exchangeable for cash
5. Present this voucher to the business to accept the offer
6. Pre booked games only
7. £1 OFF per player for up to 10 people

BIG DUNK'S Paintball

At Big Dunk's play paintball or Outdoor Digital Laser Tag on a purpose built UKPSF accredited site with 9 game zones set in 20 acres. Full instruction and organised games from £10 per player, twilight and night games also available.

Great fun for family groups and birthday parties too.

Big Dunk's Paintball

Blue Reef Aquarium
Towan Promenade, Newquay
Cornwall TR7 1DU.
Tel: 01637 878134

Terms & Conditions

1. Only one voucher per transaction
2. Defaced, torn or photocopied vouchers will not be accepted
3. Not to be used in conjunction with any other offer
4. Not exchangeable for cash
5. Present this voucher to the business to accept the offer
6. 15% OFF the admission price
7. Voucher valid upto 6 people

Enjoy close encounters with our seahorses, tropical sharks, stingrays, giant octopus and hundreds of incredible aquatic creatures. At the Aquarium's heart is the giant ocean tank where an underwater tunnel offers incredible views of reef sharks and shoals of colourful fish.

OPEN DAILY FROM 10AM

Blue Reef Aquarium

Callestick Farm
Callestick Farm,Callestick,Truro
Cornwall,TR4 9LL
Tel: 01872 5731126

Terms & Conditions

1. Only one voucher per transaction
2. Defaced, torn or photocopied vouchers will not be accepted
3. Not to be used in conjunction with any other offer
4. Not exchangeable for cash
5. Present this voucher to the business to accept the offer
6. 15% OFF when you buy 2 one litre tubs or bigger of ice cream

Callestick Farm
Cornish Dairy Ice Cream

Flavours to tempt all -including award winning Clotted Cream Vanilla with bourbon bean, Butterscotch Pecan and over twenty more flavours. Available in retail and catering sizes.

Carnglaze Caverns
St Neot, Liskeard, Cornwall
PL14 6HQ
Tel: 01579 320251

Terms & Conditions

1. Only one voucher per transaction
2. Defaced, torn or photocopied vouchers will not be accepted
3. Not to be used in conjunction with any other offer
4. Not exchangeable for cash
5. Present this voucher to the business to accept the offer
6. 10% OFF full priced tickets, voucher not valid in August

- Concerts Underground ~ Classical to Rock
- Weddings in 4 locations
- Open all year Monday - Saturday 10am till 5pm

Carnglaze Caverns

Falmouth, Cornwall, TR11 5JA
Tel: 01326 250258

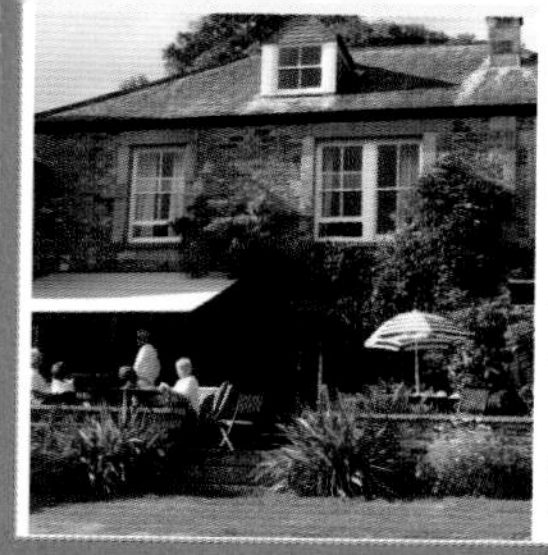

Carwinion
Cornwall's Bamboo Garden

FN6

Carwinion House is a beautiful 18th Century manor house tucked away in its own private estate in the lush North Helford area of Cornwall, only a stone's throw from Falmouth. Jane's cream teas, served on Carwinion's garden terrace, are said to be the best in Cornwall and simply must be sampled.

SAVE
2 FOR 1

See reverse for more information

Valid from 01.01.10 to 31.12.10

Cornwall, PL26 8XG
Tel: 01726 850362

FN7

Discover for yourself how Cornwall's china clay industry literally shaped the environment and communities of the heart of Cornwall at this preserved Victorian clay-works set in 26 acres of woodland.

See reverse for more information

Valid from 01.01.10 to 31.12.10

TR20 8XA.
Tel: 07831 757934

ENGLISH HERITAGE
Chysauster Ancient Village

FN8

Almost at the very tip of the country you will discover Celtic Cornwall at Chysauster. The Original inhabitants of this ancient settlement occupied the site almost 2000 years ago.

FREE

See reverse for more information

Valid from 01.04.10 to 31.10.10

Tel: 01208 821469

FN9

Colliford's Kids Kingdom is a 30,000 square foot, all-weather, action packed adventure playground. We have so much for you to do. You can play in the mega ball pool, get lost in the never ending net mazes, wiz along on

SAVE

See reverse for more information

Valid from 01.01.10 to 31.12.10

Tel: 01637 880544

THE CORNISH BIRDS OF PREY CENTRE & ANIMAL PARK

FN10

The Cornish Birds of Prey Centre has a large collection of birds of prey and owls, as well as a variety of other birds and animals. Flying displays are held daily at 12, 2 and 4, subject to weather conditions.

SAVE
2 FOR 1

See reverse for more information

Valid from Good Friday to 31.10.10

Carwinion
Carwinion Road, Mawnan Smith
Falmouth, Cornwall, TR11 5JA
Tel: 01326 250258

Terms & Conditions

1. Only one voucher per transaction
2. Defaced, torn or photocopied vouchers will not be accepted
3. Not to be used in conjunction with any other offer
4. Not exchangeable for cash
5. Present this voucher to the business to accept the offer
7. 2 for1 cream teas are served from April 1st to September 30 – please check availability at other times of the year

Carwinion House is a beautiful 18th Century manor house tucked away in its own private estate in the lush North Helford area of Cornwall, only a stone's throw from Falmouth. Jane's cream teas, served on Carwinion's garden terrace, are said to be the best in Cornwall and simply must be sampled.

Carwinion
www.carwinion.co.uk

China Clay Country Park
Wheal Martyn, Carthew, St Austell
Cornwall, PL26 8XG
Tel: 01726 850362

Terms & Conditions

1. Only one voucher per transaction
2. Defaced, torn or photocopied vouchers will not be accepted
3. Not to be used in conjunction with any other offer
4. Not exchangeable for cash
5. Present this voucher to the business to accept the offer
6. Children Under 16 **FREE**

The modern industry is revealed with a view of a massive working pit.

China Clay Country Park
Email: info@chinaclaycountry.co.uk

Chysauster Ancient Village
4 miles north of Penzance of B3311
TR20 8XA.
Tel: 07831 757934

Terms & Conditions

1. Only one voucher per transaction
2. Defaced, torn or photocopied vouchers will not be accepted
3. Not to be used in conjunction with any other offer
4. Not exchangeable for cash
5. Present this voucher to the business to accept the offer
6. 2 children go **FREE** with an accompanying paying adult
7. All rights of admission reserved by English Heritage
8. Redemption code SWKCC

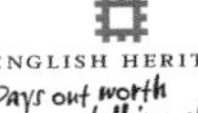

Explore a cluster of unique homesteads found only in this area, set amongst wild and rugged surroundings, wild flowers and windswept heather. Ponder at the entrance to the 'fogou' what it might once have been used for?

Chysauster Ancient Village

Colliford Lake Park
Bolventor, Bodmin Moor
Cornwall, Pl14 6PZ
Tel: 01208 821469

Terms & Conditions

1. Only one voucher per transaction
2. Defaced, torn or photocopied vouchers will not be accepted
3. Not to be used in conjunction with any other offer
4. Not exchangeable for cash
5. Present this voucher to the business to accept the offer
6. Half price entry for up to 2 children

on the infamous toboggan run, spin through the wicked rollers and more!

Colliford Lake Park

The Cornish Birds of Prey Centre
Winnards Perch, St Columb Major
Cornwall TR9 6DH.
Tel: 01637 880544

Terms & Conditions

1. Only one voucher per transaction
2. Defaced, torn or photocopied vouchers will not be accepted
3. Not to be used in conjunction with any other offer
4. Not exchangeable for cash
5. Present this voucher to the business to accept the offer
6. 2 for 1 on enrty

THE CORNISH BIRDS OF PREY CENTRE & ANIMAL PARK

Falconry courses / experiences are run throughout the year. Gift vouchers are available.

The Cornish Birds of Prey Centre

www.countryskittles.com

Country Skittles is a great fun experience whether for a family get-together or a night out with friends. It has everything you need to have a really good night out.

See reverse for more information

Valid from 01.01.10 to 31.12.10

SAVE UPTO £4.50

Cornwall, TR27 6ER
Tel: 01736 850209

At 15 metres tall and frighteningly fast, The Beast towers high in the sky, looming above those too scared to ride! Climb aboard the Viking Warrior Ship, swinging high through the air, slide down the Raging Rivers raft ride to the biggest splash of your life and whoosh down the rapids of Thunder Falls - Cornwall's only double drop log flume!

See reverse for more information

Valid from 01.01.10 to 31.12.10

PL27 7RA
Tel: 01841 540276

Come and enjoy the fun of an all-weather attraction, providing a day's entertainment for all ages. There is so much to do including Bull Pen indoor play area, drop slides, mini tractors, pat-a-pet, raging bull rides, adventure playgrounds and much more!

See reverse for more information

Valid from 01.01.10 to 31.12.10

Tel: 01872 510349 or 01872 510246

greenleisure.co.uk
experience the country ... enjoy the difference

Would you like to try your hand at off-road driving in one of our environmentally friendly biodiesel landrovers under the watchful eye of an expert? Well now you can with this gift voucher from greenleisure.co.uk

See reverse for more information

Valid from 01.01.10 to 31.12.10

Tel: 07773 255426

The Isles of Scilly, just 28 miles south west of Cornwall offer a unique getaway. This idyllic group of sub-tropical islands provide the perfect day out for singles, families, friends and couples with a wide variety of activities.

See reverse for more information

Valid from 01.01.10 to 31.12.10

Tel: 0845 710 5555

Country Skittles
Bunkers Hill, Townshend, Hayle
Cornwall, TR27 6ER
Tel: 01736 850209

Terms & Conditions

1. Only one voucher per transaction
2. Defaced, torn or photocopied vouchers will not be accepted
3. Not to be used in conjunction with any other offer
4. Not exchangeable for cash
5. Present this voucher to the business to accept the offer
6. **FREE** entrance for up to 6 people
   Usually 75p per person

At Country Skittles, there are 4 automated skittle alleys, a fantastic restaurant serving delicious home-made meals, great games, a shooting gallery, crazy golf, pool tables and video games. There is also a well-stocked bar to quench your thirst!

Country Skittles

Cornwall's Crealy
Tredinnick, Wadebridge, Cornwall
PL27 7RA
Tel: 01841 540276

Terms & Conditions

1. Only one voucher per transaction
2. Defaced, torn or photocopied vouchers will not be accepted
3. Not to be used in conjunction with any other offer
4. Not exchangeable for cash
5. Present this voucher to the business to accept the offer
6. Normal opening times apply
7. £1 OFF per person for a maximum of four people

Visit Cornwall's Crealy for Maximum Fun Guaranteed at the County's biggest family attraction. Venture into the Realms of Magic, Action, Wild Water, Enchantment, Nature and Animals with hundreds of the county's cuddliest furry friends to meet and feed!

Cornwall's Crealy

DairyLand Farm World
Nr Newquay, Cornwall,
TR8 5AA
Tel: 01872 510349 or 01872 510246

Terms & Conditions

1. Only one voucher per transaction
2. Defaced, torn or photocopied vouchers will not be accepted
3. Not to be used in conjunction with any other offer
4. Not exchangeable for cash
5. Present this voucher to the business to accept the offer
6. £1 OFF entry per ticket
7. Valid for upto 6 people

Our philosophy has always been to encourage visitors to the farm and promote a better understanding between town and country.

DairyLand Farm World

---

greenleisure.co.uk
Sunny Corner Farmhouse, Tregony
Cornwall, TR2 5TE
Tel: 07773 255426

Terms & Conditions

1. Only one voucher per transaction
2. Defaced, torn or photocopied vouchers will not be accepted
3. Not to be used in conjunction with any other offer
4. Not exchangeable for cash
5. Present this voucher to the business to accept the offer
6. 4x4 gift experience - normal price for 1 person is £99
   Book for 2 and pay £118 SAVING £80

Cornwall's premier provider of stimulating, land-based environmentally friendly leisure activities. Delivered by experts and set against the backdrop of some of the most spectacular countryside and coastline in the world. Choose from a variety of spectacular locations across Cornwall.

greenleisure.co.uk

Isles Of Scilly Travel
Scillonian / Skybus, QuayStreet
Penzance, Cornwall, TR18 4BZ
Tel: 0845 710 5555

Terms & Conditions

1. Only one voucher per transaction - Not exchangeable for cash
2. Defaced, torn or photocopied vouchers will not be accepted
3. Not to be used in conjunction with any other offer
4. Present this voucher to the business to accept the offer
5. £5 reduction on day trip tickets only (excludes Air and sea tickets)
6. Valid for travel during 2010 excluding 30th April to 3rd May and public holidays
7. Scillonian sails from 27.03.10 to 30.10.10
8. Bookings must be made by telephone at least 24 hour prior to travel
9. Subject to availability

Day Trip passengers can fly with Skybus from Land's End and Newquay* Airports or alternatively Scillonian III sails from Penzance to St Marys

*Passengers departing from Newquay Airport will be charged a £5 Airport Development Fee per person, payable on departure (aged 16 and above).

Isles Of Scilly Travel

FN16

Kidzworld is St. Austell's biggest, bounciest, slidiest indoor children's venue. Newly refurbished with even more to enjoy. Open all year; the ideal party venue for the perfect birthday.

See reverse for more information

Valid from 01.01.10 to 31.12.10

FREE HOT MEAL

FN17

The King Harry Ferry is an iconic part of Cornwall's history. Established in 1888, it connects St Mawes and the Roseland Peninsula with Feock, Truro and Falmouth by avoiding the alternative 27 mile route through Truro & Tresillian.

See reverse for more information

Valid from 01.01.10 to 31.12.10

SAVE 50p OFF

ENGLISH HERITAGE
Launceston Castle

FN18

Discover a thousand years of history at Launceston Castle, once a great stronghold, a town 'gaol' and a hospital, visit the exhibition that reveals the long and varied past.

See reverse for more information

Valid from 01.04.10 to 31.10.10

FREE 2 CHILDREN GO FREE

FN19

Come on an exhilarating wildlife watching boat trip from Penzance. Not only astonishingly beautiful, this area is home to an amazing array of sealife.

See reverse for more information

Valid from 01.01.10 to 31.12.10

SAVE 10% OFF

FN20

See reverse for more information

Valid from 01.01.10 to 31.12.10

SAVE ADULTS PAY CHILD PRICE

KEEP IT... FUN

Kidzworld
Stadium Retail Park, Par Moor Rd
St Austell, Cornwall, PL25 3RP
Tel: 001726 815 553

Terms & Conditions

1. Only one voucher per transaction
2. Defaced, torn or photocopied vouchers will not be accepted
3. Not to be used in conjunction with any other offer
4. Not exchangeable for cash
5. Present this voucher to the business to accept the offer
6. **FREE** meal for each paying child
7. Not valid in school holiday periods

Situated next to Cornish Market World, there is plenty of **FREE** parking and you can do your shopping too! Kidzworld is perfect fun for children from 2-12 with ball ponds, waverider slides, climbing frames and so much more. Hot & cold food available.

Kidzworld
Email: info@kidzwallcornwall.co.uk

King Harry Ferry
www.kingharry.net
Tel: 01872 862312

Terms & Conditions

1. Only one voucher per transaction
2. Defaced, torn or photocopied vouchers will not be accepted
3. Not to be used in conjunction with any other offer
4. Not exchangeable for cash
5. Present this voucher to the business to accept the offer
6. 50p OFF a return ticket

One of only five chain ferries in England, it departs every 20 minutes from each side, 7 days a week and the ferry is a key transport link for visitors and locals alike. The King Harry Ferry offers its passengers the chance to avoid miles of congested roads and once aboard you can get out and enjoy the slow river crossing which takes in one of Cornwall's deepest and most beautiful rivers – The River Fal.

Launceston Castle
On the edge of Launceston town centre
PL15 7DR
Tel: 01566 772365

Terms & Conditions

1. Only one voucher per transaction
2. Defaced, torn or photocopied vouchers will not be accepted
3. Not to be used in conjunction with any other offer
4. Not exchangeable for cash
5. Present this voucher to the business to accept the offer
6. 2 children go **FREE** with an accompanying paying adult
7. All rights of admision reserved by English Heritage
8. Redemption code **SWKCL**

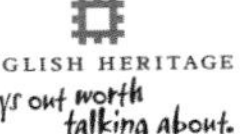

Climb to the top of the windswept tower to take in the views of the town and countryside that the castle once controlled. Browse our shop for great gifts, books and souvenirs.

Launceston Castle

Marine Discovery
Penzance Harbour
Tel: 07749 277110

Terms & Conditions

1. Only one voucher per transaction
2. Defaced, torn or photocopied vouchers will not be accepted
3. Not to be used in conjunction with any other offer
4. Not exchangeable for cash
5. Present this voucher to the business to accept the offer
6. Trips are undertaken at your own risk
7. We will do our utmost to seek out wildlife for your trip, but due to the nature of wild animals, sightings cannot be guaranteed
8. To ensure your place, booking in advance is essential. You will also need to phone 2 days in advance to confirm your place
9. Trips are weather dependent and undertaken at the skippers discretion. we reserve the right to cancel / pospone trips at short notice

Join us in search of seals, seabirds, dolphins, porpoises, basking sharks and more along the stunning West Cornwall coastline. We hope to see you soon.

Marine discovery

The Flora Cinema
Wendron Street, Helston, TR13 8PT
Tel: 01326 569977

Terms & Conditions

1. Only one voucher per transaction
2. Defaced, torn or photocopied vouchers will not be accepted
3. Not to be used in conjunction with any other offer
4. Not exchangeable for cash
5. Present this voucher to the business to accept the offer
6. Adults pay a child price, upto 4 adults
7. Not valid on FLS films (Free List Suspended)
8. Valid Sundays to Thursdays only

The Flora Cinema is situated inside the Flora centre on Wendron Street, just 50 yards from the main central crossroads in Helston, at the junction of coinagehall and Meneage Street.

There are Pay & Display car parks off Trengrouse Way and opposite the cinema. There is also some free parking in Godolphin Road, a short walk from the cinema.

The Flora Cinema

TR11 3PL Tel: 01326 313072

FN21

KEEP IT CORNISH

The Phoenix Cinema

See reverse for more information

Valid from 01.01.10 to 31.12.10

SAVE
ADULTS PAY CHILD PRICE

TR26 2ND Tel: 01736 796843

FN22

KEEP IT CORNISH

The Royal Cinema

See reverse for more information

Valid from 01.01.10 to 31.12.10

SAVE
ADULTS PAY CHILD PRICE

Cornwall, TR15 2AZ Tel: 01209 216278

FN23

KEEP IT CORNISH

The Regal Cinema

See reverse for more information

Valid from 01.01.10 to 31.12.10

SAVE
ADULTS PAY CHILD PRICE

Tel: 01736 363330

FN24

KEEP IT CORNISH

The Savoy Cinema

See reverse for more information

Valid from 01.01.10 to 31.12.10

SAVE
ADULTS PAY CHILD PRICE

Tel: 01503 262 532

FN25

KEEP IT CORNISH

The Monkey Sanctuary is a world-renowned centre caring for unwanted and ex-pet primates. Its doors open to visitors from April to October, offering the opportunity to see and learn about these beautiful animals and the issues jeopardising their survival.

See reverse for more information

Valid from 28.03.10 to 30.09.10

FREE HOT DRINK

KEEP IT... FUN

The Phoenix Cinema
11 Berkeley Vale, Falmouth, Cornwall
TR11 3PL
Tel: 01326 313072

Terms & Conditions

1. Only one voucher per transaction
2. Defaced, torn or photocopied vouchers will not be accepted
3. Not to be used in conjunction with any other offer
4. Not exchangeable for cash
5. Present this voucher to the business to accept the offer
6. Adults pay a child price, upto 4 adults
7. Not valid on FLS films (Free List Suspended)
8. Valid Sundays to Thursdays only

The Phoenix Cinema a state of the Art 5 Screen Cinema including 3 Luxury Licensed Screens with waiter service offering snacks & drinks. The cinema also has a Cafe/Bar open to cinema and non-cinema customers.

The Cinema is situated at the corner of Berkeley Vale & Brook Street. A large car park [Quarry Car Park] is only two minutes walk.

The Phoenix Cinema
www.merlincinema.co.uk

The Royal Cinema
Royal Sqaure, St. Ives, Cornwall,
TR26 2ND
Tel: 01736 796843

Terms & Conditions

1. Only one voucher per transaction
2. Defaced, torn or photocopied vouchers will not be accepted
3. Not to be used in conjunction with any other offer
4. Not exchangeable for cash
5. Present this voucher to the business to accept the offer
6. Adults pay a child price, upto 4 adults
7. Not valid on FLS films (Free List Suspended)
8. Valid Sundays to Thursdays only

The Royal Cinema is situated at the bottom of The Stennack in Royal Square, opposite the Co-op.

The Malakoff bus station and St Ives railway station are a few minutes walk from the cinema if you go down Tregenna Hill and turn left at the Nat West bank.

Most buses stop in Royal Square or at the bus station

There is a large car park two minutes walk from the cinema, up the Stennack; the car park entrance is next to a launderette and the St Ives health Centre.

The Royal Cinema

The Regal Cinema
Regal Cinema, Fore St, Redruth,
Cornwall, TR15 2AZ
Tel: 01209 216278

Terms & Conditions

1. Only one voucher per transaction
2. Defaced, torn or photocopied vouchers will not be accepted
3. Not to be used in conjunction with any other offer
4. Not exchangeable for cash
5. Present this voucher to the business to accept the offer
6. Adults pay a child price, upto 4 adults
7. Not valid on FLS films (Free List Suspended)
8. Valid Sundays to Thursdays only

The Regal Cinema is at the bottom of Fore Street (WEST END), the main shopping street and just two minutes walk from the railway station and town centre bus-stops.

The cinema is easily accessible from the A30 and so serves a large part of West Cornwall. Follow the signs for Redruth, the cinema is less than a mile from the A30 turn off.

The Regal Cinema

The Savoy Cinema
Causewayhead, Penzance, Cornwall,
TR18 2SN
Tel: 01736 363330

Terms & Conditions

1. Only one voucher per transaction
2. Defaced, torn or photocopied vouchers will not be accepted
3. Not to be used in conjunction with any other offer
4. Not exchangeable for cash
5. Present this voucher to the business to accept the offer
6. Adults pay a child price, upto 4 adults
7. Not valid on FLS films (Free List Suspended)
8. Valid Sundays to Thursdays only

The Savoy Cinema and Restaurant is situated in Causewayhead, half way up the street.

Causewayhead is at the top end of Market Jew Street. The striking landmark of the domed Lloyds bank, visible as you enter Penzance, is almost at the bottom of the street.

The cinema is just 5 minutes walk from the main railway and bus station.

The Savoy Cinema

The Monkey Sanctuary
Murrayton House, St Martins, Looe
Cornwall, PL13 1NZ
Tel: 01503 262 532

Terms & Conditions

1. Only one voucher per transaction. Valid to maximum of five people.
2. Defaced, torn or photocopied vouchers will not be accepted
3. Not to be used in conjunction with any other offer
4. Not exchangeable for cash
5. Present this voucher to the business to accept the offer
6. **FREE** cup of tea or coffee from the shop or cafe

Features wildlife gardens, award-winning café, ethical gift shop and play area.

The Monkey Sanctuary

FN26

Recently voted the South West's Visitor Attraction of the Year, the National Maritime Museum Cornwall is a new generation of museum offering a lot more than you might expect.

See reverse for more information

Valid from 01.01.10 to 31.12.10

SAVE 10% OFF

TR11 3QY
Tel: 01326 313388

newquay harbour boatmens association

FN27

Welcome to our fishing and angling trips, one of the best experiences Newquay has to offer! Newquay Boatmens Association have the top 2 angling boats, the Mystique and the Che Sara Sara, both of which are MCA licensed and insured up to 60 miles offshore.

See reverse for more information

Valid from 01.01.10 to 31.12.10

SAVE £20 OFF

Newquay, Cornwall
Tel: 07772196845/07836335903

FN28

Situated just 10 minutes from the town centre and set in the beautiful Cornish countryside. Newquay Paintball has a mixture of speedball and woodland zones with bunkers, fortified positions and natural cover giving an exciting and atmospheric combination.

See reverse for more information

Valid from 01.01.10 to 31.12.10

FREE 50 FREE PAINTBALLS

FN29

Experience the world's wildlife with hundreds of animals set in sub-tropical lakeside gardens. Enjoy fascinating talks and feeding times. See our exotic animals in the Tropical House, penguins swimming in their pool and much much more. There's fun for all age groups.

See reverse for more information

Valid from 01.01.10 to 31.12.10

SAVE UPTO £6

Tel: 01637 873342

Ocean Bowl is a 12 lane tenpin bowling centre incorporating a restaurant, bar and diner. Also within the centre are 5 pool tables, air hockey and numerous video games. We have a large screen showing sporting events.

See reverse for more information

Valid from 01.01.10 to 31.12.10

SAVE UPTO £4

Tel: 01326 313130

National Maritime Museum Cornwall
Discovery Quay, Falmouth, Cornwall
TR11 3QY
Tel: 01326 313388

Terms & Conditions

1. Only one voucher per transaction
2. Defaced, torn or photocopied vouchers will not be accepted
3. Not to be used in conjunction with any other offer
4. Not exchangeable for cash
5. Present this voucher to the business to accept the offer
6. Receive a 10% discount on the full admission price with this voucher

Roll up your sleeves with fun filled activities to suit all ages, take in the breathtaking views from the 29 metre tower, marvel at one of only three natural underwater viewing windows in the world and explore the amazing interactive hands-on exhibits.

National Maritime Museum Cornwall

Newquay Boatmans Association
South Quay, The Harbour
Newquay, Cornwall
Tel: 07772196845/07836335903

Terms & Conditions

1. Only one voucher per transaction
2. Defaced, torn or photocopied vouchers will not be accepted
3. Not to be used in conjunction with any other offer
4. Not exchangeable for cash
5. Present this voucher to the business to accept the offer
6. £20 off a charter. The normal charter price is £240 for a 4 hour trip
7. Boat can hold upto a maximum of 12 people

The boats have separate toilet compartments, colour fishfinders radar and G.P.S navigation equipment. All bait and tackle is provided free of charge and you get to keep what you catch!

Newquay Boatmans Association

Newquay Paintball
See back for directions
Tel: 01637 873988 / 07838215784

Terms & Conditions

1. Only one voucher per transaction
2. Defaced, torn or photocopied vouchers will not be accepted
3. Not to be used in conjunction with any other offer
4. Not exchangeable for cash
5. Present this voucher to the business to accept the offer
6. There is a minimum group size of 8 people.
7. All players must be over 12
8. Offer not valid during peak periods- I.e. through the summer. Please phone to check availability

NEWQUAY PAINTBALL
KERNOW LEISURE LTD.

We are one of the best sites for paintball in Cornwall. We have had players ranging from 12 years of age to 70 both male and female. Not wannabe Rambo's but normal people from all walks of life. Ok and maybe a few wannabe Rambo's as well!

To reach our cornish paintball site, take the A3058 or A392 to Quintrell Downs on the outskirts of Newquay. Take the road to Indian Queens, approximately 1 mile further on, turn left for mountjoy. Turn right at the bottom of the road and Newquay Paintball is just under 1 mile down the road on the left.

Newquay Paintball

Newquay Zoo
Trenance Gardens, Newquay
Cornwall TR7 2LZ
Tel: 01637 873342

Terms & Conditions

1. Only one voucher per transaction
2. Defaced, torn or photocopied vouchers will not be accepted
3. Not to be used in conjunction with any other offer
4. Not exchangeable for cash
5. Present this voucher to the business to accept the offer
6. Save £1 per person for up to 6 people

Experience the world's wildlife with hundreds of animals set in sub-tropical lakeside gardens. Enjoy fascinating talks and feeding times. See our exotic animals in the Tropical House, penguins swimming in their pool and much much more. There's fun for all age groups.

Newquay Zoo

Ocean Bowl
Falmouth Docks Station, Falmouth
Cornwall, TR11 4L
Tel: 01326 313130

Terms & Conditions

1. Only one voucher per transaction
2. Defaced, torn or photocopied vouchers will not be accepted
3. Not to be used in conjunction with any other offer
4. Not exchangeable for cash
5. Present this voucher to the business to accept the offer
6. £1 off bowling for upto 4 people

On site is a pro shop selling the latest in bowling equipment. We have many special evening events, childrens parties and meal deals including bowling. We are open 7 days a week from 11am to 11pm. We have a large car park and are situated right beside a train station.

Orca Sea Safaris run a wide range of wildlife watching cruises from Falmouth aboard its fast, purpose built Rigid Inflatable Boat (RIB). The Orca team aims to introduce you to the outstanding beauty of the Cornish coastline, while looking for a selection of the marine wildlife that inhabits the area.

See reverse for more information

Valid from 01.01.10 to 31.12.10

SAVE
15% OFF

Tel: 01326 214928

Paradise Park

This award-winning sanctuary is home to exotic birds, otters and red pandas. Daily events give opportunities to get up close. Kids love the big 'JungleBarn' indoor play centre and 'Paradise Island' outdoor play.

See reverse for more information

Valid from 01.01.10 to 31.10.10

SAVE
UPTO £5

TR27 4HB Tel: 01736 751020

Pencarrow

Pencarrow is the much-loved home of the Molesworth family, an award-winning Georgian gem set in 50 acres of light woodland and informal gardens. There's an Iron Age fort, Victorian grotto, lake and ancient Cornish cross to discover.

See reverse for more information

Valid from 01.03.10 to 31.10.10

SAVE
2 FOR 1

Tel: 01208 841369

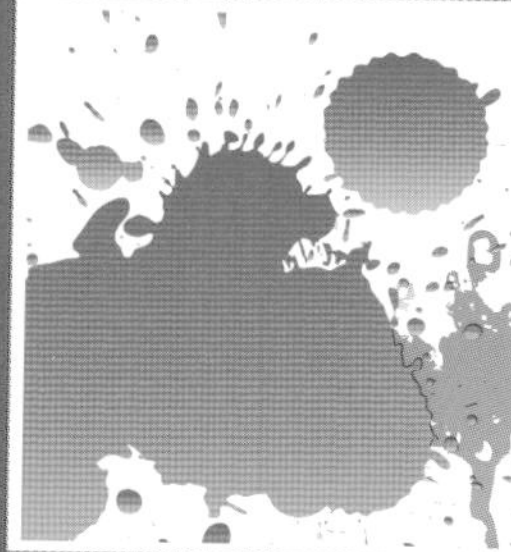

Paintball is a fast and furious game and where better to start than Pirate Paintball. The prices are cheap and we have fantastic playing arenas with Fort, Speedball and lots more.

See reverse for more information

Valid from 01.01.10 to 31.12.10

SAVE
£2.50

Tel: 01872 241 303 / 07779 794 159

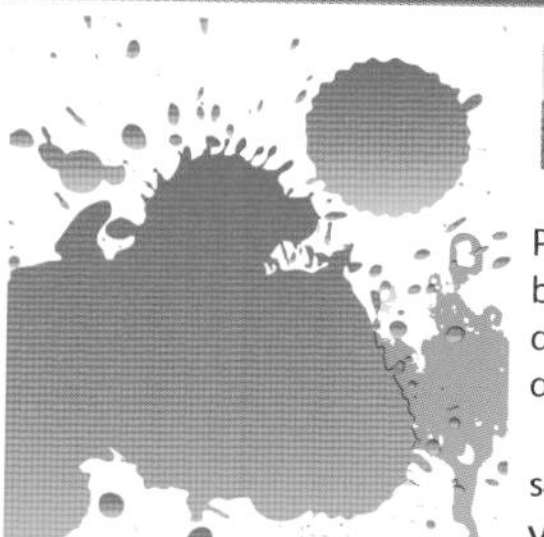

Paintball is a fast and furious game and where better to start than Pirate Paintball. The prices are cheap and we have fantastic playing arenas with Fort, Speedball and lots more.

See reverse for more information

Valid from 01.01.10 to 31.12.10

SAVE
£2.50

Tel: 01872 241 303 / 07779 794 159

Orca Sea Safaris
www.orcaseasafaris.co.uk
Tel: 01326 214928

Terms & Conditions

1. Only one voucher per transaction
2. Defaced, torn or photocopied vouchers will not be accepted
3. Not to be used in conjunction with any other offer
4. Not exchangeable for cash
5. Present this voucher to the business to accept the offer
6. All sailings subject to weather & circumstances. Full refund given if sailing cancelled
7. Offer not valid for trips in July and August

Our experienced skipper is extremely knowledgeable about the wildlife and local area and will provide a cheery face and informative commentary, describing fascinating facts about the wildlife, shipwrecks, smugglers tales, local history and marine environment. We have so much to share with you that every trip is individual.

Orca Sea Safaris

Paradise Park
16 Trelissick Road, Hayle, Cornwall
TR27 4HB
Tel: 01736 751020

Terms & Conditions

1. Only one voucher per transaction
2. Defaced, torn or photocopied vouchers will not be accepted
3. Not to be used in conjunction with any other offer
4. Not exchangeable for cash
5. Present this voucher to the business to accept the offer
6. £1 OFF entry from standard prices for up to 5 people
7. Not valid with any other discounts or saver tickets

Paradise Park

Gift shop and café. Great value Return Tickets if you run out of time to fit everything into one day!

Paradise Park

Pencarrow
Pencarrow, Washaway, Bodmin
PL30 3AG
Tel: 01208 841369

Terms & Conditions

1. Only one voucher per transaction
2. Defaced, torn or photocopied vouchers will not be accepted
3. Not to be used in conjunction with any other offer
4. Not exchangeable for cash
5. Present this voucher to the business to accept the offer
6. Offer 2 for1 garden admission daily from March 1st to October 31st 2010, 9.30am to 5.30pm

Pencarrow

While inside, be amazed at the antique furniture, family portraits, ceramics and memorabilia from another age. Cafe, shop, dog friendly (off leads in woodlands), free parking.

Pencarrow

Pirate Paintball
Nansavallan Farm, Kea, Truro
Cornwall, TR3 6AD
Tel: 01872 241 303 / 07779 794 159

Terms & Conditions

1. Only one voucher per transaction
2. Defaced, torn or photocopied vouchers will not be accepted
3. Not to be used in conjunction with any other offer
4. Not exchangeable for cash
5. Present this voucher to the business to accept the offer
6. Save £2.50 OFF the entry on a half day package at £12.50
7. One voucher per person, must come with player

All the latest equipment, semi-auto markers, full face and head protection, well trained staff, paintball shop on site, changing rooms, and toilets. Corporate entertainment, birthday groups, Stag and Hen parties or just for fun.

Pirate Paintball

Pirate Paintball
Nansavallan Farm, Kea, Truro
Cornwall, TR3 6AD
Tel: 01872 241 303 / 07779 794 159

Terms & Conditions

1. Only one voucher per transaction
2. Defaced, torn or photocopied vouchers will not be accepted
3. Not to be used in conjunction with any other offer
4. Not exchangeable for cash
5. Present this voucher to the business to accept the offer
6. Save £2.50 OFF the entry on a half day package at £12.50
7. One voucher per person, must come with player

All the latest equipment, semi-auto markers, full face and head protection, well trained staff, paintball shop on site, changing rooms, and toilets. Corporate entertainment, birthday groups, Stag and Hen parties or just for fun.

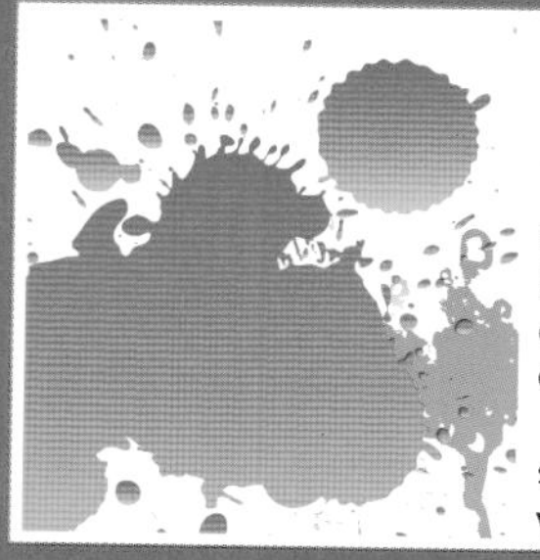

Paintball is a fast and furious game and where better to start than Pirate Paintball. The prices are cheap and we have fantastic playing arenas with Fort, Speedball and lots more.

SAVE £2.50

See reverse for more information

Valid from 01.01.10 to 31.12.10

Tel: 01872 241 303 / 07779 794 159

Paintball is a fast and furious game and where better to start than Pirate Paintball. The prices are cheap and we have fantastic playing arenas with Fort, Speedball and lots more.

SAVE £2.50

See reverse for more information

Valid from 01.01.10 to 31.12.10

Tel: 01872 241 303 / 07779 794 159

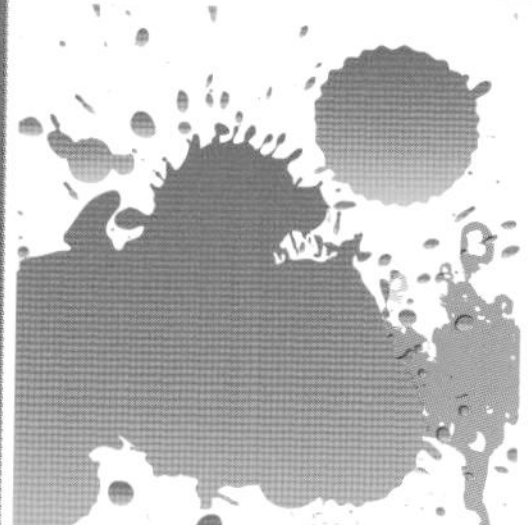

Paintball is a fast and furious game and where better to start than Pirate Paintball. The prices are cheap and we have fantastic playing arenas with Fort, Speedball and lots more.

SAVE £2.50

See reverse for more information

Valid from 01.01.10 to 31.12.10

Tel: 01872 241 303 / 07779 794 159

Here is something for the whole family! Multi-level mega play frame giving exercise in disguise, Baby and Toddler zones, two Laser tag arenas and amusements. Book a birthday in one of our three themed rooms.

SAVE 2 FOR 1

See reverse for more information

Valid from 01.01.10 to 31.12.10 (see reverse)

Tel: 01326 377481

ENGLISH HERITAGE

Restormel Castle

Explore this splendid castle ruin, set high on a hill. A former stronghold it was used as a mini palace to provide lavish entertainment for the Duke and his honoured guests.

FREE 2 CHILDREN GO FREE

See reverse for more information

Valid from 01.04.10 to 31.10.10

Tel: 01208 872687

KEEP IT... FUN

www.keepitcornish.co.uk

Pirate Paintball
Nansavallan Farm, Kea, Truro
Cornwall, TR3 6AD
Tel: 01872 241 303 / 07779 794 159

Terms & Conditions

1. Only one voucher per transaction
2. Defaced, torn or photocopied vouchers will not be accepted
3. Not to be used in conjunction with any other offer
4. Not exchangeable for cash
5. Present this voucher to the business to accept the offer
6. Save £2.50 OFF the entry on a half day package at £12.50
7. One voucher per person, must come with player

All the latest equipment, semi-auto markers, full face and head protection, well trained staff, paintball shop on site, changing rooms, and toilets. Corporate entertainment, birthday groups, Stag and Hen parties or just for fun.

Pirate Paintball

Pirate Paintball
Nansavallan Farm, Kea, Truro
Cornwall, TR3 6AD
Tel: 01872 241 303 / 07779 794 159

Terms & Conditions

1. Only one voucher per transaction
2. Defaced, torn or photocopied vouchers will not be accepted
3. Not to be used in conjunction with any other offer
4. Not exchangeable for cash
5. Present this voucher to the business to accept the offer
6. Save £2.50 OFF the entry on a half day package at £12.50
7. One voucher per person, must come with player

All the latest equipment, semi-auto markers, full face and head protection, well trained staff, paintball shop on site, changing rooms, and toilets. Corporate entertainment, birthday groups, Stag and Hen parties or just for fun.

Pirate Paintball

Pirate Paintball
Nansavallan Farm, Kea, Truro
Cornwall, TR3 6AD
Tel: 01872 241 303 / 07779 794 159

Terms & Conditions

1. Only one voucher per transaction
2. Defaced, torn or photocopied vouchers will not be accepted
3. Not to be used in conjunction with any other offer
4. Not exchangeable for cash
5. Present this voucher to the business to accept the offer
6. Save £2.50 OFF the entry on a half day package at £12.50
7. One voucher per person, must come with player

All the latest equipment, semi-auto markers, full face and head protection, well trained staff, paintball shop on site, changing rooms, and toilets. Corporate entertainment, birthday groups, Stag and Hen parties or just for fun.

Pirate Paintball

Raze the Roof
30a Parkengue, Kernick Road Industrial
Estate, Penryn, Cornwall TR10 9EP
Tel: 01326 377481

Terms & Conditions

1. Only one voucher per transaction
2. Defaced, torn or photocopied vouchers will not be accepted
3. Not to be used in conjunction with any other offer
4. Not exchangeable for cash
5. Present this voucher to the business to accept the offer
6. 2 for1 on entry
7. Valid Monday to Friday, 9.30 a.m. to 3p.m.
8. Excludes school holidays

Comfortable café, fresh food and drink menu and complete with complementary Wi-Fi.

Raze the Roof

Restormel Castle
1 mile North of Lostwithiel off A390
PL22 0EE
Tel: 01208 872687

Terms & Conditions

1. Only one voucher per transaction
2. Defaced, torn or photocopied vouchers will not be accepted
3. Not to be used in conjunction with any other offer
4. Not exchangeable for cash
5. Present this voucher to the business to accept the offer
6. 2 children go FREE with an accompanying paying adult
7. All rights of admission reserved by English Heritage
8. Redemption code SWKCR

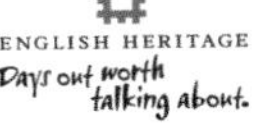

A fantastic place for children to explore and imagine themselves in the castle of Edward, the Black Prince. In the summer, Restormel is one of the best picnic spots in Cornwall and boasts panoramic views of the peaceful countryside.

FN41

Screech Owl Sanctuary is home to over 140 owls of over 30 different species. * Children's Play area * Tearooms * Close encounters *Flying displays * Guided tours * Owl hospital unit (not on public display).

See reverse for more information

Valid from 01.03.10 to 31.10.10

£2

Tel: 01726 860182

FN42

Set in 40 acres on Cornwall's beautiful Helford estuary, the National Seal Sanctuary is Europe's busiest seal rescue centre. Every year the sanctuary rescues and releases over 30 injured or abandoned seal pups, providing a refuge for the seals / sea lions that are unable to be returned to the wild.

See reverse for more information

Valid from 01.01.10 to 31.12.10

SAVE

2 FOR 1

FN43

KEEP IT CORNISH

Fun-packed leisure pool open daily for a family fun-time. With wave machine, river run, 70 metre flume, spa pools, water geysers, bubble mats and a shallow area for little ones.

See reverse for more information

Valid from 01.01.10 to 31.12.10

SAVE

Tel: 01326 212129

FN44

Located on the North Cornwall Coast (between Newquay & Padstow), St. Eval Kart Circuit is the culmination of 12 years planning and construction and as a result is the Largest, Fastest and Most Exciting race circuit in the South West.

See reverse for more information

Valid from 01.01.10 to 31.12.10

SAVE

10% OFF

Tel: 01637 860160

St Ives
ceramica

FN45

Ceramica is St Ives' paint-your-own pottery studio situated in the heart of this beautiful seaside town. We offer a fun and relaxing environment for people of all ages to come and express their creativity.

See reverse for more information

Valid from 01.01.10 to 31.12.10

FREE

HOT
DRINK

Screech Owl Sanctuary
Goss Moor, St Columb, Cornwall
TR9 6HP
Tel: 01726 860182

Terms & Conditions

1. Only one voucher per transaction
2. Defaced, torn or photocopied vouchers will not be accepted
3. Not to be used in conjunction with any other offer
4. Not exchangeable for cash
5. Present this voucher to the business to accept the offer
6. Save £2 per person
7. Not valid on family ticket

Take this wonderful opportunity to come and meet our owls and even get up close and stroke them if you wish to.

Take a guided tour with a friendly staff member who can tell you lots of interesting facts.

Screech Owl Sanctuary

National Seal Sanctuary
Gweek, Helston, TR12 6UG
Tel: 0871 423 2110

Terms & Conditions

1. Only one voucher per transaction
2. Defaced, torn or photocopied vouchers will not be accepted
3. Not to be used in conjunction with any other offer
4. Not exchangeable for cash
5. Present this voucher to the business to accept the offer
6. 2 for 1 on entry

Set in 40 acres on Cornwall's beautiful Helford estuary, the National Seal Sanctuary is Europe's busiest seal rescue centre. Every year the sanctuary rescues and releases over 30 injured or abandoned seal pups, providing a refuge for the seals / sea lions that are unable to be returned to the wild.

National Seal Sanctuary

Ships & Castles Leisure Centre
Castle Drive, Falmouth, Cornwall
TR11 4NG
Tel: 01326 212129

Terms & Conditions

1. Only one voucher per person
2. Photocopied vouchers will not be accepted
3. Not to be used in conjunction with any other offer
4. Not exchangeable for cash
5. Present this voucher to the business to accept the offer
6. Spaces subject to availability

Ships & Castles
CLL

Fun-packed leisure pool open daily for a family fun-time. With wave machine, river run, 70 metre flume, spa pools, water geysers, bubble mats and a shallow area for little ones.

Call or check website for fun session times. Children to adult ratio in water. Under 5's 1:1, under 8's 2:1

Ships & Castles Leisure Centre

St Eval Kart Circuit
St Eval, Wadebridge, Cornwall
PL27 7UN
Tel: 01637 860160

Terms & Conditions

1. Only one voucher per transaction
2. Defaced, torn or photocopied vouchers will not be accepted
3. Not to be used in conjunction with any other offer
4. Not exchangeable for cash
5. Present this voucher to the business to accept the offer
6. Valid Monday to Friday and Saturday depending on the season

Offering 800m/1000m/1200m tracks including a flyover. The 1200m circuit has been very carefully designed with the assistance of some of the UK's top racing drivers and constructed using the very best materials. So whether you decide to visit the circuit for a quick practice or opt for one of our great race events you can be assured to receive the very best service by a highly trained team.

St Ives Ceramica
6 Tregenna Place, St Ives
Cornwall, TR26 1SD
Tel: 01736 791 581

Terms & Conditions

1. Only one voucher per transaction
2. Defaced, torn or photocopied vouchers will not be accepted
3. Not to be used in conjunction with any other offer
4. Not exchangeable for cash
5. Present this voucher to the business to accept the offer
6. **FREE** hot drink for all 'Pottery Painters' (this could be tea, coffee or hot chocolate)

St Ives
ceramica

The studio at Tregenna is the perfect place to spend time with friends, celebrate with colleagues, unwind after work or have a treat with the kids! We have a large selection of ceramics to choose from, full range of paint colours, stamps, design books and all the tools you need to create your very own unique work of art. Whether you're painting a present for someone, or painting yourself a full dinner service, you are sure to have fun!

The St Mawes Ferry connects the old world fishing harbour of St Mawes with the bustling port of Falmouth. The ferry provides an all year round service to over 100,000 visitors a year and is an absolute must for anyone visiting Cornwall.

See reverse for more information

Valid from 01.01.10 to 31.12.10

SAVE

50p OFF

Trethorne
Leisure Park

FN47

Trethorne has something for all ages, whatever the weather. The wide range of activities offered include a dropslide, ball pool, ball-blaster, bungee-run, crazy golf, paddleboats and much more.

See reverse for more information

Valid from 01.01.10 to 31.12.10

FREE

ONE FREE ENTRY

FN48

Whitesands Hotel, B & B accommodation in Lands End Cornwall is a unique family Hotel having luxury ensuite rooms, with fluffy robes, scented toiletries, hairdryers and tea and coffee making facilities.

See reverse for more information

Valid from 01.01.10 to 31.12.10

FREE

SECOND PERSON STAYS FREE

FN49

Our family, group and back packers self-catering accommodation at Lands End in Sennen has a fully equipped self catering kitchen with oven, fridge, microwave and tea and coffee making facilities. All cutlery, crockery and cooking utensils are supplied.

See reverse for more information

Valid from 01.01.10 to 31.12.10

FREE

HALF DAY
SURFING LESSON

KEEP IT
CORNISH

FN50

Whitesands camping in tipi's accommodation at Lands End, Sennen has three American Indian Sioux tipi's and two yurts in their own privately enclosed hedged garden. They have wooden deck flooring internally and you're provided with fold provided with fold out futon chairs that turn into mattresses for added comfort.

See reverse for more information

Valid from 01.01.10 to 31.12.10

FREE

4th NIGHT

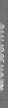

St Mawes Ferry
www.stmawesferry.co.uk
Tel: 01872 681 910

Terms & Conditions

1. Only one voucher per transaction
2. Defaced, torn or photocopied vouchers will not be accepted
3. Not to be used in conjunction with any other offer
4. Not exchangeable for cash
5. Present this voucher to the business to accept the offer
6. All sailing subject to weather and circumstances
7. 50p OFF a return ticket

Passing the impressive castles of St Mawes & Pendennis, the ferry route takes you on a magical journey across the Carrick Roads. As well as the castles you will see many large ships, the working docks of Falmouth, Black Rock (a local isolated shipping hazard) and, if you're lucky, some of the dolphins and basking sharks that regularly visit the harbour.

St Mawes Ferry

Trethorne Leisure Park
Kennards House, Launceston
Cornwall, PL15 8QE
Tel: 01566 86324

Terms & Conditions

1. Only one voucher per transaction
2. Defaced, torn or photocopied vouchers will not be accepted
3. Not to be used in conjunction with any other offer
4. Not exchangeable for cash
5. Present this voucher to the business to accept the offer
6. One **FREE** entry with 2 full paying adults

You can feed the lambs, milk the cow and hold the smaller animals. We have bars, amusement arcade and a licensed restaurant.

From 8th of Novermber 2009 - 5th of February we are only open weekends from 10am - 5pm

Trethorne Leisure Park

Whitesands Hotel
Sennen, Nr. Land's End
Cornwall, TR19 7AR
Tel: 01736 871776

Terms & Conditions

1. Only one voucher per transaction
2. Defaced, torn or photocopied vouchers will not be accepted
3. Not to be used in conjunction with any other offer
4. Not exchangeable for cash
5. Present this voucher to the business to accept the offer
6. Valid Monday to Thursday throughout the year except for Easter, May bank holidays , July & August
7. Second person stays free when one person pays full price

White Sands hotel, b&b & restaurant

All our Hotel rooms are themed under different capital cities from London, Washington, Nairobi, Rome, to romantic Paris with luxury corner bath big enough for two! (Va va voom!) Making this bed and breakfast accommodation in Lands End, an obvious choice!

Whitesands Lodge
Sennen, Nr. Land's End
Cornwall, TR19 7AR
Tel: 01736 871776

Terms & Conditions

1. Only one voucher per transaction
2. Defaced, torn or photocopied vouchers will not be accepted
3. Not to be used in conjunction with any other offer
4. Not exchangeable for cash
5. Present this voucher to the business to accept the offer
6. **FREE** half day surfing lesson when booked into the lodge for 4 nights
7. Valid Monday to Thursday (cost £72.00 for 4 nights)
8. Minimum amount of people 4. Upto a maximum of 15 sharing three different dorm rooms

Piping hot showers and separate men's and ladies WC's are all fitted to a high standard. All you need to bring is a towel!

Whitesands Lodge
Sennen, Nr. Land's End
Cornwall, TR19 7AR
Tel: 01736 871776

Terms & Conditions

1. Only one voucher per transaction
2. Defaced, torn or photocopied vouchers will not be accepted
3. Not to be used in conjunction with any other offer
4. Not exchangeable for cash
5. Present this voucher to the business to accept the offer
6. 4th night **FREE** when you pay for 3 nights in one of our tipis or yurts

You still bring everything you would do for a conventional camping holiday apart from the tent!

KEEP IT SHOPPING

Penzance

- Boa S6-7
- Books Plus S10
- Destine Designs S19
- Dishotay S22
- East of Here S23
- Fishboy S27-31
- Fishing Tackle Box S32
- Flowers by Cindy S34
- Fur, Feathers & Flowers S38
- Granary Healthfoods S40
- Jean Barry Soap Company S50
- Market House Galleries S60-62
- Mounts Bay Wine Company S64
- Music Box S66-67
- Newlyn Art Gallery S100
- Number 36 S71
- Olive Farm Deli S73
- Perfect Pictures S77-78
- Pure Nuff Stuff S79
- South Shore S89
- South Shore Kids S90
- St Justin S93
- Walkers S106

Hayle

- Bee Inspired S3
- Blushhh Lingerie S5
- Flowertime S35
- Wharf S108

St Ives

- Cornish Deli S16
- Fabulous Kids S25
- Floral Shop S33
- Harbour Bookshop S42
- I Should Coco S46
- Natural Balance Surf S68
- St Ives Silver S91
- St Ives Valeting S92
- Wheal Sara Flowers S109
- Yumi S110

Newquay

- Boardwalk Surf S8
- By Design S12
- Emoceanl Surf S24
- Fore Street Deli S36
- Korner Kabin S54
- Newline Blinds & Interiors S69
- Newquay Sports S70
- Overhead Surf S76
- Sugar Loaf S95
- True S102

Truro

- Attla S2
- Boardwalk Surf S9
- Casa Fina S13
- Cascade S14
- Cheese Shop S15
- Design Thoughts S18
- Gift S39
- Guild of Ten S41
- Hendra Health Store S44
- In 2 Connections S47
- Inhabit S48
- Inscriptions S49
- Madame Butterfly Lingerie S58
- Mallets S59
- Mums and Little Ones S65
- Old Jeans Store S72
- Scentstore S83
- Shoozze S86
- SJ's Skateshop S87
- Soup Gallery S88
- Surfside S96-98
- Tilly Mint Bakery S101
- Truro Tea & Coffee Co S103

MORE OVERLEAF

SHOPPING

17% OFF all fancy dress

Ribticklers

8 Market Strand, Falmouth,
Cornwall,TR11 3DB

T 01326 211713
www.ribticklers.co.uk

Opening Hours.
Monday - Saturday 9am - 5.30pm
Sunday 10am - 2pm
Extended opening hours during Christmas, Halloween & other events

Terms and conditions

- This voucher offer entitles you to 17% off your bill.
- See voucher for terms and conditons.

...t us help you with your party plans from colours ... set themes we have endless possibilities.

...nvite you to visit our new shop and take a look at our massive choice of costumes and accessories spread over two ...s with everything for all your party needs including eyelashes, wigs, hats, tights, make up and contact lenses. We also ... a new collection of party favours and party bags that can be made to order.

...hase with the confidence that you are getting the best service, quality and value available from a professional and ...dly team who are always happy to help.

...re guaranteed to be the best value in Cornwall! Why pay more elsewhere?

10% OFF

Newline blinds & interiors

6 Station Parade, Cliff Road, Newquay, Cornwall, TR7 2NF

T 01637 854800
www.newline-interiors.co.uk

Opening Hours.
Mon - Sat, 9am - 5pm

- This voucher offer entitles you to 10% OFF bespoke blinds and curtains
- See voucher for full terms and conditions

Newline Blinds & Interiors is Cornwall's leading supplier, manufacturer and installer of curtains, blinds and all other types of window dressings and soft furnishings.

At Newline Interiors we not only pride ourselves in supplying a wide range of products to suit all tastes and budgets but are dedicated to providing high quality customer service, from initial enquiry through to final installation and after care.

A warm welcome awaits you in our beautiful Newquay store, where you can view our extensive range of curtains, blinds, fabrics, wallpapers, soft furnishings and tasteful gifts. Feel free to browse and get inspiration from our displays, or if you would like help and advice, our experienced and friendly staff are always happy to help. Free consultations in your home or place of work are also available.

The combination of high quality products and a first class professional service from our highly experienced team means that whatever your requirements, we can offer you a truly inspirational solution. It is our dedication to every aspect of the business that has enabled Newline Interiors to develop an enviable reputation for quality.

S71

Number 36

5% OFF under £100,
10% OFF over £100

ber 36 is a feast to the eyes. Located on the cobbled streets of ewayhead it has a vast and unusual range of jewellery, clothes, scarves and . If your house needs sprucing up we have a quirky and stylish range of gifts e home. There is a treat for every girl whether buying a present for that al someone or simply feel like treating yourself. We aim to brighten up your vith an array of colours and styles..........

Number 36

4 Causeway Head, Penzance, Cornwall, TR18 2SN

T 01736 367590

Opening Hours.
9.30 to 5,30 everyday.

Terms and conditions

- This voucher offer entitles you to 5% or 10% off your bill.
- See voucher for terms and conditions.

S106

One HALF PRICE watch battery

the top of Causewayhead, Penzance's unique run ndependent shops, you'll find Walkers, a traditional ellers with a reputation for value and service.

premise's workshop and team of goldsmiths carry out repairs, alterations, ations and bespoke designs; all provided with a smile by owner Julian and ager Hannah.

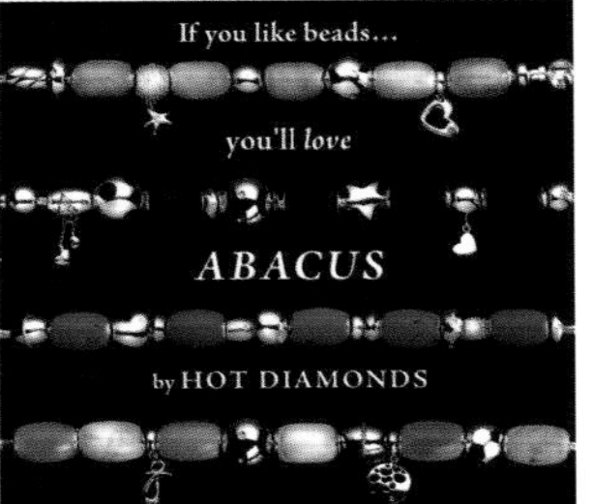

Walkers

50 Causewayhead, Penzance, TR18 2SS

T 01736 363195
www.walkers-jewellers.com

Opening Hours.
Monday - Saturday 9am - 5pm

Stockist
Hot Diamonds
Unity wedding bands
Elements gold & silver
Fiorelli Jewellery
Royal London Watches
Passione Jewellery

- This offer entitles you to one half price watch battery.
- See voucher for terms and conditions.

Blushhh has a fast growing reputation for THE place to go for measuring, fitting, amazing lingerie, service and choice.

Whether you have small curves or big curves , the lingerie at Blushhh will make the most of them. If you are one of the 80% of women wearing the wrong size bra, a trip to Blushhh is an absolute must. I offer a FREE MEASURING & FITTING SERVICE. so if you are looking for your first bra, a comfortable supporting mastectomy bra, a bounce reducing sports bra or a figure enhancing everyday bra Blushhh Lingerie has it all. With sizes AA - K and a professional and friendly service, ladies visit again and again for the amazing fit and variety of colours and flattering designs .

So for support to seduction and a shopping experience with a difference visit Blushhh.

Out of hours appointments to suit you call Bini at Blushhh 01736 753440.

Blushhh Lingerie

20% OFF

Blushhh Lingerie

49 Fore Street, Hayle, Cornwall
TR12 3AB

T 01736 753440
www.blushhhlingerie.co.uk

Opening Hours.
Mon - Sat

- This voucher offer entitles you to 20% OFF.
- See voucher for terms and conditions.

Welcome to Just Delights, inspired by the love of the simple Cornish lifestyle.

Located In the old market town of Penryn, near Falmouth, Just Delights offers a unique range of vintage and reproduction furniture and a variety of accessories and soft furnishings to make your house a home. It is also the perfect little present shop with a large selection of gifts, cards and locally made craftwork. Our team girlies all love beautiful things and will be more than happy to help you choose a perfect gift and gift wrap it. So whether you are looking to furnish your home or are looking for a gift for a special person, we would be delighted to see you and hope you have a lovely shopping experience.

Just Delights

10% OFF

see voucher for terms and conditions

Just Delights

Commercial Road, Penryn,
Cornwall, TR10 8AQ

T 01326 379075
E justdelights@hotmail.com
www.justdelights.co.uk

Opening Hours.
Mon - Sat 9.30am - 5.30pm
Sun - 12.00pm - 16.00
(Closed sundays from January till Easter weekend)
Times may vary during the months of January - March

- This voucher offer entitles you to 10% off anything in store.

S1

We offer a full & comprehensive range of cycles and electric bikes with a complete stock of accessories and parts. We also have a fully equipped workshop offering servicing and repairs to all makes of bikes.

See reverse for more information

Valid from 01.01.10 to 31.12.10

SAVE **10% OFF**

TR14 8EX
Tel: 01209 714970

attla

KEEP IT CORNISH

S2

Established in 2007 attla set out to bring the finest snowboard / skateboard / surf brands to Cornwall, UK. Our store opened in Little Castle Street, Truro in fall 2007 at the same time as we launched our online store at www.attla.co.uk.

See reverse for more information

Valid from 01.01.10 to 31.12.10

SAVE **10% OFF**

Tel: 01872 271847

Bee Inspired

S3

We are a new shop in Hayle specialising in Yankee Candles, Wax Lyrical , Bomb Cosmetics, Handmade Soap, Wildberry Incense, Flowers, Jewellery and much much more.

See reverse for more information

Valid from 01.01.10 to 31.12.10

SAVE **20% OFF**

Tel: 01736 757606

S4

Bloomsberry Flowers offers a full and comprehensive floristry service and is a traditional florist, designing creative flowers for every occasion, including wedding flowers and, of course, funeral tributes.

See reverse for more information

Valid from 01.01.10 to 31.12.10

SAVE **10% OFF**

Tel: 01326 569191

Blushhh Lingerie

S5

Blushhh has a fast growing reputation for THE place to go for measuring, fitting, amazing lingerie, service and choice. Whether you have small curves or big curves, the lingerie at Blushhh will make the most of them.

See reverse for more information

Valid from 01.01.10 to 31.12.10

SAVE **20% OFF**

Tel: 01736 753440

Aldridge Cycles
38 Cross Street, Camborne, Cornwall
TR14 8EX
Tel: 01209 714970

Terms & Conditions

1. Only one voucher per transaction
2. Defaced, torn or photocopied vouchers will not be accepted
3. Not to be used in conjunction with any other offer
4. Not exchangeable for cash
5. Present this voucher to the business to accept the offer
6. 10% off any cycle spare, accessories or bike servicing

We aim to provide an excellent service for all our customers.

Aldridge Cycles

---

attla
1 Little Castle Street, Truro
TR1 3DL
Tel: 01872 271847

Terms & Conditions

1. Only one voucher per transaction
2. Defaced, torn or photocopied vouchers will not be accepted
3. Not to be used in conjunction with any other offer
4. Not exchangeable for cash
5. Present this voucher to the business to accept the offer
6. 10% OFF any items in store with the voucher excluding sale items and gift vouchers

Since then attla has been steadily growing into the boardstore it is today. Founded by seasonaires and now staffed and run by qualified ski technicians, pro riders, seasonaires and friends, the mission remains the same: namely to bring the freshest snow, skateboard and surf brands to you, constantly serving up the finest new collections from some of the more sought-after brands alongside timeless classics from the best known names.

attla

Bee Inspired
57 Fore Street, Copperhouse, Hayle
TR27 4DX
Tel: 01736 757606

Terms & Conditions

1. Only one voucher per transaction
2. Defaced, torn or photocopied vouchers will not be accepted
3. Not to be used in conjunction with any other offer
4. Not exchangeable for cash
5. Present this voucher to the business to accept the offer
6. 20% off any purchase excluding sale items

Bee Inspired

We can even host a party night for you and your friends, there's something special in store for everyone.

Bloomsberry Flowers
Fore Street, Porthleven, Helston
Cornwall, TR13 9HJ
Tel: 01326 569191

Terms & Conditions

1. Only one voucher per transaction
2. Defaced, torn or photocopied vouchers will not be accepted
3. Not to be used in conjunction with any other offer
4. Not exchangeable for cash
5. Present this voucher to the business to accept the offer
6. Receive 10% discount on one purchase over the sum of £30
7. Not valid on wedding flowers or funeral tributes

flowers by Bloomsberry 

Friendly advice given freely, no charge for consultations just pop in or telephone to discuss your requirements. Please take a look at our website **www.bloomsberryflowers.co.uk**

Bloomsberry Flowers
Email:

Blushhh Lingerie
49 Fore Street, Hayle, Cornwall
TR27 4DX
Tel: 01736 753440

Terms & Conditions

1. Only one voucher per transaction
2. Defaced, torn or photocopied vouchers will not be accepted
3. Not to be used in conjunction with any other offer
4. Not exchangeable for cash
5. Present this voucher to the business to accept the offer
6. 20% OFF with this voucher

Blushhh Lingerie

If you are one of the 80% of women wearing the wrong size bra, a trip to Blushhh is an absolute must. I have been trained by Rigby and Peller in London & offer a FREE MEASURING & FITTING SERVICE.

S6

boa ...something special

Suppliers of quality gifts and solid wood furniture at affordable prices. Whether you're looking to furnish your home or add those finishing touches or make someone very happy with a special gift, you'll find it here. boa. . . . . . . something special.

See reverse for more information

Valid from 01.01.10 to 31.12.10

SAVE 10% OFF

Tel: 01736 360 378

S7

boa ...something special

Suppliers of quality gifts and solid wood furniture at affordable prices. Whether you're looking to furnish your home or add those finishing touches or make someone very happy with a special gift, you'll find it here. boa. . . . . . . something special.

See reverse for more information

Valid from 01.01.10 to 31.12.10

KEEP IT CORNISH

SAVE 15% OFF

Tel: 01736 360 378

S8

Established in 1985, Boardwalk Surf has been bringing you the largest range of Surf Clothing, Surfboards and advice on every aspect of Surf Lifestyle.

See reverse for more information

Valid from 01.01.10 to 31.12.10

Tel: 01637 878880

S9

Established in 1985, Boardwalk Surf has been bringing you the largest range of Surf Clothing, Surfboards and advice on every aspect of Surf Lifestyle.

See reverse for more information

Valid from 01.01.10 to 31.12.10

Tel: 01872 479222

Books Plus is an independent bookshop, with a wide and varied stock, and friendly, helpful staff. Books of Cornish interest are a strong feature and we also have a great kids corner.

See reverse for more information

Valid from 01.01.10 to 31.12.10

SAVE

Tel: 01736 365607

boa
34 Market Jew Street Penzance
TR18 2HT
Tel: 01736 360 378

Terms & Conditions

1. Only one voucher per transaction
2. Defaced, torn or photocopied vouchers will not be accepted
3. Not to be used in conjunction with any other offer
4. Not exchangeable for cash
5. Present this voucher to the business to accept the offer

boa
...something special

Suppliers of quality gifts and solid wood furniture at affordable prices. Whether you're looking to furnish your home or add those finishing touches or make someone very happy with a special gift, you'll find it here. boa. . . . . . . something special.

boa
34 Market Jew Street Penzance
TR18 2HT
Tel: 01736 360 378

Terms & Conditions

1. Only one voucher per transaction
2. Defaced, torn or photocopied vouchers will not be accepted
3. Not to be used in conjunction with any other offer
4. Not exchangeable for cash
5. Present this voucher to the business to accept the offer
6. 15% OFF when you spend over £100 on furniture

boa
...something special

Suppliers of quality gifts and solid wood furniture at affordable prices. Whether you're looking to furnish your home or add those finishing touches or make someone very happy with a special gift, you'll find it here. boa . . . . . . something special.

Boardwalk
17 Cliff Road, Newquay, Cornwall
TR7 2NE
Tel: 01637 878880

Terms & Conditions

1. Only one voucher per transaction
2. Defaced, torn or photocopied vouchers will not be accepted
3. Not to be used in conjunction with any other offer
4. Not exchangeable for cash
5. Present this voucher to the business to accept the offer
6. Buy any new surfboard and get a bag, leash and a block of wax worth £55 for only £20

If you are shopping for a new Surfboard and Wetsuit or want to refresh your wardrobe, stop off at one of our stores or check us out online.

Boardwalk
Lemon Quay, Truro, Cornwall
TR1 2LW
Tel: 01872 479222

Terms & Conditions

1. Only one voucher per transaction
2. Defaced, torn or photocopied vouchers will not be accepted
3. Not to be used in conjunction with any other offer
4. Not exchangeable for cash
5. Present this voucher to the business to accept the offer
6. Buy any new surfboard and get a bag, leash and a block of wax worth £55 for only £20

If you are shopping for a new Surfboard and Wetsuit or want to refresh your wardrobe, stop off at one of our stores or check us out online.

Books Plus
23, Market Jew St., Penzance
TR182HR
Tel: 01736 365607

Terms & Conditions

1. Only one voucher per transaction
2. Defaced, torn or photocopied vouchers will not be accepted
3. Not to be used in conjunction with any other offer
4. Not exchangeable for cash
5. Present this voucher to the business to accept the offer
6. £5 Shop voucher

There are many special offers on new books and all bestselling paperbacks are discounted by £1. Browsers are always welcome.

S11

The Bottle Bank is an independent retailer of wine, beer and spirits based in Falmouth. We're located on Discovery Quay adjacent to the maritime museum and right next to the maritime car park.

See reverse for more information

Valid from 01.01.10 to 31.12.10

SAVE **10% OFF**

Falmouth TR11 3XP
Tel: 01326 218 319

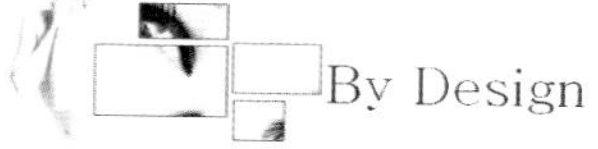

KEEP IT CORNISH

S12

As well as our stock clothing we sell hand made clothing made by new designers and are happy to showcase any work from graduating designers as well as having an alterations service. Most pieces are one offs and will be made to order to suit customers requirements.

See reverse for more information

Valid from 01.01.10 to 31.12.10

SAVE **10% OFF**

Tel: 01637 852777

S13

Wonderful selection of lamps & lighting, home accessories, cushions, silk flowers, glassware and ceramics, sofas & sofabeds by Tetrad & Duresta Bedding & accessories by Designers Guild Fabrics & Wallpapers with full interior design service.

See reverse for more information

Valid from 01.01.10 to 31.12.10

SAVE **15% OFF**

Tel: 01872 270818

Cascade

S14

Cascade has something for everyone, for all budgets and tastes. Stocking a fantastic range of Handbags, Workbags, & Accessories, from well known brands such as Ameribag (Healthy Back Bags), Tula, Hidesign, Mywalit, Ri2K, and Smith & Canova, etc.

See reverse for more information

Valid from 01.01.10 to 31.12.10

Tel: 01872 222547

Sample our vast range of cheese or try some oils and vinegars in handmade, reusable bottles. Sample Cornish, crellow chutneys and preserves, Vicky's breads, Cornish Charcuterie and Tregothnan teas. We stock Cornish, European and new world wines.

See reverse for more information

Valid from 01.01.10 to 31.12.10

SAVE **10% OFF**

Tel: 01872 270742

The Bottle Bank
2 Tidemill House Discovery Quay
Falmouth TR11 3XP
Tel: 01326 218 319

Terms & Conditions

1. Only one voucher per transaction
2. Defaced, torn or photocopied vouchers will not be accepted
3. Not to be used in conjunction with any other offer
4. Not exchangeable for cash
5. Present this voucher to the business to accept the offer
6. 10% OFF all still table wine

the bottle bank

The Bottle Bank is an independent retailer of wine, beer and spirits based in Falmouth. We're located on Discovery Quay adjacent to the maritime museum and right next to the maritime car park.

By Design
23 Cliff Road, Newquay, Cornwall
TR7 2NE
Tel: 01637 852777

Terms & Conditions

1. Only one voucher per transaction
2. Defaced, torn or photocopied vouchers will not be accepted
3. Not to be used in conjunction with any other offer
4. Not exchangeable for cash
5. Present this voucher to the business to accept the offer
6. 10% OFF clothing

As well as our stock clothing we sell hand made clothing made by new designers and are happy to showcase any work from graduating designers as well as having an alterations service. Most pieces are one offs and will be made to order to suit customers requirements.

Simply precious...... Simply beautiful...... Simply by design

Casa Fina
29 River Street, Truro, Cornwall
TR1 2SJ
Tel: 01872 270818

Terms & Conditions

1. Only one voucher per transaction
2. Defaced, torn or photocopied vouchers will not be accepted
3. Not to be used in conjunction with any other offer
4. Not exchangeable for cash
5. Present this voucher to the business to accept the offer
6. 15% OFF on single sale of £40 and over

Beautiful French painted & cherry furniture from Grange. Plus La Bevanda our superb licensed, continental coffee shop/restaurant.

Cascade
7 Pydar Mews, Truro, Cornwall
TR1 2UX
Tel: 01872 222547

Terms & Conditions

1. Only one voucher per transaction
2. Defaced, torn or photocopied vouchers will not be accepted
3. Not to be used in conjunction with any other offer
4. Not exchangeable for cash
5. Present this voucher to the business to accept the offer

Cascade

We also stock gorgeous hand bags from local designer Kelly Nash, which are all hand made in Cornwall.

The Cheese Shop
29 Ferris Town, Truro, Cornwall
TR1 3JH
Tel: 01872 270742

Terms & Conditions

1. Only one voucher per transaction
2. Defaced, torn or photocopied vouchers will not be accepted
3. Not to be used in conjunction with any other offer
4. Not exchangeable for cash
5. Present this voucher to the business to accept the offer

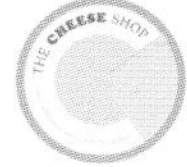

The Cheese Shop, Truro is between the Truro Museum and the Railway Station.

The Cornish Deli

The Cornish Deli exists to bring the **best** quality Cornish and regional produce to its customers. It offers fantastic quality, local meats, cheeses, seafood, gourmet hampers, beach picnics and regional specialities.

See reverse for more information

Valid from 01.01.10 to 31.12.10

SAVE **10% OFF**

Tel: 01736 795100

CAVENDISH THECOURTYARDDELI

Discover our beautiful deli and enjoy our wide selection of cheeses, salamis, olives, pickles, jams and home baked breads. Or join us in the cosy café and treat yourself to some of our home-made delights.

See reverse for more information

Valid from 01.01.10 to 31.12.10

SAVE **10% OFF**

Tel: 01326 319526

design thoughts

Every design starts with a thought.....

Design thoughts is a freelance graphic designer offering business clients a fresh approach to graphic design that works outside the box.

See reverse for more information

Valid from 01.01.10 to 31.12.10

SAVE **15% OFF**

Tel: 07732 103597

Destine Designs

Whether you are looking for web design, posters, brochures, logo design, frontpage presentation, etc, you need look no further for top quality results. Uncannily, we seem to know exactly what you want and talk on the same level.

See reverse for more information

Valid from 01.01.10 to 31.12.10

SAVE **20% OFF**

Tel: 01736 365747 or 07970 349363

Diamond Oceans Jewellers

Diamond Oceans Jewellers prides itself on being Cornwall's only high-class jewellers boutique in a marina setting. Instore open workshop, where you can watch the goldsmith at work.

See reverse for more information

Valid from 01.01.10 to 31.12.10

SAVE **10% OFF**

The Cornish Deli
3 Chapel Street, St. Ives, Cornwall
TR26 2LR.
Tel: 01736 795100

Terms & Conditions

1. Only one voucher per transaction
2. Defaced, torn or photocopied vouchers will not be accepted
3. Not to be used in conjunction with any other offer
4. Not exchangeable for cash
5. Present this voucher to the business to accept the offer
6. 10% OFF Cornish cheeses

Incorporated within the Cornish Deli is the Deli Café, offering hot and cold drinks, brunches, lunches, afternoon tea, and evening meals.

The Cornish Deli

The Courtyard deli
2 Bells Court, falmouth
Cornwall, TR11 3AZ
Tel: 01326 319526

Terms & Conditions

1. Only one voucher per transaction
2. Defaced, torn or photocopied vouchers will not be accepted
3. Not to be used in conjunction with any other offer
4. Not exchangeable for cash
5. Present this voucher to the business to accept the offer
6. 10% OFF when you spend over £20

BESPOKE BUFFETS, CAKES AND HAMPERS ALSO AVAILABLE.

Have you discovered us?

The Courtyard Deli

Design thoughts
www.designthoughts.co.uk
Tel: 07732 103597

Terms & Conditions

1. Only one voucher per transaction
2. Defaced, torn or photocopied vouchers will not be accepted
3. Not to be used in conjunction with any other offer
4. Not exchangeable for cash
5. Present this voucher to the business to accept the offer
6. 15% OFF for all new clients

design thoughts

Design thoughts provide; editorial, branding, stationary, logo design and consumer photography in preprint format to cover all business requirements.

Design thoughts

Destine Designs
www.destinedesigns.co.uk
Tel: 01736 365747 or 07970 349363

Terms & Conditions

1. Only one voucher per transaction
2. Defaced, torn or photocopied vouchers will not be accepted
3. Not to be used in conjunction with any other offer
4. Not exchangeable for cash
5. Present this voucher to the business to accept the offer
6. 20% OFF all Web Design packages

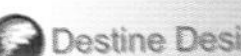

Our designs reflect exactly what you want to get across to the public, get you results and hopefully make you money.

Destine Designs

Diamond Oceans Jewellers
9 Tidemill House, Discovery Quay
Falmouth, Cornwall, TR11 3XP
Tel: 01326 210484

Terms & Conditions

1. Only one voucher per transaction
2. Defaced, torn or photocopied vouchers will not be accepted
3. Not to be used in conjunction with any other offer
4. Not exchangeable for cash
5. Present this voucher to the business to accept the offer

We offer a large selection of unique pearls, silver, gold and platinum jewellery. Free bespoke design service. Repairs and Commissions undertaken.
"Inspire your desires"

Tel: 01326 211650

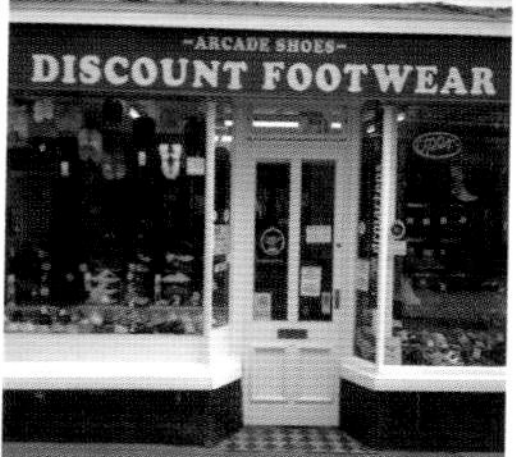

Discount Footwear

S21

We opened our business in the town on 1993, we sell a very large range of shoes, specialising in Dr Martens at a discount price. Also we do stock Wrangler Sketchers and many more. We also do a wide range of industrial footwear.

See reverse for more information

Valid from 01.01.10 to 31.12.10

SAVE £5

Tel: 01736 367497

Fine teas, coffee and accessories

S22

Dishotay, our specialist tea and coffee shop situated in the famous Chapel Street, Penzance in the far west of Cornwall, would like customers far and wide to be able to sample our wares any time of the year, not just on visiting this beautiful part of the country.

See reverse for more information

Valid from 01.01.10 to 31.12.10

SAVE 10% OFF

Tel: 01736 359076

eastofhere

S23

We trade in Indian antiques - oriental rugs and carpets from Iran, India, Afhghanistan & Turkey including many older tribal pieces - salt bags - saddle bags. A fantastic selection of new vegetable dyed Afghan Kilims and tribal weavings.

See reverse for more information

Valid from 01.01.10 to 31.12.10

SAVE 10% OFF ANY RUG

Tel: 01637 851121 or 07737 598032

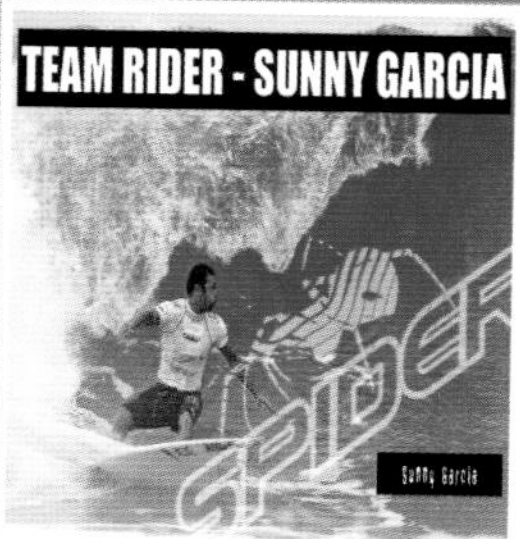

S24

Established in 1997, Emoceanl Surf has proven to be a favourite of local surfers and shoppers. Stockists of Spider surfboards and clothing, Protest clothing, Sanuk shoes and sandals, Kuccia clothing, Saltrock clothing and accessories.

See reverse for more information

Valid from 01.01.10 to 31.12.10

SAVE 10% OFF

S25

Fabulous Kids has a passion for sourcing the best funky fashion, fantastic footwear, gorgeous gifts and toys. Our extensive range of products come from all over the world, including many ethical and organic gifts. The one stop shop for those gorgeous presents and treats you simply have to have.

See reverse for more information

Valid from 01.01.10 to 31.12.10

SAVE 10% OFF

Discount Footwear
22 Arwenack Street, Falmouth
Cornwall, TR11 3JL
Tel: 01326 211650

Terms & Conditions

1. Only one voucher per transaction
2. Defaced, torn or photocopied vouchers will not be accepted
3. Not to be used in conjunction with any other offer
4. Not exchangeable for cash
5. Present this voucher to the business to accept the offer
6. £5 OFF with any purchase over £75

Discount Footwear

We opened our business in the town in 1993, we sell a very large range of shoes, specialising in Dr Martens at a discount price. Also we do stock Wrangler Sketchers and many more. We also do a wide range of industrial footwear.

Discount Footwear

Dishotay
Chapel Street, Penzance, Cornwall
TR18 4AE
Tel: 01736 367497

Terms & Conditions

1. Only one voucher per transaction
2. Defaced, torn or photocopied vouchers will not be accepted
3. Not to be used in conjunction with any other offer
4. Not exchangeable for cash
5. Present this voucher to the business to accept the offer

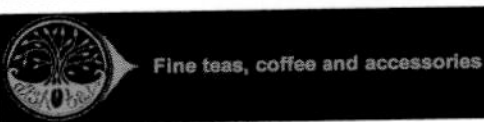

Teas from India, China, Sri Lanka and the famous Tregothnan tea, the first tea to be grown in the UK. Coffee roasted in Cornwall from Columbia, Brazil, India, Nicaragua and Indonesia just to mention a few. Along with our accessories will give you a complete package to enjoy tea or coffee at its best.

Dishotay

east of here
2-3 Chapel Street, Penzance
TR18 4AJ
Tel: 01736 359076

Terms & Conditions

1. Only one voucher per transaction
2. Defaced, torn or photocopied vouchers will not be accepted
3. Not to be used in conjunction with any other offer
4. Not exchangeable for cash
5. Present this voucher to the business to accept the offer
6. 10% OFF any rug

eastofhere

All this mixed with newly upholstered traditional English hand made furniture creates a truly '1 off' shopping experience.

east of here

Emoceanl Surf
2-4 Gover Lane, Newquay
Cornwall, TR71ER
Tel: 01637 851121 or 07737 598032

Terms & Conditions

1. Only one voucher per transaction
2. Defaced, torn or photocopied vouchers will not be accepted
3. Not to be used in conjunction with any other offer
4. Not exchangeable for cash
5. Present this voucher to the business to accept the offer
6. 10% OFF clothing only, excludes hardwear, accessories, wetsuits or shoes
7. Excludes all sale items

West wetsuits, Hurricane surf accessories, Bondiblu sunglasses, Fossil watches and a unique Emoceanl clothing range.

Emoceanl Surf

Fabulous Kids
28 Fore Street, St Ives, Cornwall
TR26 1HE
Tel: 01736 791900

Terms & Conditions

1. Only one voucher per transaction
2. Defaced, torn or photocopied vouchers will not be accepted
3. Not to be used in conjunction with any other offer
4. Not exchangeable for cash
5. Present this voucher to the business to accept the offer
6. 10% OFF non sale clothes and shoes

Fabulous Kids has a passion for sourcing the best funky fashion, fantastic footwear, gorgeous gifts and toys. Our extensive range of products come from all over the world, including many ethical and organic gifts. The one stop shop for those gorgeous presents and treats you simply have to have.

Tel: 01326 565707

S26

feeline

CLOTHING

Feeline fleecewear is suitable for any occasion, from everyday to weddings, as evening wear, for gardening, walking the dog, skiing. Design your own unique outfit from the many colours and styles to choose from.

See reverse for more information

Valid from 01.01.10 to 31.12.10

SAVE 5% OFF

Tel: 01736 331846

S27

fishboy specialises in the production of limited edition printed t-shirts inspired by all things rural with a modern twist, hand printed in Penzance. Set alongside an evolving range of international mens and womens labels.

See reverse for more information

Valid from 01.01.10 to 31.12.10

Tel: 01736 331846

S28

fishboy specialises in the production of limited edition printed t-shirts inspired by all things rural with a modern twist, hand printed in Penzance. Set alongside an evolving range of international mens and womens labels.

See reverse for more information

Valid from 01.01.10 to 31.12.10

Tel: 01736 331846

S29

fishboy specialises in the production of limited edition printed t-shirts inspired by all things rural with a modern twist, hand printed in Penzance. Set alongside an evolving range of international mens and womens labels.

See reverse for more information

Valid from 01.01.10 to 31.12.10

fishboy specialises in the production of limited edition printed t-shirts inspired by all things rural with a modern twist, hand printed in Penzance. Set alongside an evolving range of international mens and womens labels.

See reverse for more information

Valid from 01.01.10 to 31.12.10

Feeline clothing
Salt cellar workshops, Salt cellar hill
Porthleven, Nr helston, TR13 9DN
Tel: 01326 565707

Terms & Conditions

1. Only one voucher per transaction
2. Defaced, torn or photocopied vouchers will not be accepted
3. Not to be used in conjunction with any other offer
4. Not exchangeable for cash
5. Present this voucher to the business to accept the offer

feeline CLOTHING

Bespoke orders are my speciality ensuring the best fit and most flattering effect. Look great and feel comfortable!

Feeline clothing

---

fishboy
64 Chapel Street, Penzance
TR18 4AD
Tel: 01736 331846

Terms & Conditions

1. Only one voucher per transaction
2. Defaced, torn or photocopied vouchers will not be accepted
3. Not to be used in conjunction with any other offer
4. Not exchangeable for cash
5. Present this voucher to the business to accept the offer
6. £5 OFF a fishboy handprinted item

Open 11-6 Monday to Saturday, occasionally open Sundays.

fishboy

---

fishboy
64 Chapel Street, Penzance
TR18 4AD
Tel: 01736 331846

Terms & Conditions

1. Only one voucher per transaction
2. Defaced, torn or photocopied vouchers will not be accepted
3. Not to be used in conjunction with any other offer
4. Not exchangeable for cash
5. Present this voucher to the business to accept the offer
6. £5 OFF a fishboy handprinted item

Open 11-6 Monday to Saturday, occasionally open Sundays.

fishboy

---

fishboy
64 Chapel Street, Penzance
TR18 4AD
Tel: 01736 331846

Terms & Conditions

1. Only one voucher per transaction
2. Defaced, torn or photocopied vouchers will not be accepted
3. Not to be used in conjunction with any other offer
4. Not exchangeable for cash
5. Present this voucher to the business to accept the offer
6. £5 OFF a fishboy handprinted item

Open 11-6 Monday to Saturday, occasionally open Sundays.

fishboy

---

fishboy
64 Chapel Street, Penzance
TR18 4AD
Tel: 01736 331846

Terms & Conditions

1. Only one voucher per transaction
2. Defaced, torn or photocopied vouchers will not be accepted
3. Not to be used in conjunction with any other offer
4. Not exchangeable for cash
5. Present this voucher to the business to accept the offer
6. £5 OFF a fishboy handprinted item

Open 11-6 Monday to Saturday, occasionally open Sundays.

fishboy specialises in the production of limited edition printed t-shirts inspired by all things rural with a modern twist, hand printed in Penzance. Set alongside an evolving range of international mens and womens labels.

See reverse for more information

Valid from 01.01.10 to 31.12.10

SAVE £5

Tel: 01736 331846

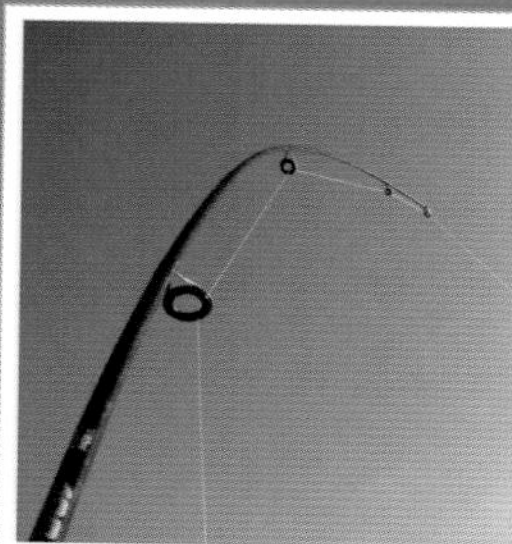

TheFishingTackleBox.co.uk
sea, coarse & game fishing tackle

Quality fishing tackle at affordable prices. Whatever fishing tackle you need, we have it, sea fishing, coarse fishing, fly fishing etc., 'ready to go' kits, even nets for the kids. The Fishing Tackle Box, catching fish on a shoestring!

See reverse for more information

Valid from 01.01.10 to 31.12.10

FREE GIFT

Tel: 01736 360 378

The Floral Shop

A friendly local service from St Ives, we offer a range of flowers for every occasion including plants, balloons, chocolates and teddy bears. We also stock a large selection of quality fruit and veg.

See reverse for more information

Valid from 01.01.10 to 31.12.10

FREE BOX OF CHOCOLATES

Tel: 01736 797286

We are a family run business with qualified florists supplying wedding and funeral flowers, in fact ANY occasion flowers!
We might be the smallest florists in Penzance but we are BIG on quality!

See reverse for more information

Valid from 01.01.10 to 31.12.10

SAVE 10% OFF

Tel: 01736 364442

FLOWERTIME FLORIST

S35

KEEP IT CORNISH

Flowertime Florist Limited was founded in 1989, and are the highest qualified florists in Devon and Cornwall, we are into flowers in a big way. Flowertime Florist is a family run company and believes in giving excellent personal service.

See reverse for more information

Valid from 01.01.10 to 31.12.10

Tel: 0800 056 0711

KEEP IT... SHOPPING

www.keepitcornish.co.uk

fishboy
64 Chapel Street, Penzance
TR18 4AD
Tel: 01736 331846

Terms & Conditions

1. Only one voucher per transaction
2. Defaced, torn or photocopied vouchers will not be accepted
3. Not to be used in conjunction with any other offer
4. Not exchangeable for cash
5. Present this voucher to the business to accept the offer
6. £5 OFF a fishboy handprinted item

Open 11-6 Monday to Saturday, occasionally open Sundays.

The Fishing Tackle Box
34 Market Jew Street, Penzance
TR18 2HT
Tel: 01736 360 378

Terms & Conditions

1. Only one voucher per transaction
2. Defaced, torn or photocopied vouchers will not be accepted
3. Not to be used in conjunction with any other offer
4. Not exchangeable for cash
5. Present this voucher to the business to accept the offer
6. **FREE** gift with any order placed in person in store

TheFishingTackleBox.co.uk
sea, coarse & game fishing tackle

Quality fishing tackle at affordable prices. Whatever fishing tackle you need, we have it, sea fishing, coarse fishing, fly fishing etc., 'ready to go' kits, even nets for the kids. The Fishing Tackle Box, catching fish on a shoestring!

The Floral Shop
Tregenna Hill, St Ives, Cornwall
TR26 1SF
Tel: 01736 797286

Terms & Conditions

1. Only one voucher per transaction
2. Defaced, torn or photocopied vouchers will not be accepted
3. Not to be used in conjunction with any other offer
4. Not exchangeable for cash
5. Present this voucher to the business to accept the offer
6. Not valid at Christmas, valentines day or mothers day
7. **FREE** box of chocolates with any local order over £40

The Floral Shop

We are open from 8:30 - 5:00 Monday - Saturday

Flowers by Cindy
Albert Street Penzance, Cornwall
TR18 2LR
Tel: 01736 364442

Terms & Conditions

1. Only one voucher per transaction
2. Defaced, torn or photocopied vouchers will not be accepted
3. Not to be used in conjunction with any other offer
4. Not exchangeable for cash
5. Present this voucher to the business to accept the offer
6. 10% OFF any flower or plant

Daily deliveries to Penzance, Helston and all surrounding areas including the Isles of Scilly.

Flowertime Florist
17 Penpol Terrace, Hayle, Cornwall
TR27 4BQ
Tel: 0800 056 0711

Terms & Conditions

1. Only one voucher per transaction
2. Defaced, torn or photocopied vouchers will not be accepted
3. Not to be used in conjunction with any other offer
4. Not exchangeable for cash
5. Present this voucher to the business to accept the offer
6. **FREE** delivery to Hayle area, Lelant, Carbis Bay, St Ives, Connor Downs, St Erth, Cannontowns when you spend £25.00 and over in Store or by calling 0800 056 0711. **Worth up to £5.00**

If you wish to call and speak to us that's not a problem just call us on the number provided. Flowertime Florist competes in many floral competitions and is a Chelsea Gold Medalist.

fore street deli
& wholefood shop

S36

We are stockists of a range of cooks ingredients, Organic and Fairtrade items as well as ready prepared and chef inspired sauces, savoury pies, quiches, olives, cheeses and a multitude of treats from our extensive deli fridge.

SAVE **10% OFF**

See reverse for more information

Valid from 01.01.10 to 31.12.10

Cornwall, TR7 1LP Tel: 01637 851465

FREERIDERS

S37

Freeriders was born from a passion, a youth spent on the beach, dreaming of a life in the water. An independent surf shop located in the heart of Falmouth endeavoring to bring you the most comprehensive range of surfing equipment possible.

SAVE **10% OFF**

See reverse for more information

Valid from 01.01.10 to 31.12.10

Tel: 01326 313456

Fur, Feathers & Flowers

S38

Why not visit Fur, Feathers & Flowers where you can purchase all of the things you need to keep your pet happy! Choose from a wide range of animal feed and accessories.

SAVE **10% OFF**

See reverse for more information

Valid from 01.01.10 to 31.12.10

Tel: 01736 368530

gift

S39

We are a small but gorgeous gift shop in River Street Truro, look for the museum we are opposite. If you are looking for a luxury gift you will find it here.

SAVE **10% OFF**

See reverse for more information

Valid from 01.01.10 to 31.12.10

Tel: 01872 270033

THE GRANARY

S40

A shop full of character and charm where a smiley face always greets you at the door. We sell organic vegetables (the ones that come in all shapes and sizes, and colours!), fresh breads, a huge range of herbs and spices, and much much more.

SAVE **10% OFF**

See reverse for more information

Valid from 01.01.10 to 31.12.10

Tel: 01736 361869

Fore Street Deli & Wholefood Shop
40 Fore Street, Newquay,
Cornwall, TR71LP
Tel: (01637) 851465

Terms & Conditions

1. Only one voucher per transaction
2. Defaced, torn or photocopied vouchers will not be accepted
3. Not to be used in conjunction with any other offer
4. Not exchangeable for cash
5. Present this voucher to the business to accept the offer
6. 10% OFF with every £10 spent

fore street deli
& wholefood Shop

Bringing local, low-carbon quality produce to Newquay. The very best in Cornish produce on our shelves.

Fore Street Deli & Wholefood Shop

Freeriders
The Moor, Falmouth, Cornwall
TR11 3PN
Tel: 01326 313456

Terms & Conditions

1. Only one voucher per transaction
2. Defaced, torn or photocopied vouchers will not be accepted
3. Not to be used in conjunction with any other offer
4. Not exchangeable for cash
5. Present this voucher to the business to accept the offer
6. 10% OFF
7. Excludes hardware and sale items

From novice to pro, we offer professional and honest advice to ensure you get the most out of your water time. Freeriders now brings its unsurpassed service to the web with the launch of our online shop.

Freeriders

Fur, Feathers & Flowers
61, Causewayhead, Penzance
TR18 2SS
Tel: 01736 368530

Terms & Conditions

1. Only one voucher per transaction
2. Defaced, torn or photocopied vouchers will not be accepted
3. Not to be used in conjunction with any other offer
4. Not exchangeable for cash
5. Present this voucher to the business to accept the offer

Fur, Feathers & Flowers

We also cover all aspects of floristry design, whether you need something for a birthday, wedding or just to put a smile on the face of someone special we can make an arrangement to suit your needs.

gift
19 River Street Truro Cornwall
TR1 2SQ
Tel: 01872 270033

Terms & Conditions

1. Only one voucher per transaction
2. Defaced, torn or photocopied vouchers will not be accepted
3. Not to be used in conjunction with any other offer
4. Not exchangeable for cash
5. Present this voucher to the business to accept the offer
6. 10% OFF. Excludes sale items

gift

Although small we stock a number of high end brands, we like to think our gifts are designer led. We stock Durance en Provence, Parlane International - design led products for the home, Savon de Marseille - beautiful french soap, alongside Trevarno's Organic skincare and Jo Edwards designer bags.

We open from Tuesday to Saturday 10.00 - 5.00.

The Granary Healthfoods
15d Causewayhead, Penzance
TR18 2SN
Tel: 01736 361869

Terms & Conditions

1. Only one voucher per transaction
2. Defaced, torn or photocopied vouchers will not be accepted
3. Not to be used in conjunction with any other offer
4. Not exchangeable for cash
5. Present this voucher to the business to accept the offer
6. 10% OFF when you spend £20 or more in one transaction

THE GRANARY

Daily tasty treats are available for vegans, vegetarians and pretty much any dietary requirement out there! The bread usually sells out very quickly too, so go early!

THE·GUILD·OF·TEN

The Guild of Ten is a contemporary craft and art gallery run by a group of designer/makers living in Cornwall to present their work directly to the public. You can find there the best in jewellery, glass, ceramics, wood, women and children's clothing.

See reverse for more information

Valid from 01.01.10 to 31.12.10

SAVE 10% OFF

Tel: 01872 274681

Harbour Bookshop

Great range of books for all ages on two floors including local history and maps. Friendly and helpful service, next day order service, including CDs and DVDs, many special offers, World-wide mail order, greetings cards, customer loyalty scheme.

See reverse for more information

Valid from 01.01.10 to 31.12.10

SAVE 10% OFF

Tel: 01736 794973

S43

Helston Toy shop is Helstons only independent toy retailer. We are dedicated to supplying toys that are fun, educational and good value for money.

See reverse for more information

Valid from 01.01.10 to 31.12.10

SAVE 10% OFF

Tel: 01326 561779

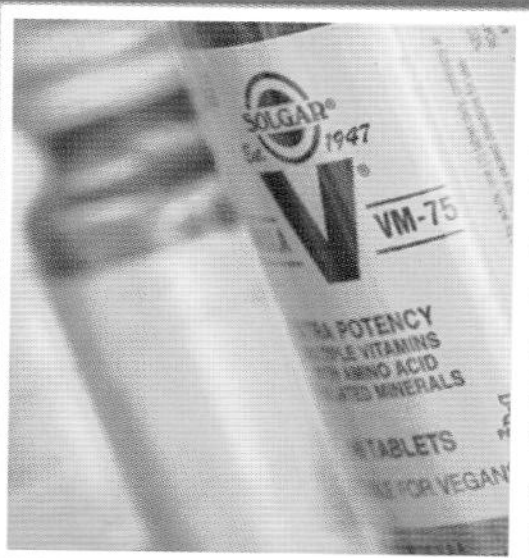

HENDRA HEALTH

KEEP IT CORNISH

S44

Complementary and alternative remedies, quality supplements and vitamins, natural skin and beauty products, organic / health foods. Specialist diets including - gluten free, sugar free, vegetarian and much more!

See reverse for more information

Valid from 01.01.10 to 31.12.10

SAVE 10% OFF

Tel: 01872 223799

S45

The sister shop to Bristol's award winning Here Gallery. We host exhibitions every month showcasing local students and more established artists. We stock a wide range of original artwork, prints and cards.

See reverse for more information

Valid from 01.01.10 to 31.12.10

SAVE 10% OFF

Guild of Ten
19 Old Bridge Street Truro
Cornwall, TR1 2AH
Tel: 01872 274681

Terms & Conditions

1. Only one voucher per transaction
2. Defaced, torn or photocopied vouchers will not be accepted
3. Not to be used in conjunction with any other offer
4. Not exchangeable for cash
5. Present this voucher to the business to accept the offer
6. 10% OFF one item

THE · GUILD · OF · TEN

The Guild of Ten is a contemporary craft and art gallery run by a group of designer/makers living in Cornwall to present their work directly to the public. You can find there the best in jewellery, glass, ceramics, wood, women and children's clothing.

Harbour Bookshop
2 Tregenna Place, St Ives
Cornwall, TR26 1SD
Tel: 01736 794973

Terms & Conditions

1. Only one voucher per transaction
2. Defaced, torn or photocopied vouchers will not be accepted
3. Not exchangeable for cash
4. Not to be used in conjunction with existing loyalty scheme

Harbour Bookshop

Great range of books for all ages on two floors including local history and maps, friendly and helpful service, next day order service, including CDs and DVDs, many special offers, world-wide mail order, greetings cards and customer loyalty scheme.

Helston Toyshop
16a Meneage Street, Helston
Cornwall, TR13 8AB
Tel: 01326 561779

Terms & Conditions

1. Only one voucher per transaction
2. Defaced, torn or photocopied vouchers will not be accepted
3. Not to be used in conjunction with any other offer
4. Not exchangeable for cash
5. Present this voucher to the business to accept the offer
6. 10% OFF when you spend over £20

Toys are our passion and we love finding new and exciting products for all ages and we pride ourselves in having friendly and knowledgeable staff.

Hendra Health Store
6-8 Lemon Street Market, Truro
TR1 2LQ
Tel: 01872 223799

Terms & Conditions

1. Only one voucher per transaction
2. Defaced, torn or photocopied vouchers will not be accepted
3. Not to be used in conjunction with any other offer
4. Not exchangeable for cash
5. Present this voucher to the business to accept the offer
6. 10% OFF. Offer does not include discounted or items on promotion

HENDRA HEALTH

We stock quality brands including; Solgar, Quest, Bioforce, Neal's Yard Remedies and Burt's Bees to name a few!

Here and Now Gallery
41a Killigrew Street, Falmouth
Cornwall. TR11 3PW
Tel: 01326 211505

Terms & Conditions

1. Only one voucher per transaction
2. Defaced, torn or photocopied vouchers will not be accepted
3. Not to be used in conjunction with any other offer
4. Not exchangeable for cash
5. Present this voucher to the business to accept the offer
6. 10% OFF on purchases over £10

Small press books, comics and zines from around the world, lots of unusual gifts and much more besides. Submissions welcome.

I Should Coco
ARTISAN CHOCOLATE - HAND MADE IN ST. IVES

S46

I Should Coco is an Award Winning Artisan Chocolatier and a Haven of Chocolate Activity! All our Chocolates are Hand-Crafted, Filled and Wrapped, here in our Glass Walled Workshop in St Ives, using as many Local Cornish Ingredients as possible.

See reverse for more information

Valid from 01.01.10 to 31.12.10

FREE V.I.P TREATMENT

Tel: 01736 798 756

S47

Here at In 2 Connections and Flowers we aim to fulfill every brides dream day. With our reputation second to none, and helpful personal attention to every one, we aim to make her day extra special.

See reverse for more information

Valid from 01.01.10 to 31.12.10

SAVE 10% OFF

Tel: 01872 262177

INHABIT

S48

Inhabit is an Independent family retail business started 10 years ago. A fantastic gift shop full of stylish fashion accessories, unique and unusual gifts, contemporary interior products with something gorgeous for everyone.

See reverse for more information

Valid from 01.01.10 to 31.12.10

SAVE 10% OFF

Tel: 01872 222 231

Inscriptions

S49

Inscriptions Glass Engravers supply unique, personalised, hand and machine engraved glass while the customer waits. With probably the largest selection of glass and crystal in Cornwall, there's something for all budgets and every occasion.

See reverse for more information

Valid from 01.01.10 to 31.12.10

FREE GIFT WRAP

Tel: 01872 223757

jb

S50

Jean makes the natural handmade soaps from quality ingredients in her beautifully restored barn. After lovingly nurturing them to maturity, the soap is then hand cut, wrapped in beautiful handmade paper and displayed in her shop.

See reverse for more information

Valid from 01.01.10 to 31.12.10

SAVE 10% OFF

I Should Coco
39 Fore Street, St Ives, Cornwall
TR26 1HE
Tel: 01736 798 756

Terms & Conditions

1. Only one voucher per transaction
2. Defaced, torn or photocopied vouchers will not be accepted
3. Not to be used in conjunction with any other offer
4. Not exchangeable for cash
5. Present this voucher to the business to accept the offer
6. Exclusive VIP treatment where you can meet the chocolatiers and have a FREE pot luck taste of what ever is being made in the kitchen that day

Fresh Cream Truffles a speciality. Watch the Chocolatiers at Work - and with this voucher claim your Free Taste of whatever they're making! Could be our Gold Award winning Nutmeg and Vanilla chocolate or the Chilli and Tequila Truffles recently featured in Jamie Oliver Magazine. As a VIP customer, you can also ask the Chocolatier any questions you may have.

In 2 Connections & FLowers
3 Little Castle, Street, Truro
TR1 3DL
Tel: 01872 262177

Terms & Conditions

1. Only one voucher per transaction
2. Defaced, torn or photocopied vouchers will not be accepted
3. Not to be used in conjunction with any other offer
4. Not exchangeable for cash
5. Present this voucher to the business to accept the offer
6. 10% OFF everything for you wedding day

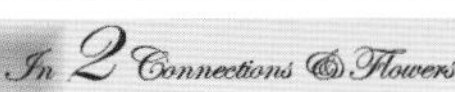

With our Bridal suite and in-house florist through to our recommendation wall, every need is catered for.

Inhabit
Green street mews, Green street, Truro
Cornwall , TR1 2LH
Tel: 01872 222 231

Terms & Conditions

1. Only one voucher per transaction
2. Defaced, torn or photocopied vouchers will not be accepted
3. Not to be used in conjunction with any other offer
4. Not exchangeable for cash
5. Present this voucher to the business to accept the offer

INHABIT

The bright atmosphere and friendly staff make this a must see destination when shopping in Truro.

Inscriptions
Pannier Market, Lemon Quay, Truro
Cornwall, TR1 2LL
Tel: 01872 223757

Terms & Conditions

1. Only one voucher per transaction
2. Defaced, torn or photocopied vouchers will not be accepted
3. Not to be used in conjunction with any other offer
4. Not exchangeable for cash
5. Present this voucher to the business to accept the offer
6. Free luxury gift wrap on each item costing £15 or more

Inscriptions

Weddings, birthdays, retirements, anniversaries, christenings, graduations, whatever! All engraved with your special message and choice of design.

Jean Barry Soap Company
25 Causewayhead, Penzance
Cornwall, TR18 2SP
Tel: 01736 361888

Terms & Conditions

1. Only one voucher per transaction
2. Defaced, torn or photocopied vouchers will not be accepted
3. Not to be used in conjunction with any other offer
4. Not exchangeable for cash
5. Present this voucher to the business to accept the offer
6. 10% OFF on all purchases over £15

jb

Jean makes the natural handmade soaps from quality ingredients in her beautifully restored barn. After lovingly nurturing them to maturity, the soap is then hand cut, wrapped in beautiful handmade paper and displayed in her shop where you can purchase a large range of luxurious gifts and natural ingredients.

Just Delights

S51

KEEP IT CORNISH

Welcome to Just Delights, inspired by the love of the simple Cornish lifestyle. Located In the old market town of Penryn, near Falmouth, Just Delights offers a unique range of vintage and reproduction furniture and a variety of accessories and soft furnishings to make your house a home.

See reverse for more information

Valid from 01.01.10 to 31.12.10

SAVE 10% OFF

Cornwall, TR10 8AQ Tel: 01326 379075

Just Like This

S52

Our unique and interesting store is full of colour and vibrance. We stock bags, Desigual womenswear, funky brollies, Irregular choice shoes, tights, bags, jewellery, tuk shoes and lots more bags. So come and give us a visit and enjoy a whole new shopping experience......

See reverse for more information

Valid from 01.01.10 to 31.12.10

SAVE 10% OFF

Tel: 01326 212895

KIT

S53

Kit is a quirky lifestyle boutique, stocking a wide range of colourful gifts, homewares and ladies clothes. We have 2 shops in Falmouth where you can find an original mix of vintage and new from brands such as Rice, Greengate and Motel.

See reverse for more information

Valid from 01.01.10 to 31.12.10

SAVE 10% OFF

Tel: 01326 313050

Korner Kabin

S54

Situated in the heart of Newquay at Central Square is the Korner Kabin Bag Co. With a huge variety of different brands and styles, many have been known to say this is the best bag shop in the country!

See reverse for more information

Valid from 01.01.10 to 31.12.10

SAVE 10% OFF

Tel: 01637 877187

S55

Lily the pink is a popular girlies shop, with a good selection of clothes for all ages. We have some beautiful beaded necklaces and bracelets in a large variety of colours and at affordable prices.

See reverse for more information

Valid from 01.01.10 to 31.12.10

SAVE 10% OFF

Tel: 01326 57 33 99

Just Delights
Commercial Road, Penryn
Cornwall, TR10 8AQ
Tel: 01326 379075

Terms & Conditions

1. Only one voucher per transaction
2. Defaced, torn or photocopied vouchers will not be accepted
3. Not to be used in conjunction with any other offer
4. Not exchangeable for cash
5. Present this voucher to the business to accept the offer
6. 10% OFF, excludes sale items

Just Delights

It is also the perfect little present shop with a large selection of gifts, cards and locally made craftwork. Our team of girlies all love beautiful things and will be more than happy to help you choose a perfect gift and gift wrap it.

JUST LIKE THIS
37 High Street, Falmouth, Cornwall
TR11 2AF
Tel: 01326 212895

Terms & Conditions

1. Only one voucher per transaction
2. Defaced, torn or photocopied vouchers will not be accepted
3. Not to be used in conjunction with any other offer
4. Not exchangeable for cash
5. Present this voucher to the business to accept the offer
6. Not including sale items

Just Like This

Our unique and interesting store is full of colour and vibrance. We stock bags, Desigual womenswear, funky brollies, Irregular choice shoes, tights, bags, jewellery, tuk shoes and lots more bags. So come and give us a visit and enjoy a whole new shopping experience......

Kit
3 Arwenack St, Falmouth
Cornwall, TR11 3HZ
Tel: 01326 313050

Terms & Conditions

1. Only one voucher per transaction
2. Defaced, torn or photocopied vouchers will not be accepted
3. Not to be used in conjunction with any other offer
4. Not exchangeable for cash
5. Present this voucher to the business to accept the offer

Kit is a quirky lifestyle boutique, stocking a wide range of colourful gifts, homewares and ladies clothes. We have 2 shops in Falmouth where you can find an original mix of vintage and new from brands such as Rice, Greengate and Motel.

Korner Kabin
7, Central Square, Newquay
Cornwall, TR7 1EX
Tel: 01637 877187

Terms & Conditions

1. Only one voucher per transaction
2. Defaced, torn or photocopied vouchers will not be accepted
3. Not to be used in conjunction with any other offer
4. Not exchangeable for cash
5. Present this voucher to the business to accept the offer
6. 10% OFF purchases over £40
7. Does not include sale items

Korner Kabin

Among the many designers in stock are: Radley, Fiorelli, Suzy Smith and Vendula London. Not forgetting the Mary Frances, Littlearth and Rocio Collections which are works of art! Other stock includes luggage/ man-bags/ purses/ wallets.

Everything is now also available online from **www.kornerkabin.co.uk**.

Lily the Pink
5 The Parade, Trengrouse Way
Helston, Cornwall, TR13 8AH
Tel: 01326 57 33 99

Terms & Conditions

1. Only one voucher per transaction
2. Defaced, torn or photocopied vouchers will not be accepted
3. Not to be used in conjunction with any other offer
4. Not exchangeable for cash
5. Present this voucher to the business to accept the offer
6. 10% OFF when you spend £50 or over
7. Excludes sale items

We also have a nice selection of fashionable bags, silver jewellery and gift items so why not pop in and see for yourself?

Lolo is a children's lifestyle boutique stocking an eclectic collection of clothes and gifts including a unique selection of baby goods.

See reverse for more information

Valid from 01.01.10 to 31.12.10

THE LONG & THE SHORT

Why not come & take a look at our range of ladies' fashion clothing, bags, shoes & jewellery. We offer something different at an affordable price. Go on treat yourself! (or better still let someone treat you!).

SAVE

10% OFF

See reverse for more information

Valid from 01.01.10 to 31.12.10

Madame Butterfly Lingerie

We stock a variety of corsets, hosiery and elegant lingerie sets in sizes 6-24. We also keep a large selection of adult products - toys, gifts and fetishwear. In store catalogue ordering is available.

SAVE

10% OFF

See reverse for more information

Valid from 01.01.10 to 31.12.10

Tel: 01872 274441

Malletts **home**hardware

£5 OFF
WHEN YOU SPEND
£25 ON TOYS
TOYMASTER

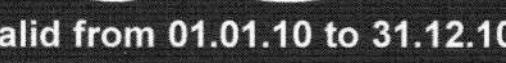

Valid from 01.01.10 to 31.12.10

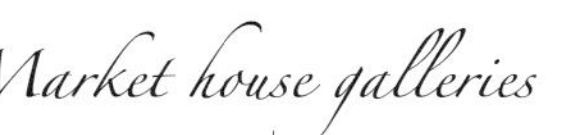

We are an independent retailer in Penzance. Our listing is endless - Neal's Yard, beautiful clothes, fair trade & ethically sourced bags, beads & bangles, gifts, local art, craft, jewellery & pocket money toys.

SAVE

10% OFF

See reverse for more information

Valid from 01.01.10 to 31.12.10

Lolo
31 High Street, Falmouth
Cornwall, TR11 2AD
Tel: 01326 212306

Terms & Conditions

1. Only one voucher per transaction
2. Defaced, torn or photocopied vouchers will not be accepted
3. Not to be used in conjunction with any other offer
4. Not exchangeable for cash
5. Present this voucher to the business to accept the offer

Lolo little ones

For fun pressies to dazzle your friends, for funky threads to explore coast and country in style or functional gear to create the feeling of home for your little ones visit Lolo, we are fun, funki, funktionaliti.

The Long & The Short
22 High Street, Falmouth, Cornwall
TR11 2AB.
Tel: 01326 218600

Terms & Conditions

1. Only one voucher per transaction
2. Defaced, torn or photocopied vouchers will not be accepted
3. Not to be used in conjunction with any other offer
4. Not exchangeable for cash
5. Present this voucher to the business to accept the offer
6. The management have the right to refuse this voucher & can end this offer at any time

THE LONG & THE SHORT

Why not come & take a look at our range of ladies' fashion clothing, bags, shoes & jewellery. We offer something different at an affordable price. Go on treat yourself! (or better still let someone treat you!).

Madame Butterfly Lingerie
Shop 4/11 Green Street Mews
Green Street, Truro, Cornwall TR1 2LH
Tel: 01872 223555

Terms & Conditions

1. Only one voucher per transaction
2. Defaced, torn or photocopied vouchers will not be accepted
3. Not to be used in conjunction with any other offer
4. Not exchangeable for cash
5. Present this voucher to the business to accept the offer
6. 10% OFF when you spend £50 or over in store

Madame Butterfly Lingerie

We are located at shop 4/11 Green Street (entrance opposite Truro Bus station).

Terms & Conditions

1. Only one voucher permitted per transaction.
2. Photocopied vouchers will not be excepted.
3. Cannot be used in conjunction with other offers, vouchers and sale products.
4. Only available on Toymaster products in-store.

Malletts **home**hardware

6 & 7 Victoria Square, Truro, Cornwall, TR1 2RT Tel: 01872 274441 Fax: 01872 240664

Market House Galleries
Market Place, Penzance
TR18 2JE
Tel: 01736 363284

Terms & Conditions

1. Only one voucher per transaction
2. Defaced, torn or photocopied vouchers will not be accepted
3. Not to be used in conjunction with any other offer
4. Not exchangeable for cash
5. Present this voucher to the business to accept the offer
6. 10% OFF any purchases over £20

Market house galleries

OPEN: Monday to Saturday 10 til 5 - come along & see for yourselves...

Market house galleries

We are an independent retailer in Penzance. Our listing is endless - Neal's Yard, beautiful clothes, fair trade & ethically sourced bags, beads & bangles, gifts, local art, craft, jewellery & pocket money toys.

See reverse for more information

Valid from 01.01.10 to 31.12.10

SAVE 10% OFF

Tel: 01736 363284

Market house galleries

We are an independent retailer in Penzance. Our listing is endless - Neal's Yard, beautiful clothes, fair trade & ethically sourced bags, beads & bangles, gifts, local art, craft, jewellery & pocket money toys.

See reverse for more information

Valid from 01.01.10 to 31.12.10

SAVE 10% OFF

Tel: 01736 363284

mondo trasho

Mondo Trasho is a hip new vintage clothing boutique situated in Arwenack Street, Falmouth. We offer a varied range of handpicked vintage and retro clothing and accessories for guys and gal's at affordable prices.

See reverse for more information

Valid from 01.01.10 to 31.12.10

SAVE 10% OFF

Tel: 01326 210053

Mounts Bay Wine Company

Mount's Bay Wine Company is a long established independent wine business serving both retail and trade customers in the west of Cornwall.

See reverse for more information

Valid from 01.01.10 to 31.12.10

SAVE 10% OFF

Tel: 01736 364118

Mums and little ones

Cornwall's unique gift store from conception to pre school. Mums and little ones the cute little shop tucked away just off lemon quay in the heart of the city of Truro where you are sure to find that special gift for mums to be and little ones 0-3.

See reverse for more information

Valid from 01.01.10 to 31.12.10

SAVE 10% OFF

Market House Galleries
Market Place, Penzance
TR18 2JE
Tel: 01736 363284

Terms & Conditions

1. Only one voucher per transaction
2. Defaced, torn or photocopied vouchers will not be accepted
3. Not to be used in conjunction with any other offer
4. Not exchangeable for cash
5. Present this voucher to the business to accept the offer
6. 10% OFF any purchases over £20

Market house galleries

OPEN: Monday to Saturday 10 til 5 - come along & see for yourselves…

Market House Galleries
Market Place, Penzance
TR18 2JE
Tel: 01736 363284

Terms & Conditions

1. Only one voucher per transaction
2. Defaced, torn or photocopied vouchers will not be accepted
3. Not to be used in conjunction with any other offer
4. Not exchangeable for cash
5. Present this voucher to the business to accept the offer
6. 10% OFF any purchases over £20

Market house galleries

OPEN: Monday to Saturday 10 til 5 - come along & see for yourselves…

Mondo Trasho
25a Arwenack St, Falmouth
Cornwall, TR11 3JE
Tel: 01326 210053

Terms & Conditions

1. Only one voucher per transaction
2. Defaced, torn or photocopied vouchers will not be accepted
3. Not to be used in conjunction with any other offer
4. Not exchangeable for cash
5. Present this voucher to the business to accept the offer

mondo trasho

We also stock levi's and imported t-shirts, sweats and jackets from the USA.

Mounts Bay Wine Company
Old Brewery Yard, Bread Street
Penzance, TR18 2EQ.
Tel: 01736 364118

Terms & Conditions

1. Only one voucher per transaction
2. Defaced, torn or photocopied vouchers will not be accepted
3. Not to be used in conjunction with any other offer
4. Not exchangeable for cash
5. Present this voucher to the business to accept the offer
6. 10% off a case of 12 bottles (single wine or mixed case)

Mounts Bay Wine Company

Service, professionalism and experience come as standard and helpful staff can ensure that your needs and requirements are met from our range of wines, spirits, liqueurs & beers.

Mums and Little Ones
Unit 4, Tinners Court, Black Quay
Truro, Cornwall, TR1 2LL
Tel: 01872 242446

Terms & Conditions

1. Only one voucher per transaction
2. Defaced, torn or photocopied vouchers will not be accepted
3. Not to be used in conjunction with any other offer
4. Not exchangeable for cash
5. Present this voucher to the business to accept the offer
6. 10% OFF when you spend over £20 in store

We have practical ideas from gro-group, hippy chick and handy sitt. Not to mention a gorgeous range of gifts from Kaloo, Moulin Roty, Haba, Brio,Taggies, and many more.

Tel: 01736 360867

KEEP IT CORNISH

We are situated in the busy town of Penzance in Cornwall, just off the main shopping street, and not too hard to find. We are a family run business with over 30 years experience in the music industry.

See reverse for more information

Valid from 01.01.10 to 31.12.10

SAVE **10% OFF**

Tel: 01736 360867

KEEP IT CORNISH

We are situated in the busy town of Penzance in Cornwall, just off the main shopping street, and not too hard to find. We are a family run business with over 30 years experience in the music industry.

See reverse for more information

Valid from 01.01.10 to 31.12.10

FREE **STRINGS, STRAP & LEAD**

Tel: 01736 793264

NATURAL BALANCE SURF Co.

Established in 1992. We cater for all your surfing needs both in and out of the water.

We stock a large range of clothing, footwear and accessories for men, women and children.

See reverse for more information

Valid from 01.01.10 to 31.12.10

SAVE **10% OFF**

Tel: 01637 854 800

Bespoke curtains, blinds, soft furnishings and shutters for the domestic and commercial markets from Newline.

See reverse for more information

Valid from 01.01.10 to 31.12.10

SAVE **10% OFF**

Massive range of footwear and clothing from brands such as Nike, Adidas, Vans, DC, 6.0, KSwiss, Lacoste, Osiris, DVS, Globe, Puma and many more, including limited editions. Call in to view the best fashion footwear range in Cornwall.

See reverse for more information

Valid from 01.01.10 to 31.12.10

SAVE **10% OFF**

The Music Box
60 Adelaide Street, Penzance
Cornwall, TR18 2ES
Tel: 01736 360867

Terms & Conditions

1. Only one voucher per transaction
2. Defaced, torn or photocopied vouchers will not be accepted
3. Not to be used in conjunction with any other offer
4. Not exchangeable for cash
5. Present this voucher to the business to accept the offer
6. 10% OFF any purchase over £5

Ring us or call in for a friendly chat.

The Music Box

The Music Box
60 Adelaide Street, Penzance,
Cornwall, TR18 2ES
Tel: 01736 360867

Terms & Conditions

1. Only one voucher per transaction
2. Defaced, torn or photocopied vouchers will not be accepted
3. Not to be used in conjunction with any other offer
4. Not exchangeable for cash
5. Present this voucher to the business to accept the offer
6. Free pack of strings, strap and lead with any electric guitar or electro/ acoustic guitar

The Music Box

Ring us or call in for a friendly chat.

The Music Box

Natural Balance Surf Co.
15 Fore Street, St.Ives, Cornwall
TR26 1AB
Tel: 01736 793264

Terms & Conditions

1. Only one voucher per transaction
2. Defaced, torn or photocopied vouchers will not be accepted
3. Not to be used in conjunction with any other offer
4. Not exchangeable for cash
5. Present this voucher to the business to accept the offer
6. 10% OFF if you spend £30 or more
7. Not available on sale items

Established in 1992. We cater for all your surfing needs both in and out of the water.

We stock a large range of clothing, footwear and accessories for men, women and children.

Natural Balance Surf Co.

Newline Blinds & Interiors
6 Station Parade, Cliff Road, Newquay
Cornwall TR7 2NF
Tel: 01637 854 800

Terms & Conditions

1. Only one voucher per transaction
2. Defaced, torn or photocopied vouchers will not be accepted
3. Not to be used in conjunction with any other offer
4. Not exchangeable for cash
5. Present this voucher to the business to accept the offer
6. 10% discount on bespoke blinds and curtains

newline
blinds & interiors

Visit our beautiful store in Newquay, where you can chose from thousands of designs and pick up tasteful gifts, or take advantage of our Interior design service and free home or business consultation.

Newquay Sports
2 Crantock Street, Newquay
Cornwall, TR7 1JA
Tel: 01637 874101

Terms & Conditions

1. Only one voucher per transaction
2. Defaced, torn or photocopied vouchers will not be accepted
3. Not to be used in conjunction with any other offer
4. Not exchangeable for cash
5. Present this voucher to the business to accept the offer
6. 10% OFF non sale goods

Massive range of footwear and clothing from brands such as Nike, Adidas, Vans, DC, 6.0, KSwiss, Lacoste, Osiris, DVS, Globe, Puma and many more, including limited editions. Call in to view the best fashion footwear range in Cornwall.

Number 36

S71

Number 36 is a feast to the eyes. Located on the cobbled streets of Causewayhead it has a vast and unusual range of jewellery, clothes, scarves and bags. If your house needs sprucing up we have a quirky and stylish range of gifts for the home.

SAVE UPTO 10%

See reverse for more information

Valid from 01.01.10 to 31.12.10

TR18 2SN Tel: 01736 367590

The Old Jeans Store Ltd

S72

The Jeans Store, has been established for over 14yrs. We stock male and female jeans/tops and accessories from brands such as: Levis, G-star, Pepe, Lee, Wrangler, Sonneti, Fly53, Jakes and others.

SAVE 15% OFF

See reverse for more information

Valid from 01.01.10 to 31.12.10

Tel: 01872 261961

The OLIVE FARM

MEDITERRANEAN EATING HOUSE AND DELI

S73

The Olive Farm has been serving delicious deli food with a southern flavour at Wharfside since 2000. Offering over 20 varieties of olives from Greece and Spain, a wide selection of cheeses from Cornwall, England and Europe, plus roasted peppers, sun-dried tomatoes, artichokes, chillies and all the other products.

SAVE 10% OFF

See reverse for more information

Valid from 01.01.10 to 31.12.10

Tel: 01736 359009

OLIVERS

S74

Olivers of Helston in Cornwall was established in 1860. This traditional, Cornish, family business started as a butchers. In the 1950's the business diversified into a delicatessen including cheese and then into fine wines and spirits.

SAVE 10% OFF

See reverse for more information

Valid from 01.01.10 to 31.12.10

Tel: 01326 572420

S75

Outback Trading should be your first stop for all your outdoor clothing, footwear and camping needs. We are stockists of brands including Vango, Force 10, Scarpa, Oakley and North Face but to name a few.

SAVE 10% OFF

See reverse for more information

Valid from 01.01.10 to 31.12.10

Tel: 01326 569569

Number 36
4, Causeway Head, Penzance
TR18 2SN
Tel: 01736 367590

Terms & Conditions

1. Only one voucher per transaction
2. Defaced, torn or photocopied vouchers will not be accepted
3. Not to be used in conjunction with any other offer
4. Not exchangeable for cash
5. Present this voucher to the business to accept the offer
6. 5% OFF on purchases upto £100 and 10% OFF when you spend £100 or more

Number 36

There is a treat for every girl whether buying a present for that special someone or simply feel like treating yourself. We aim to brighten up your day with an array of colours and styles……

The Old Jeans Store Ltd
14A Kenwyn Street, Truro, Cornwall
TR1 3DJ
Tel: 01872 261961

Terms & Conditions

1. Only one voucher per transaction
2. Defaced, torn or photocopied vouchers will not be accepted
3. Not to be used in conjunction with any other offer
4. Not exchangeable for cash
5. Present this voucher to the business to accept the offer

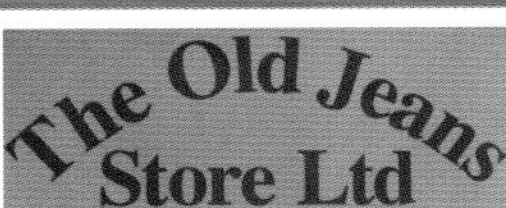

Our knowledgeable and friendly staff, are here to assist customers in finding that illusive 'perfect fitting jean'.

The Olive Farm Deli
Units 17/18, Wharfside Shopping Centre
Penzance, Cornwall, TR18 2GB
Tel: 01736 359009

Terms & Conditions

1. Only one voucher per transaction
2. Defaced, torn or photocopied vouchers will not be accepted
3. Not to be used in conjunction with any other offer
4. Not exchangeable for cash
5. Present this voucher to the business to accept the offer
6. 10% OFF fresh deli goods

The OLIVE FARM
MEDITERRANEAN EATING HOUSE AND DELI

The Olive Farm has been serving delicious deli food with a southern flavour at Wharfside since 2000. Offering over 20 varieties of olives from Greece and Spain, a wide selection of cheeses from Cornwall, England and Europe, plus roasted peppers, sun-dried tomatoes, artichokes, chillies and all the other products which have made the Olive Farm indispensable to Penzance.

Olivers
65 Meneage Street, Helston
Cornwall, TR13 8RB
Tel: 01326 572420

Terms & Conditions

1. Only one voucher per transaction
2. Defaced, torn or photocopied vouchers will not be accepted
3. Not to be used in conjunction with any other offer
4. Not exchangeable for cash
5. Present this voucher to the business to accept the offer
6. 10% OFF any purchase. Does not include spirits

OLIVERS

A large selection of jams, marmalades, honey, curds, sauces, pickles and dips are available. Olivers offer high quality products including local Cornish brands. Olivers wine merchants, offer some classic vintages that are imported directly. These are available by the bottle or case.

Outback Trading
The Angel Centre, Tyacke Road
Helston, Cornwall TR13 8RR
Tel: 01326 569569

Terms & Conditions

1. Only one voucher per transaction
2. Defaced, torn or photocopied vouchers will not be accepted
3. Not to be used in conjunction with any other offer
4. Not exchangeable for cash
5. Present this voucher to the business to accept the offer

Haven't got time to pop into our Helston store then why not visit our comprehensive Website!

www.outbacktrading.co.uk

Overhead Surf is based at our Cliff Road store in the UK's surf capital Newquay and at our sister store in Saltash - Cornwall. We stock a wide range of surfboards, bodyboards, wetsuits, surf fashion & accessories, from some of the top surfing brands.

See reverse for more information

Valid from 01.01.10 to 31.12.10

SAVE 10% OFF

TR7 1SG Tel: 01637 850808 or 01752 845522

PERFECT PICTURES

Based in Penzance specializing in popular types of cameras and optical equipment. High quality printing including standard, large format & canvas is available. We sell photographic accessories, picture frames and most film types, offer a repair service, and good sound advice is provided by our experienced staff.

See reverse for more information

Valid from 01.01.10 to 31.12.10

5% OFF
BINOCULARS

Cornwall TR18 2SN Tel: 01736 364407

PERFECT PICTURES

KEEP IT CORNISH

Based in Penzance specializing in popular types of cameras and optical equipment. High quality printing including standard, large format & canvas is available. We sell photographic accessories, picture frames and most film types, offer a repair service, and good sound advice is provided by our experienced staff.

See reverse for more information

Valid from 01.01.10 to 31.12.10

ENLARGEMENT

Tel: 01736 364407

pure nuff stuff

Pure Nuff Stuff are passionate about making the finest natural skincare products. We're committed to bringing you the most comprehensive range of products for the whole family.

See reverse for more information

Valid from 01.01.10 to 31.12.10

10% OFF

Tel: 01736 366008

S80

CORNISH

Red Ella is a boutique specialising in bespoke clothing, hand-made from pre-loved garments and vintage fabrics. We are far from the means of traditional sewing, with our unique Red Ella style.

See reverse for more information

Valid from 01.01.10 to 31.12.10

SAVE 10% OFF

Tel: 07859759757

Overhead Surf
19 Cliff Road, Newquay, Cornwall
TR7 1SG
Tel: 01637 850808 or 01752 845522

Terms & Conditions

1. Only one voucher per transaction
2. Defaced, torn or photocopied vouchers will not be accepted
3. Not to be used in conjunction with any other offer
4. Not exchangeable for cash
5. Present this voucher to the business to accept the offer
6. 10% OFF excluding sale items and surf boards

Surfing brands: – RipCurl, Animal, Hurley, Nike, Reef, Sola, NMD, VS, Pride, Clayton, Chris Harris, and many many more. With a daily surf report uptodate surf news from "Surfers Village", and new products added daily, www.overheadsurf.co.uk is set to be one of the fastest growing surf wear E-commerce sites in the UK.

Perfect Pictures
14 Causewayhead Penzance
Cornwall TR18 2SN
Tel: 01736 364407

Terms & Conditions

1. Only one voucher per transaction
2. Defaced, torn or photocopied vouchers will not be accepted
3. Not to be used in conjunction with any other offer
4. Not exchangeable for cash
5. Present this voucher to the business to accept the offer
6. Save 5% OFF binoculars

PERFECT PICTURES

Based in Penzance specializing in popular types of cameras and optical equipment. High quality printing including standard, large format & canvas is available. We sell photographic accessories, picture frames and most film types, offer a repair service, and good sound advice is provided by our experienced staff.

Perfect Pictures
14 Causewayhead Penzance
Cornwall TR18 2SN
Tel: 01736 364407

Terms & Conditions

1. Only one voucher per transaction
2. Defaced, torn or photocopied vouchers will not be accepted
3. Not to be used in conjunction with any other offer
4. Not exchangeable for cash
5. Present this voucher to the business to accept the offer
6. Free picture enlargement with every frame purchased

PERFECT PICTURES

Based in Penzance specializing in popular types of cameras and optical equipment. High quality printing including standard, large format & canvas is available. We sell photographic accessories, picture frames and most film types, offer a repair service, and good sound advice is provided by our experienced staff.

Pure Nuff Stuff
The Egyptian House, 6 Chapel Street
Penzance, Cornwall, TR18 4AJ
Tel: 01736 366008

Terms & Conditions

1. Only one voucher per transaction
2. Defaced, torn or photocopied vouchers will not be accepted
3. Not to be used in conjunction with any other offer
4. Not exchangeable for cash
5. Present this voucher to the business to accept the offer
6. 10% OFF when you spend over £30

They're all made here in Cornwall from the purest oils and butters Nature has to offer, all sustainably sourced and cruelty free.

Red Ella
No.1 Old Brewery Yard, High Street
Falmouth, TR11 2BY
Tel: 07859759757

Terms & Conditions

1. Only one voucher per transaction
2. Defaced, torn or photocopied vouchers will not be accepted
3. Not to be used in conjunction with any other offer
4. Not exchangeable for cash
5. Present this voucher to the business to accept the offer

We offer a commission based service, tailoring garments to suit your personality. In our authentic boutique you will find corset bustles and other fancy frocks, as well as a special kind of day wear.

Get the party started at Falmouth's professional party shop where our experienced and friendly team are always happy to help you choose from our extensive range of costumes, masks, wigs, hats, make up, eyelashes, contact lenses, tights and lots of accessories.

See reverse for more information

Valid from 01.01.10 to 31.12.10

S81

SAVE 17% OFF

Cornwall TR11 3DB
Tel: 01326 211713

Salt Cellar Hats

Hats made by Claire Francis.
Fabulous handmade hats.
On display in our harbourside workshops.
Hats also made to order.

See reverse for more information

Valid from 01.01.10 to 31.12.10

S82

SAVE 10% OFF

Porthleven, Cornwall TR13 9DP
Tel: 01326 565707

scentstore®

Scentstore is a large independent perfumery situated in the Cathedral City of Truro. Trading since 1996, Scentstore is renowned locally for being the cheapest supplier of fragrance; many items are less than duty free!

See reverse for more information

Valid from 01.01.10 to 31.12.10

S83

SAVE 10% OFF

Tel: 01872 263663

Sea Holly Arts & Crafts

We are a small art and craft shop selling beads, papercraft, glass and ceramic paint, manga markers and general art supplies. We also sell a small amount of locally made craft.

See reverse for more information

Valid from 01.01.10 to 31.12.10

S84

SAVE 20% OFF

Tel: 01326 558869

sheoak acoustics

Sheoak Acoustics is an independent guitar shop located in The Old High Street, Falmouth; specialising in quality solid top steel-string and classical guitars. You will also find a select range of ukuleles, banjos and mandolins plus all related musical accessories.

See reverse for more information

Valid from 01.01.10 to 31.12.10

S85

SAVE 10% OFF

Tel: 01326 312078

Ribticklers
8 Market Strand, Falmouth
Cornwall TR11 3DB
Tel: 01326 211713

Terms & Conditions

1. Only one voucher per transaction
2. Defaced, torn or photocopied vouchers will not be accepted
3. Not to be used in conjunction with any other offer
4. Not exchangeable for cash
5. Present this voucher to the business to accept the offer

Get the party started at Falmouth's professional party shop where our experienced and friendly team are always happy to help you choose from our extensive range of costumes, masks, wigs, hats, make up, eyelashes, contact lenses, tights and lots of accessories.

Ribticklers

Salt Cellar Hats
Saltcellar workshops Saltcellar hill
porthleven, cornwall TR139DP
Tel: 01326 565707

Terms & Conditions

1. Only one voucher per transaction
2. Defaced, torn or photocopied vouchers will not be accepted
3. Not to be used in conjunction with any other offer
4. Not exchangeable for cash
5. Present this voucher to the business to accept the offer

Salt Cellar Hats

From sweeping brims to funky berets.

Hats can be formal or fun.

Scentstore
10-11 Cathedral Lane, Truro
Cornwall, TR1 2QS
Tel: 01872 263663

Terms & Conditions

1. Only one voucher per transaction
2. Defaced, torn or photocopied vouchers will not be accepted
3. Not to be used in conjunction with any other offer
4. Not exchangeable for cash
5. Present this voucher to the business to accept the offer
6. 10% OFF all purchases over £30

scentstore

They also provide great customer service, offer free gift wrapping and an internet/mail order service.

Scentstore

Sea Holly Arts & Crafts
12 Wendron Street, Helston
Cornwall, TR13 8PS
Tel: 01326 558869

Terms & Conditions

1. Only one voucher per transaction
2. Defaced, torn or photocopied vouchers will not be accepted
3. Not to be used in conjunction with any other offer
4. Not exchangeable for cash
5. Present this voucher to the business to accept the offer
6. 20% OFF sales over £10 with this voucher
7. This does not include previously discounted items or locally made crafts

Sea Holly Arts & Crafts

Stockists of Winsor and Newton, Pebeo, Copic, Sakura, Fimo, dufex, craftime, K&co, beadalon, beadsmith. We have a wide range of bead stock which changes frequently throughout the year.

Sheoak Acoustics
34 High St, Falmouth, Cornwall
TR11 2AD
Tel: 01326 312078

Terms & Conditions

1. Only one voucher per transaction
2. Defaced, torn or photocopied vouchers will not be accepted
3. Not to be used in conjunction with any other offer
4. Not exchangeable for cash
5. Present this voucher to the business to accept the offer
6. 10% discount on accessories (excluding sale items)

Come and pay us a visit for friendly, expert advice.

SHOOZZE

KEEP IT CORNISH

S86

From heels, to boots, to bags we stock everything a woman could wish for! If you would like to visit our shop why not come to the delightful town of Truro, where our staff will be waiting to give you first class service.

See reverse for more information

Valid from 01.01.10 to 31.12.10

SAVE **10% OFF**

Cornwall. TR1 3DL
Tel: 01872 277200

S87

SJ'Z Skateshop of Truro first opened it's doors in 1989 and more than 20 years later is still going strong! SJ'z is situated in St Marys Street and offers the latest in Skateboarding equipment, clothing and footwear.

See reverse for more information

Valid from 01.01.10 to 31.12.10

SAVE **10% OFF**

Cornwall, TR1 2BE
Tel: 01872 223533

The Soup Gallery

S88

The Soup Gallery is Truro's hottest urban Art Gallery, showcasing Graffiti and Contemporary Art. Opened by Graffiti Artist Mark Polglase in May 2008, The Soup Gallery aims to promote and exhibit the work of contemporary illustrators and street artists based both locally and further a field.

See reverse for more information

Valid from 01.01.10 to 31.12.10

SAVE **10% OFF**

Tel: 01872 278135

S89

South Shore has a large collection of street brands that sit with both surf & skate life style images. Here at South Shore we have been specialising in surf and skate for over 20 years and supply both hardwear and soft goods.

See reverse for more information

Valid from 01.01.10 to 31.12.10

SAVE **10% OFF**

Tel: 01736 365757

South Shore Kids

S90

Newly opened and full of must have childrens casual clothing. Quiksilver, Animal, Billabong, Ripcurl, Etnies and much more. A large range of responsibly priced baby wear in our baby department.

See reverse for more information

Valid from 01.01.10 to 31.12.10

SAVE **10% OFF**

Tel: 01736 361615

Shoozze
2 Little Castle Street, Truro
Cornwall. TR1 3DL
Tel: 01872 277200

Terms & Conditions

1. Only one voucher per transaction
2. Defaced, torn or photocopied vouchers will not be accepted
3. Not to be used in conjunction with any other offer
4. Not exchangeable for cash
5. Present this voucher to the business to accept the offer
6. 10% OFF any purchase

SHOOZZE

If you want to talk to someone from the shop then give us a call or why not visit our Website.

Shoozze

Sj'z Skate Shop
1 St Marys Mews, Truro
Cornwall, TR1 2BE
Tel: 01872 223533

Terms & Conditions

1. Only one voucher per transaction
2. Defaced, torn or photocopied vouchers will not be accepted
3. Not to be used in conjunction with any other offer
4. Not exchangeable for cash
5. Present this voucher to the business to accept the offer
6. Offer expires 31 May 2010
7. 10% OFF any purchase £50 or over with this voucher

SJ'z is an authorized stockist of Nike SB, Fallen, Plan B, Independent, Girl, Thrasher and loads more!

Sj'z Skate Shop

The Soup Gallery
106 Kenwyn Street, Truro, Cornwall
TR1 3BX
Tel: 01872 278135

Terms & Conditions

1. Only one voucher per transaction
2. Defaced, torn or photocopied vouchers will not be accepted
3. Not to be used in conjunction with any other offer
4. Not exchangeable for cash
5. Present this voucher to the business to accept the offer
6. 10% OFF any print or piece of original artwork

The Soup Gallery

The Soup Gallery is Truro's hottest urban Art Gallery, showcasing Graffiti and Contemporary Art. Opened by Graffiti Artist Mark Polglase in May 2008, The Soup Gallery aims to promote and exhibit the work of contemporary illustrators and street artists based both locally and further a field.

The Soup Gallery

South Shore
Unit 13, Wharfside Centre,
Market Jew Street, Penzance TR18 2GB
Tel: 01736 365757

Terms & Conditions

1. Only one voucher per transaction
2. Defaced, torn or photocopied vouchers will not be accepted
3. Not to be used in conjunction with any other offer
4. Not exchangeable for cash
5. Present this voucher to the business to accept the offer
6. 10% OFF, given as a credit voucher for your next visit

We carry a large range of all the top boards, wet suits, clothes, shoes and accessories. Stocked brands include: Roxy, Art, Rocket Dog, Da Kine, Alder, Quiksilver, Billabong, Rip Curl, DC, Etnies, ES, Emerica, Nikita, Skull Candy, m WE, Analog, Matrix, DVS, Fenchurch, Reef, Oakley.

South Shore Kids
Unit 2a Wharfeside Shopping Centre,
Penzance, TR18 2GB
Tel: 01736 361615

Terms & Conditions

1. Only one voucher per transaction
2. Defaced, torn or photocopied vouchers will not be accepted
3. Not to be used in conjunction with any other offer
4. Not exchangeable for cash
5. Present this voucher to the business to accept the offer
6. 10% OFF, given as a credit voucher for your next visit

South Shore Kids

Newly opened and full of must have childrens casual clothing. Quiksilver, Animal, Billabong, Ripcurl, Etnies and much more. A large range of reasonibly priced baby wear in our baby department.

Beautiful handcrafted silver and gemstone jewellery ethically sourced from around the world.

SAVE 15% OFF

See reverse for more information

Valid from 01.01.10 to 31.12.10

TR26 1AB
Tel: 01736 793724

ST IVES VALETING.COM
FOR ALL YOUR VALETING NEEDS

Car, commercial, classic and special vehicle valeting. Private, trade and contracts. Mini and full valets. Upholstery, shampooing and leather care. Paint renovation and protection. Odour removal. Evening and weekends collection and delivery.

FREE UPGRADE

See reverse for more information

Valid from 01.01.10 to 31.12.10

www.stivesvaleting.com
Tel: 01736 797941 / 07969073179

St Justin

St Justin designs and manufactures jewellery, gifts and accessories for retailers all over the world as well as their own shop in Penzance. Celtic design predominates but there is also a choice of contemporary pieces.

SAVE 10% OFF

See reverse for more information

Valid from 01.01.10 to 31.12.10

Cornwall, TR20 8HX
Tel: 01736 360001

STICK WITH IT

Cambornes craft shop specializing in scrap-booking and card-making. Stockists of all the major papercraft brands including Do-crafts, DCWV and Dufex.

SAVE 10% OFF

See reverse for more information

Valid from 01.01.10 to 31.12.10

Cornwall. TR14 8AL
Tel: 01209 613733

SUGAR LOAF

Sugarloaf offers a range of exclusive Brazilian surf and streetwear brands for both men and women. As we import the brands directly from Brazil you will not find them anywhere else.

SAVE 20% OFF

See reverse for more information

Valid from 01.01.10 to 31.12.10

Tel: 01637 852535

St Ives Silver
1 Fore Street, St. Ives, Cornwall
TR26 1AB
Tel: 01736 793724

Terms & Conditions

1. Only one voucher per transaction
2. Defaced, torn or photocopied vouchers will not be accepted
3. Not to be used in conjunction with any other offer
4. Not exchangeable for cash
5. Present this voucher to the business to accept the offer
6. 15% of all purchases

We buy direct from individuals and small businesses, and work together with craft workers and designers to ensure a high quality of workmanship and design.

Also find us at Lemon Street Market, Truro.

St Ives Silver

St Ives Valeting
www.stivesvaleting.com
Tel: 01736 797941 / 07969073179

Terms & Conditions

1. Only one voucher per transaction
2. Defaced, torn or photocopied vouchers will not be accepted
3. Not to be used in conjunction with any other offer
4. Not exchangeable for cash
5. Present this voucher to the business to accept the offer
6. A free upgrade from what you have purchased

ST IVES VALETING.COM
FOR ALL YOUR VALETING NEEDS

Fully insured. We welcome the opportunity to earn your trust and deliver the very best service in the industry.

St Ives Valeting

St Justin Shop
58 Causewayhead, Penzance
Cornwall, TR20 8HX
Tel: 01736 360001

Terms & Conditions

1. Only one voucher per transaction
2. Defaced, torn or photocopied vouchers will not be accepted
3. Not to be used in conjunction with any other offer
4. Not exchangeable for cash
5. Present this voucher to the business to accept the offer
6. 10% OFF when you spend £25 or more

St Justin

Products are made in pewter, tin, bronze and silver.

St Justin Shop

Stick With It Ltd
79 Trelowarren Street, Camborne
Cornwall. TR14 8AL
Tel: 01209 613733

Terms & Conditions

1. Only one voucher per transaction
2. Defaced, torn or photocopied vouchers will not be accepted
3. Not to be used in conjunction with any other offer
4. Not exchangeable for cash
5. Present this voucher to the business to accept the offer
6. 10% OFF when you spend £25 or over

With one of the broadest ranges of card and paper available and 1000's of decoupage sheets the choice is exceptional. From stamps to scrapbooks you won't believe your eyes.

Stick With It

Sugar Loaf
1 Bank St, Newquay, Cornwall
TR7 1EP
Tel: 01637 852535

Terms & Conditions

1. Only one voucher per transaction
2. Defaced, torn or photocopied vouchers will not be accepted
3. Not to be used in conjunction with any other offer
4. Not exchangeable for cash
5. Present this voucher to the business to accept the offer

SUGAR LOAF

Pop in to check out the latest trends in Hoodies, art and graffiti t-shirts, boardshorts, skate shoes and much more.

Sugar Loaf

S96

Surfside was established in 2008, located in Kenwyn Street, Truro. We stock alot of the well known surf brands. You will find mens and womens clothing, Footwear, Wetsuits, Surfboards and Hardware.

See reverse for more information

Valid from 01.01.10 to 31.12.10

SAVE **10% OFF**

S97

Surfside was established in 2008, located in Kenwyn Street, Truro. We stock alot of the well known surf brands. You will find mens and womens clothing, Footwear, Wetsuits, Surfboards and Hardware.

See reverse for more information

Valid from 01.01.10 to 31.12.10

SAVE **10% OFF**

S98

Surfside was established in 2008, located in Kenwyn Street, Truro. We stock alot of the well known surf brands. You will find mens and womens clothing, Footwear, Wetsuits, Surfboards and Hardware.

See reverse for more information

Valid from 01.01.10 to 31.12.10

SAVE **10% OFF**

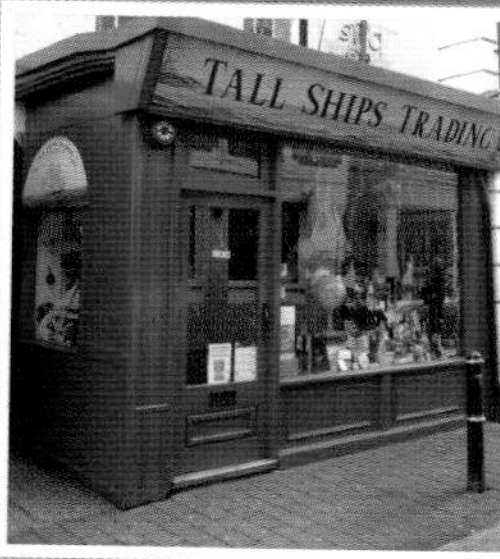

TALL SHIPS TRADING

S99

Welcome to Tall Ships Trading. We are a Maritime themed shop selling furniture, model boats , paintings, ceramics, gifts and nautical bric-a-brac. Current best sellers include Globes, Custom painted furniture, Clocks & Barometers.

See reverse for more information

Valid from 01.01.10 to 31.12.10

SAVE **10% OFF**

newlyn ART GALLERY

S100

Our shops at The Exchange and Newlyn Art Gallery provide a range of contemporary art books and art-related gifts and cards. Prior to our launch in 2007, Simon Jaques used the camera on a mobile phone to record the transformation of the old telephone exchange into a gallery.

See reverse for more information

Valid from 01.01.10 to 31.12.10

SAVE **5% OFF**

KEEP IT... SHOPPING

www.keepitcornish.co.uk

Surfside
Units 1 and 2 Truro Lanes, Kenwyn Street, Truro, TR1 3DL
Tel: 01872 278555

Terms & Conditions

1. Only one voucher per transaction
2. Defaced, torn or photocopied vouchers will not be accepted
3. Not to be used in conjunction with any other offer
4. Not exchangeable for cash
5. Present this voucher to the business to accept the offer
6. 10% OFF when you spend £50 or more
7. Please quote the code 'ss10' to also get 10% OFF online when you spend over £50

Also online at www.surfsideonline.co.uk

Surfside

Surfside
Units 1 and 2 Truro Lanes, Kenwyn Street, Truro, TR1 3DL
Tel: 01872 278555

Terms & Conditions

1. Only one voucher per transaction
2. Defaced, torn or photocopied vouchers will not be accepted
3. Not to be used in conjunction with any other offer
4. Not exchangeable for cash
5. Present this voucher to the business to accept the offer
6. 10% OFF when you spend £50 or more
7. Please quote the code 'ss10' to also get 10% OFF online when you spend over £50

Also online at www.surfsideonline.co.uk

Surfside

Surfside
Units 1 and 2 Truro Lanes, Kenwyn Street, Truro, TR1 3DL
Tel: 01872 278555

Terms & Conditions

1. Only one voucher per transaction
2. Defaced, torn or photocopied vouchers will not be accepted
3. Not to be used in conjunction with any other offer
4. Not exchangeable for cash
5. Present this voucher to the business to accept the offer
6. 10% OFF when you spend £50 or more
7. Please quote the code 'ss10' to also get 10% OFF online when you spend over £50

Also online at www.surfsideonline.co.uk

Surfside

Tall Ships Trading
49 Church Street, Falmouth
Cornwall, TR11 3DS
Tel: 01326 318888

Terms & Conditions

1. Only one voucher per transaction
2. Defaced, torn or photocopied vouchers will not be accepted
3. Not to be used in conjunction with any other offer
4. Not exchangeable for cash
5. Present this voucher to the business to accept the offer
6. 10% OFF on purchases over £10. Excludes sale and commission item

TALL SHIPS TRADING

A wide range of original artwork and prints by local artists now available in store.

Tall Ships Trading

The Newlyn Art Gallery
Princes Street, Penzance, Cornwall
TR18 2NL
Tel: 01736 363715

Terms & Conditions

1. Only one voucher per transaction
2. Defaced, torn or photocopied vouchers will not be accepted
3. Not to be used in conjunction with any other offer
4. Not exchangeable for cash
5. Present this voucher to the business to accept the offer

There is an ever changing selection from local and national artists and always something to discover for that elusive gift idea or just to treat yourself to that silk scarf or ceramic vase.

S101

KEEP IT CORNISH

Tilly Mint Bakery is where sugar meets art. Cupcakes and celebration cakes, kitsch or classic designs all freshly baked in Truro. Cupcakes available fresh every day.

There is nothing like it…

See reverse for more information

Valid from 01.01.10 to 31.12.10

FREE

4 CUPCAKES FREE

Truro, TR1 2LH
Tel: 01872 279987

S102

Situated directly above Newquay Sports, True is a much needed addition to the local shopping scene. Exclusively stocking a whole host of designer menswear including Diesel, G-Star, Superdry, Fred Perry, Polo Jeans and Religion but to name a few.

See reverse for more information

Valid from 01.01.10 to 31.12.10

10% OFF

Cornwall, TR7 1JA
Tel: 01637 874101

THE TRURO TEA & COFFEE Co

S103

We are a small, independent, specialist tea & coffee company based in Cornwall. Started in 2005, we are now pleased to be able to offer our products online.

See reverse for more information

Valid from 01.01.10 to 31.12.10

SAVE

10% OFF

Cornwall, TR1 2LL
Tel: 01872 276524

tyto

S104

Tyto is a maverick boutique and gallery on Discovery Quay in Falmouth. Established in July 09, she stocks many lovely things for ladies & gentlemen to wear, gorgeous gowns by Emily & Fin, whimsical shirts from Ria Roberts & fabulous jewellery from Stolen Thunder.

See reverse for more information

Valid from 01.01.10 to 31.12.10

SAVE

10% OFF

Falmouth, TR11 3XF
Tel: 01326 313260

VIDEO EXPRESS

S105

KEEP IT CORNISH

Extensive film library from world cinema to latest releases, booking service, confectionery and drinks. Discounts and deals available. Joining is simple, just bring along ID confirming your address and be signed up in minutes!

See reverse for more information

Valid from 01.01.10 to 31.12.10

SAVE

50p OFF

Tel: 01326 212993

Tilly Mint Bakery
Shop 5, Green St Mews, Green St
Truro, TR1 2LH
Tel: 01872 279987

Terms & Conditions

1. Only one voucher per transaction
2. Defaced, torn or photocopied vouchers will not be accepted
3. Not to be used in conjunction with any other offer
4. Not exchangeable for cash
5. Present this voucher to the business to accept the offer
6. **4 FREE** cupcakes in a gift box with every cake order over £50

There is nothing like it... we do Cupcakes with bling! Found in Green St Mews. Take the walkway next to Inhabit opposite Truro bus station. We are next door to Madame Butterfly.

Tilly Mint Bakery
www.tillymintbakery.com

True
2 Crantock Street, Newquay
Cornwall, TR7 1JA
Tel: 01637 874101

Terms & Conditions

1. Only one voucher per transaction
2. Defaced, torn or photocopied vouchers will not be accepted
3. Not to be used in conjunction with any other offer
4. Not exchangeable for cash
5. Present this voucher to the business to accept the offer
6. 10% OFF non sale goods

Why go to the City when you have all your clothing needs on your doorstep.

The Truro Tea and Coffee Co
55, Pannier Market, Back Quay, Truro
Cornwall, TR1 2LL
Tel: 01872 276524

Terms & Conditions

1. Only one voucher per transaction
2. Defaced, torn or photocopied vouchers will not be accepted
3. Not to be used in conjunction with any other offer
4. Not exchangeable for cash
5. Present this voucher to the business to accept the offer

THE TRURO TEA & COFFEE Co

We have a wide range of single origin coffee, fairtrade & organic coffee beans, loose leaf teas, herbal infusions & fruit teas which we sell at our shop in Truro and provide mail order delivery thoughout the U.K. Why not pop in and see us at the Pannier Market in Truro or place an order online!

The Truro Tea and Coffee Co

Tyto
3 Tidemill House, Discovery Quay
Falmouth, TR11 3XP
Tel: 01326 313260

Terms & Conditions

1. Only one voucher per transaction
2. Defaced, torn or photocopied vouchers will not be accepted
3. Not to be used in conjunction with any other offer
4. Not exchangeable for cash
5. Present this voucher to the business to accept the offer
6. Excluding Artwork and Locally made products

Also on offer is an assortment of wonderful gifts and carefully selected vintage items. She also offers a platform for emerging local talent to display their work and runs a monthly art space event schedule.

Tyto

Video Express
9 Berekely Vale Falmouth
TR11 3PL
01326 212993

Terms & Conditions

1. Only one voucher per transaction
2. Defaced, torn or photocopied vouchers will not be accepted
3. Not to be used in conjunction with any other offer
4. Not exchangeable for cash
5. Present this voucher to the business to accept the offer
6. 50p off One Night Film Rental with voucher

Extensive film library from world cinema to latest releases, booking service, confectionery and drinks. Discounts and deals available. Joining is simple, just bring along ID confirming your address and be signed up in minutes!

At the top of Causewayhead, Penzance's unique run of independent shops, you'll find Walkers, a traditional jewellers with a reputation for value and service.

See reverse for more information

Valid from 01.01.10 to 31.12.10

SAVE

HALF PRICE
WATCH BATTERY

TR18 2SS
Tel: 01736 363195

We are based in The beautiful seaside town of Falmouth, Cornwall. We supply watersports equipment such as towable toys like ringos & donuts, Kneeboards, & water skis from the worlds best manufactures like Body Glove &

See reverse for more information

Valid from 01.01.10 to 31.12.10

SAVE

10% OFF

TR11 3PW
Tel: 01326 219123

The Wharf

The Wharf is a small independent boutique in Hayle's Fore Street. Although it has only been open for a couple of years it is gaining a reputation for having sought-after labels such as Ugg, Fly, Fitflop, Firetrap, Noa Noa and Inwear.

See reverse for more information

Valid from 01.01.10 to 31.12.10

SAVE

10% OFF

TR27 4DY
Tel: 01736 752053

Wheal Sara Flowers, a florist shop with a difference. Young, modern and enthusiastic, specializing in wedding and party flowers but covering all aspects of floristry design, stocking a wide selection of flowers from all over the world.

See reverse for more information

Valid from 01.01.10 to 31.12.10

SAVE

10% OFF

Tel: 01736 797788

Yumi opened on Fore Street, St Ives in April 2009 and became instantly popular with its printed tunics and elaborate designs alongside high-end lace and chiffon dresses.

See reverse for more information

Valid from 01.01.10 to 31.12.10

SAVE

15% OFF

Tel: 01736 791782

Walkers
50 Causewayhead, Penzance
TR18 2SS
Tel: 01736 363195

Terms & Conditions

1. Only one voucher per transaction
2. Defaced, torn or photocopied vouchers will not be accepted
3. Not to be used in conjunction with any other offer
4. Not exchangeable for cash
5. Present this voucher to the business to accept the offer
6. Half price watch battery fitted with this voucher

The premise's workshop and team of goldsmiths carry out repairs, alterations, valuations and bespoke designs; all provided with a smile by owner Julian and manager Hannah.

Walkers

Wavelength One
39 Killigrew Street. Falmouth.
TR11 3PW
Tel: 01326 219123

Terms & Conditions

1. Only one voucher per transaction
2. Defaced, torn or photocopied vouchers will not be accepted
3. Not to be used in conjunction with any other offer
4. Not exchangeable for cash
5. Present this voucher to the business to accept the offer

Freemotion. Sit on Kayaks from top suppliers such as Ocean Kayak, Robson & FatYak , Tenders and dinghies from Southern Pacific, Wetsuits from £15 Adults from £50 Clothing from Speedo, Bailin, Black Salamnder and more.

Wavelength One

The Wharf
38 Fore Street, Hayle. Cornwall
TR27 4DY
Tel: 01736 752053

Terms & Conditions

1. Only one voucher per transaction
2. Defaced, torn or photocopied vouchers will not be accepted
3. Not to be used in conjunction with any other offer
4. Not exchangeable for cash
5. Present this voucher to the business to accept the offer
6. Save 10% when you spend over £25

The Wharf

The Wharf also has a great selection of denim from Levi and Firetrap.

Wheal Sara Flowers
2 Bedford Road, St Ives, Cornwall
TR26 1SP
Tel: 01736 797788

Terms & Conditions

1. Only one voucher per transaction
2. Defaced, torn or photocopied vouchers will not be accepted
3. Not to be used in conjunction with any other offer
4. Not exchangeable for cash
5. Present this voucher to the business to accept the offer
6. For use in store only. Not redeemable on wedding flower orders. Excluding the Christmas week, Valentines week and Mothering Sunday weekend. No cash exchanges given
7. 10% OFF on all orders over £30

Creating floral designs from simply traditional to modern and funky. Stuck for a gift idea? Wheal Sara flowers are your answer, delivering from Camborne to Lands End.

Wheal Sara Flowers

Yumi
St Ives,14 Fore Street, Cornwall
TR26 1AB
Tel: 01736 791782

Terms & Conditions

1. Only one voucher per transaction
2. Defaced, torn or photocopied vouchers will not be accepted
3. Not to be used in conjunction with reduced items or any other offer/promotion.
4. Not exchangeable for cash
5. Present this voucher to the business to accept the offer

Yumi is an internationally acclaimed brand with a celebrity following that includes Lily Allen, Fearne Cotton, Sienna Miller, Myleene Klass and Alesha Dixon. Store Manager Natty Hopkins and her team look forward to you visiting them in store soon.

Yumi

TERMS & CONDITIONS

SAVINGS, DISCOUNTS & ADVENTURE

OVER 300 OFFERS FROM ADVENTURE PARKS TO RESTAURANTS

RULES OF USE

THE FOLLOWING ARE THE RULES OF USE FOR ALL OFFERS IN THE 'KEEP IT CORNISH' BOOK. BY PURCHASING THE BOOK YOU AGREE TO ABIDE BY THESE:

Each offer has individual terms and conditions of use and we advise these are carefully checked. Read information carefully and if you have any doubts please contact the voucher promoter directly.

'Keep it Cornish' makes no assurance as to the suitability of included businesses in relation to their premises, services or products. Any dissatisfaction or complaints should be taken up directly with the provider. However we are happy to receive any reports from book users where services or products have been very poor.

'Keep it Cornish' is not responsible if any establishment breaches its contract or refuses to accept the vouchers. However every effort will be made to secure compliance.

All discounts and offers in the 'Keep it Cornish' book are valid on presentation of a valid voucher. Amended, photocopied or defaced vouchers will not be accepted. A reservation is essential when redeeming a 'Keep it Food' or 'Keep it Food - Fine Dining' section offer. Offers are void without a valid reservation unless stated otherwise by the voucher promoter. Please mention the 'Keep it Cornish' book at the time of booking and at the time of ordering. When ordering you should also present the relevant voucher. Dining offers are subject to availability.

To receive your discount present your voucher to the participating business. Unless otherwise stated you may only use the offer once, and may only use one voucher per customer. You may not combine the offer with any other promotion or offer.

Any use of an offer in violation of these rules will render the offer void.

Prices are subject to change without notice and are correct at the time of going to print.

Vouchers cannot be exchanged for cash unless otherwise stated and are not for re-sale. Voucher value 0.0001p.

'Keep it Food' and 'Keep it Food - Fine Dining' offers are not valid for use on major holidays, including Valentine's Day, Mother's Day, Father's Day, Easter Sunday, Christmas Eve/Day and New Year's Eve/Day.

A full refund will be honoured for books returned under the 30 day money back guarantee. The returned book must be unused and all vouchers fully intact.

We reserve the right to vary terms and conditions of use of the 'Keep it Cornish' book by posting changes on our Website. Please see our Website for our terms and conditions and privacy policy.

The 'Keep it Cornish' book and its offers are intended for the personal use of the individual purchaser of this book. The barter, trade sale, purchase or transfer for compensation of this book, in whole or in part or any of its offers, is strictly prohibited. The use of this book or any of its offers for advertising purposes, in any form, is strictly prohibited.

USE OF 'KEEP IT FOOD' VOUCHERS

IN ORDER TO USE YOUR 'KEEP IT CORNISH' VOUCHER YOU MUST FOLLOW THESE SIMPLE STEPS:

You must make a reservation with the restaurant in advance and advise them that you are using a 'Keep it Cornish' voucher.

You must present the voucher when ordering your meal.

Restrictions

Each restaurant allocates a number of tables for 'Keep it Cornish' customers. During busy times, such as weekends, these will be more limited so it is always best to book as far in advance as possible.

Please read the terms of each offer carefully to check if a restaurant has included any restrictions on usage.

All restaurants offers exclude certain dates throughout the year. They are Valentine's Day, Mother's Day, Father's Day, Easter Sunday, Christmas Eve/Day and New Year's Eve/Day.

Disputes

These mainly occur when 'Keep it Cornish' customers have not fully read the terms and conditions of the offers or the above rules. On the rare occasions when they do occur we will try and resolve the problem asap. Please get in touch in writing to

Keep it Cornish
12 Carrallack Mews
St Just
Penzance
Cornwall
TR19 7UL

Precious Lives appeal

MAKING THE MOST OF SHORT AND PRECIOUS LIVES

Children's Hospice South West is the only organisation in the South West providing hospice care for children with life-limiting conditions.

Sadly there are over 1,000 children in the South West with illnesses which mean they will die in childhood. Through our two children's hospices - Little Bridge House in North Devon and Charlton Farm in Somerset - we can provide care for up to 400 such children, and their families.

There is currently no such facility in Cornwall, and by building a third children's hospice in the county we will be able to reach out and support even more families, and bring our special service closer to the many families in Cornwall and Plymouth who need us.

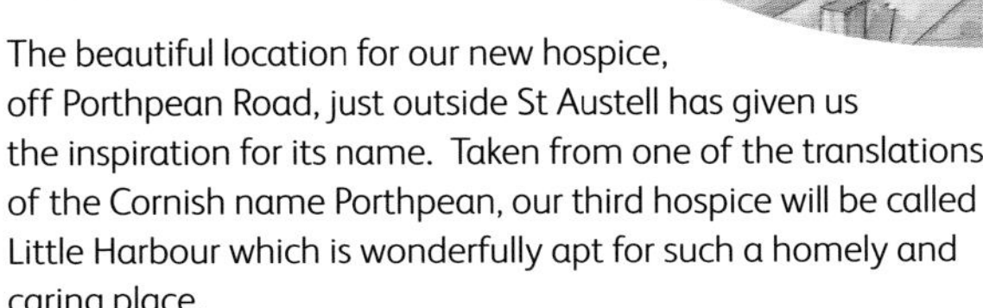

The beautiful location for our new hospice, off Porthpean Road, just outside St Austell has given us the inspiration for its name. Taken from one of the translations of the Cornish name Porthpean, our third hospice will be called Little Harbour which is wonderfully apt for such a homely and caring place.

To find out more about our plans for Little Harbour, what it will mean to local families, and the many ways in which you can help, please visit www.chsw.org.uk

Cornwall **Hospice** Care

Caring for our community

Registered Charity No. 1113140

Cornwall Hospice Care, which incorporates Mount Edgcumbe Hospice in St Austell and St Julia's Hospice in Hayle, is the charity which provides the only adult hospice care within the county. Every year thousands of people are touched by the work of the two hospices as their loved ones are given specialist palliative care to help them cope with life limiting illnesses.

Many of our patients are able to return home after a short period of care, but if this is not possible we provide people with a dignified and caring end to their lives. We exercise a truly holistic approach in the care of our patients and believe that emotional and spiritual health is as important as the physical. We care not just for the individual, but also for their families and carers.

All of our services are provided free of charge but cost £5.3 million a year or £11 a minute. With limited funding from the government we rely heavily on the generosity of the general public to ensure the survival of adult hospice care in Cornwall.

INDEX

THANKS

WE WOULD JUST LIKE TO MAKE A SPECIAL MENTION TO THE FOLLOWING

The Team:
Craig May, Richard Taylor, Hayley Marks

Special Thanks:
Gloria May, David May, Ellis May, Gareth May, Sarah Bailey, Jordan Harry Golding Talton, Justice Hattam, Grace Hattam & Yvonne May

Designers:
Creative Edge, Truro

Printers:
Pepper Print

TEL 07825 223 029
EMAIL info@keepitcornish.co.uk
ADDRESS 12 Carrallack Mews, St Just, Penzance, Cornwall TR19 7UL

www.keepitcornish.co.uk